Frampton Remembers World War I

Frampton Remembers
World War I

Rose Hewlett

with Jim Turpy

AMBERLEY

The image on the front cover shows the school gardening club *c.* 1912.

Left to right: Bill Hunt, Howard Tudor, Wallace Rowles, Fred Hitchings (pupil teacher), Charles Williams, Albert Daw, Sydney Osborn (headmaster), George Travell, [Albert Edward?] Baker, Charlie Eakett.

Frederick Robert William John Hitchings was killed in action on 12 May 1917. This book is dedicated to Fred and the other Frampton men who lost their lives during the First World War.

First published in 2016

Amberley Publishing
The Hill, Stroud,
Gloucestershire, GL5 4EP

www.amberley-books.com

Copyright © Rose Hewlett and Frampton Remembers World War One, 2016

The right of Rose Hewlett to be identified as the Author of this work has been asserted in accordance with the Copyrights, Designs and Patents Act 1988.

ISBN 978 1 4456 5198 9 (hardback)
ISBN 978 1 4456 5199 6 (ebook)

British Library Cataloguing in Publication Data. A catalogue record for this book is available from the British Library.

Typesetting and Origination by Amberley Publishing.
Printed in the UK.

CONTENTS

ACKNOWLEDGEMENTS

This book is the culmination of many thousands of hours of research by volunteers, often with the assistance of descendants of Frampton on Severn's First World War servicemen. It has not been an easy task for more than 60 per cent of the service records were destroyed during enemy bombing in 1940. Those that were saved, known as the 'burnt records', are often damaged and incomplete. Surviving medal cards contain limited information about an individual serviceman, for his number and regiment were the prime identification used by the military. We hope to have correctly identified each serviceman who is either named on the plaque in the village hall (which lists most of those who fell and those who returned), or on the war memorial. We have also included all men registered as absent military or naval voters during the war period. These three sources in themselves are inconsistent, and additional men have been found from newspaper articles. If we have inadvertently recorded the story of one serviceman against another of that name, we hope that it will serve as a fitting memorial to them both.

It has been my pleasure to bring this work together, and while it would be impossible to thank everyone individually for their contribution, I would particularly like to express my gratitude to Jim Turpy for his interpretation of the military records which lie at the heart of this book. To the rest of the research team (whether they worked on village records or those of the servicemen), and to the Frampton Remembers World War One committee and our project officer, Melanie Sherratt, I send my grateful thanks, for everyone has played an important part.

On behalf of the committee, I should like to acknowledge the use of extensive records generously shared by individual families, and also to the Williams family for the reproduction of photographs collected by the late Graham Williams, and the Mitchell family for providing access to photographs taken by the late Frank Mitchell. We have also drawn on material from Berrow's *Worcester Journal*, Cadbury Archives, Frampton Archive, Gloucestershire Archives, the Soldiers of Gloucestershire Museum, The National Archives, the Howard Beard Collection and the work of Dr Colin R. Chapman and Brian Edwards. Finally, thanks are due to the Heritage Lottery Fund and the local sponsors who have made this project possible, and to Jane Fryer for the design of our logo which is based on Frampton's war memorial.

Rose Hewlett, 2016

The plaque in Frampton Village Hall.

Inscription from the war memorial.

LIST OF SUBSCRIBERS

William and Carol Alexander
Kathleen Ballard
Joan Bateman
Sheryle and Cliff Bateman
Kevin, Hazel, Pippa and James Benn
Lawrence Birkin
David Birt
Eunice Birt
John and Mary Bowers
Daughters of Percy and nieces of Hugh Bradley
Jane and Paul Bradly
Heather Brazington
Kelvin Broad
June Clamp (descendant of Frampton Master Mariners)
The Clifford family
Ken Collier
David and Pam Daw
Andrew Downton
Mary and Maurice Durham
Mrs Peggy Evans (née Phipps)
Mike and Helen Finigan
C. E. Fryer
Rex and Marion George
Mr Ray Gillard
Ken Gleed (son of Harold Gleed)
Bill and Connie Green
Pam and David Greenfield
Mrs Joy Greenwood
Alan Richard Hale
Keith and Linda Hall (née Berry)
Phil and Mary Herbert
Edwin Hewlett
Mrs Gwen Hewlett

The descendants of Thomas and Emma Margaret Hewlett
Tim and Jennifer Hiorns
John Hitchings
Colonel Andy Hodson TD DL
Maree Hogan
Shirley Hunter (née Evans)
Gillian Keightley
Barbara and Carolyn Kidder
R. C. Lawrence
Nancy Leach (née Herbert)
Martin and Julia Lewis
Roy and Chris Lewis
Christopher Marshall
Micky O'Gorman Marshall
Mrs K. Olive Martin (née Bradley)
Susan Merrett (daughter of Ralph T. Hazell)
Derrick Millard (youngest son of John Millard)
Babs Mitchell
Reverend Canon Peter Nunn
Jessica O'Gorman
Rebecca O'Gorman
Andy and Eunice Page
Mrs B. R. Parker
Gary Peacey (great-grandson of William Wood)
Professor Anthony J. Pinching (grandson of Dr W. G. Pinching)
Sibyl Price (daughter of Timothy Sims)
Gill and Derek Rogers
Melanie Sherratt (Project Officer)
Carol Sims (granddaughter of Cecil Charles Leonard)
Ron and Dot Smale
Richard and Penny Sumsion
John Tainton
Jim Temlett
Jenny and John Treweek
Jim and Dorothy Turpy
Rosemary Walton
In memory of Charles Weaver
Sharon G. Webb
Joan Williams (née Berry)
Marg Williams
Michael and Caroline Williams
Greg Wood (great-great-grandson of William Wood)
William and Elizabeth Wood (great-great-great-grandchildren of William Wood)

INTRODUCTION

Frampton Remembers World War I is divided into two sections: life in the village, and the servicemen. An asterisk before a name indicates a Frampton serviceman whose story is told in this book. We hope that readers will use this to cross-refer for additional information. In a community such as Frampton there was much interlinking of families; we have not attempted to make every connection, only those that seem relevant to our story. Additionally, readers should note that in 1914 few of the properties had names. We have therefore used a mixture of house names from the period and from the present day to help identify where the servicemen and their families lived. This book is designed to highlight Frampton's contribution to the war effort, through the enlistment of its men and the work of its nurses, the extraction of gravel for government projects and the opening of Cadbury's factory to process milk. Because the village lies next to the Gloucester & Berkeley Canal and the River Severn, many men served at sea, helping to keep vital supply lines open. At home a considerable amount of work was undertaken by the women, and villagers were involved with war-related fundraising activities and the production of items for the troops.

The first part of this book looks at village life before the war, mainly around the time of the 1911 census. Chapters on each of the war years follow. They focus principally on what was happening in the village and locally, not only within the context of the war, but also the ordinary things that went on as normal. It is not intended to be a study of the mechanisms of central and local government, or a political commentary; those aspects of the war are beyond the scope of our project and have been dealt with in an abundance of literature. Nevertheless, in order to put life in Frampton into perspective, a short political summary appears at the beginning of each chapter, along with a brief military overview for that year. *Thomas Henry Griffin's war diary falls between 1916 and 1917, providing an insight into a soldier's life and a poignant reminder of how much our serving men missed home and their loved ones. The Armistice did not mean the instant return of all servicemen, and the final chapter of the village section reflects the long demobilisation period and a gradual return to some sense of normality. It ends with the village's acts of remembrance which continue to this day. In order to keep related subject matter together, events within each year have not necessarily been recorded chronologically.

It has been a delight to try to reconstruct village life 100 years ago, and the stories of those who stayed behind are naturally interwoven with those of the servicemen. Research has gone beyond works already published and has found out more about the day-to-day routines of villagers. We discover that they faced constant regulation and bureaucracy, had to deal with outbreaks of contagious diseases, and how they had to fight a continual battle with the education authorities when their older children were required both at school and in the fields. Who would have thought that Frampton had around a dozen cottages deemed unfit for habitation during the early part of the war, while at least 10 per cent of the available housing stock lay empty?

The war brought great social change as men learned new skills in the services and adapted to living in very different circumstances. The recruitment of women for essential war work encouraged a spirit of independence and self-reliance. Although many of their jobs disappeared after the war, the idea that women, married as well as single, could have paid employment became more acceptable. This book stops short of discussing the economic difficulties faced by Frampton people in the 1920s as the country, and indeed the world, recovered from a costly war; this is a decade of further change and adjustment, but one which falls outside the brief of our project.

When telling the stories of each serviceman (whose biographies appear under their registered birth names) we have kept to a simple format: his life before the war, his service in the forces, and his life after the war. Available records have generally been more fruitful pre-war; without the help of direct descendants it has often proved difficult to give anything other than a brief outline post-war. For a few men positive identification has proved impossible, and inevitably there are those who fall somewhere in between as the preferred name of many village men often differed according to circumstances. The military interpretations allow us to understand where our men saw action and should be treated as a guide to a particular serviceman's activities. Only in exceptional circumstances can his individual role be ascertained. It has not been possible to consult all the regimental diaries, but we have made use of them where they have been readily accessible.

The loss of records during a German bombing raid in the Second World War has made it impossible to form an overall picture of who enlisted where and when, but from those records that did survive it is evident that Framptonians percolated many different parts of the Armed Forces during the First World War. Men from the village were answering the call in a number of capacities. *Walter Henry Tainton and his son *Ernest Walter Henry enlisted with the Gloucestershire Regiment during the early stages of the war. *Frederick Charles Gardner and *Thomas George Halling found their way to the Royal Flying Corps. *Francis Henry Franklin and *Cyril Vick were gunners with the Royal Garrison Artillery and Royal Field Artillery respectively, and *Frank Thomas Sims served as a farrier with the Army Service Corps; others, such as *Jacob Jonas Godwin and *Clevedon Wells Fryer, were deployed to the Royal Engineers or Royal Field Artillery as drivers. *Peter Gandy joined one of the 'Pals' regiments, designed to attract men with similar interests and connections. Frampton's servicemen were scattered across Europe and beyond. Those that had recently settled abroad played their part too. *Thomas Hart Brinkworth enlisted at Brisbane, *Gerald

Prout and *Wells Alexander Watkins attested at Calgary within days of each other, and *Victor Charles Lawrence joined the US Army.

The village boasted numerous families whose menfolk worked on the canals and in coastal waters, and many of these served in either the Royal Navy or the Mercantile Marine (later named the Merchant Navy). *Herbert Charles Drayton and *Frederick George Simmons were already Royal Navy career-men; they were to see the service for which they had been prepared and both continued beyond the end of the war. *Stephen John Dark joined them early in 1915. His brother, *George Edward, saw wartime service with the Mercantile Marine, as did the two Wilks brothers, *Ernest Henry and *Victor William.

During the course of our research, we have used several genealogical and military websites. Where these have enabled us to inspect original records this has been an enjoyable task and brought considerably more information to the project than would have been possible even just a few years ago. However, a word of caution is needed when using such websites, for often mistakes in indexing have been made, thus leading to unfortunate wrong conclusions on the public family trees that are posted. Habitual repetition of these errors is disappointing and unhelpful.

The war brought about displacement of families, particularly as wives (with or without young children) returned home to live with their parents. This meant the influx of some to Frampton, and the movement of others away from the village. The heroism of Frampton's servicemen, including several who, through wartime family displacement, became temporarily associated with the village, has remained largely unrecorded. The exceptions are *Arthur Harry Sutton, DCM, whose bravery was recognised on a number of occasions, and three who were mentioned in despatches, *Henry Francis Clifford, *Percy Strahan and *Charles Alexander Weller. The courage of others, largely in the ranks, who witnessed the terrible scenes of comrades perishing beside them, is beyond words: fourteen men from Frampton were killed in action or died of wounds, while a further three succumbed to influenza. We hope that this book will serve as a permanent reminder of the sacrifices made by all the men, women and children of Frampton during the First World War.

The stories of the Frampton servicemen feature on our website. We welcome any additional information that may result from the publication of this book and the website gives our contact details.

www.framptonremembersww1.org.uk

I

BEFORE THE WAR

It may be hard to imagine what everyday life was like in Frampton on Severn before the First World War. Back then, news travelled by word of mouth, letters or newspapers, and urgent messages could be relayed by telegraph, carrier or on horseback. There were no residential telephones in Frampton, but there was a kiosk in the neighbouring village of Saul where, in a small wooden hut, a three-minute telephone call could be made for 2*d*. Education was provided at the National School, and the many shops and tradesmen ensured a reasonable degree of self-sufficiency in the village, which also boasted allotments, privately owned orchards and many gardens, which were often large enough to support a pig and certainly a few chickens. Entertainment was primarily local, with concerts at the school and the recently opened church Institute (now the village hall). Frampton Feast was held in August, and the annual Frampton Horse Show was also a summer treat. Football and cricket thrived, and the Berkeley hounds met regularly

Approach to Frampton with the Bell Hotel in the background.

on the village green. Religious needs were served by the church of St Mary and the Congregational church (known as the chapel), whose traditional celebrations at Harvest and Christmas were popular too.

Frampton was very accessible. Bordering the Bristol road and with regular steam packet services on the Gloucester & Berkeley Canal (renamed in 1935), communication was relatively easy. The nearest railway stations were within reasonable walking or cycling distance at Stonehouse, and were visited daily by the local carriers. There, the station in Burdett Road served the Great Western Railway for connections to London; those wishing to travel to Bristol or Birmingham used the Midland Railway in Oldends Lane. Trains to Cardiff stopped at the Great Western Railway station in Newnham, but Frampton passengers had to be mindful of the tides and weather conditions as they crossed the River Severn on the passage boat from Arlingham to make their connection.

The parish boundary mostly followed that of today, with the addition of some meadow to the east of the Bristol road. To the west of the parish, the old formal division remained at Tobacco Box and beyond Lake Lane, although most people informally considered the boundary to be the canal, which had annexed a small part of Fretherne-with-Saul parish when it opened in 1827. The Clifford family owned a large estate, much of which was rented out. Among their farms were Advowsons, Church, Denfurlong, Nastfield, Netherhills, Parks, Tanhouse and Townfield, together with Manor Farm beside the long village green. Opposite was the Estate-owned Frampton Court, and scattered around the parish were over fifty of its properties, including the Bell Hotel. *Henry Francis Clifford managed the Frampton Court Estate and was also lord of the manor, his family able to trace their roots back to the time of the Norman Conquest and to his ancestor, 'Fair Rosamund', the favourite mistress of Henry II, whose father had been lord of the manor during the twelfth century. In 1911 Major Clifford lived with his widowed mother and three of his sisters in The Grange at the south-eastern end of the village green. A cook, parlourmaid and housemaid completed their household.

The 1911 census return provides a pre-war snapshot of the village which then comprised some 224 dwellings, of which twenty-one were uninhabited. This may appear a large proportion but, as we shall see through the stories of the servicemen, several families had emigrated in search of a 'better life', particularly to Australia and Canada, during the early years of the twentieth century. Many youngsters also had left the village for other parts of the country, especially Gloucester. The total population in 1911 was 730, a drop of sixty-seven since 1901. The majority of the houses were situated around The Green and on The Street, which led to Church End and Splatt. To the north of Bridge Road were The Lake and The Walks, and in the hamlet of Fromebridge, cottages clustered around the mill. About a quarter of the properties had only two or three rooms, many of them belonging to the Estate or private landlords. Paying the rent was often a worry and it was not unusual for tenants to ask for more time to catch up with their arrears. Around 40 per cent of the housing stock had more than six rooms.

The records suggest that nearly 300 villagers found employment locally. The greatest number worked in domestic service as cooks, housekeepers, various types of maids and laundresses, and as gardeners, grooms, chauffeurs and house boys. More than fifty were involved in farming and over thirty had jobs connected with the river or canal. Thriving dressmaking and tailoring businesses accounted for

Boaz Green and Charlie Eaketts delivering bread *c.* 1912.

another twenty-three, and seven of those living in Fromebridge were employed in cloth manufacture, presumably at the factory in the neighbouring parish of Eastington. Tradesmen included builders, carpenters, a plumber, a blacksmith, a farrier, engineers, coach builders, a wheelwright, carriers and a chimney sweep. These were supported by around fifteen general labourers. Several youngsters held apprenticeships at the numerous grocery and bakery businesses which provided work for at least twenty-five people. This image shows Boaz Green, one of the bakers, with his errand boy, Charles Eaketts, whose older brothers, *Willoughby Thomas and *James, both served in the war.

Although essentially a rural community, Frampton had recently witnessed five years of extraction from the extensive gravel terraces underlying the village. These had been exploited until 1908 by Messrs Aird & Co. during the construction of the Royal Edward Dock at Avonmouth. At that time a mile-long railway had taken gravel from workings on the southern side of Perryway to the canal at Splatt, where a jetty had been built. The mill at Fromebridge produced animal feed, and the grain ready for processing was stored in a warehouse alongside the canal to the north of Fretherne Bridge.

Frampton came under the control of Wheatenhurst Rural District Council. It was in the Tewkesbury Parliamentary Division, represented by Michael Hugh Hicks-Beach, Viscount Quenington, who opened the Institute in 1907. There were more than 140 men on the electoral register in 1911, as well as several women who were householders in their own right, but were entitled to vote only in local elections. Parish council minutes indicate that there was little business to discuss, though in 1909 the council agreed to take over responsibility for the Jubilee Bridge (now usually referred to as the lych gate) which needed major repair.

This had been installed just twelve years earlier to commemorate Queen Victoria's Diamond Jubilee, and crossed Buckle Brook at the north end of The Narles.

Local government, then as now, was financed by a property tax (the rates) and paid for the county, district and parish council and for the poor law. The local police station was at Whitminster, and this also housed the magistrates' court where Petty Sessions were held. Some Frampton cases and inquests, however, were held at the Bell Hotel, the school or the Institute. For minor offences such as riding a bicycle without lights (a common occurrence), the fines were often 5s. For serious cases of assault, periods of hard labour were handed down; the punishment for breaking a window could be fourteen days. In 1911 the parish council wrote to the county council Watch Committee requesting a resident policeman, as they were concerned about the numerous petty thefts, straying dogs and unlit bicycles and horses and carts being driven at night; their request was turned down in January 1912.

There was no mains water in the village. The larger houses typically had their own well and pump, but most residents had to collect water from one of the communal village pumps. The one at the end of Vicarage Lane also served the school. The pumps drew water from the gravel terraces underlying Frampton, but there were concerns about water quality. It could be contaminated with salt from the river if the tide flaps failed, or be muddy after heavy rain, and snails and worms often dropped from the pumps. Sometimes the wells dried up in summer and had to be deepened. Many were poorly built and often they were too close to the privy. This, for most cottages, was down the garden and had to be dug out. The resultant 'manure', used liberally as a fertiliser, was prone to seep back into the water supply. The terrace of Hart's Cottages (near the Institute) had a row of privies beside number four, and the contents of their chamber pots, called by some 'upstairs music', was used on nearby vegetable plots.

The Street looking south *c.* 1913.

Homes were heated by coal or wood fires and lighting was by candle or oil lamp. Cooking was either on a cast iron range fuelled by coal, or on a paraffin stove. Those living in thatched cottages knew that care had to be taken in case a spark from the fire went up the chimney and endangered the roof. Washing was hard physical work for the housewife, scrubbing the clothes on a short plank of wood; villagers recount how their mothers were worn out at the end of a wash-day. In wealthier homes, hot water for washing came from a copper boiler; in poorer households, without a copper boiler, water was boiled in a kettle or pan over an open fire. Flat-irons were heated on a trivet in front of the fire and were swapped as they cooled. To save fuel, clothes were ironed after a fire had been used to cook a meal. The village had several laundresses, and they numbered both the better and less well-off among their clients, for many of the cottages were so tiny that there was no space to launder the bedclothes.

There were village charities to help the needy. The Ann Wicks Charity had been founded in 1829 for the aged and infirm poor of Frampton over fifty-five years of age. Two pensions were still being allocated just before the war to those considered in particular need, and grants were also made when people were ill. Although very small, these sums did provide a lifeline. Similarly, the Phillimore Charity had been set up in the nineteenth century to provide bread for poor families. In 1910 the Charity Commission suggested that this was a rather outmoded benefit and it was agreed that the two charities be combined. (These were, in turn, amalgamated with the Pinching Memorial Trust in 2000, which still honours the annual pension arrangements in force at that date.)

Dr Charles Joseph Weller was the general practitioner and lived in Russell House, from where he ran his surgery. He was also medical officer to the Wheatenhurst Union workhouse at Eastington. Dr Weller provided many of the treatments for

Russell House (left); Goodman's shop (right).

which patients would be taken to hospital today. More serious problems were treated at the Gloucester Royal Infirmary in Southgate Street, where the hospital had 140 beds. (Until the 1911 National Insurance Act, treatment in hospital or by the doctor had to be paid for, and many people joined insurance schemes. This Act set up national schemes which covered most wage earners, although not their dependants, for medical treatment, maternity and sanatorium care and twenty-six weeks' sick pay.) Dr Weller was one of only three people in the village to own a motor car before the war; he preferred the French Darracq model, owning three in succession between 1906 and 1912. In 1911 his chauffeur was the eighteen-year-old *Frederick Gilbert Alexander Cook. Dr Weller retired in 1912, and Russell House became the surgery and home of his successor, Dr William Guy Pinching, who also owned a car. Mrs Ethel Donne, the tenant of Frampton Court, owned a Wolseley Landaulette.

During this period there was a growing movement to provide district nurses, and the Estate supplied Sarah Child who lived in a terraced cottage near Roe's Pool and, in 1914, at Oatfield Cottage in Whitminster Lane. She helped with minor ailments for those families who could not afford the doctor, and she also provided maternity services, for most births were at home. With large families in small cottages, infectious diseases were common and included measles, diphtheria, chicken pox, whooping cough, scabies and scarlet fever. If there was a serious outbreak, the medical officer closed the school for days or even weeks to minimise contagion; in 1911 an outbreak of diphtheria closed the school early for Christmas but, despite this, six children died. When the school reopened in January, the children's throats were examined in order to isolate any who might be carrying the disease.

Most Frampton children were educated at the village school although some went to Saul. There was a local committee of managers which included the vicar, who also provided daily religious teaching. As the population decreased the number of pupils fell too, and in 1911 did not exceed 120. They were divided into infants and six standards according to performance, not age. The curriculum covered English, handwriting, arithmetic, geography, history, sewing and art, and the school's logbook records that on one fine day there was an 'exploration of the fields'. The attendance officer made regular visits to check the register and also visited the parents of habitual absentees, for older children were often kept away either to help at home or on a farm. To encourage attendance, the whole school was given a half-day holiday if the number present achieved 95 per cent in any month.

The headmaster, Sydney Thomas Osborn, and his wife, Phoebe, also provided some extra-curricular activities. Mrs Osborn taught the girls household skills, for which a kitchen range was installed in 1913; the boys enjoyed a gardening club two afternoons a week on plots adjacent to the school, the site of today's allotments. There was a continuous turnover of teachers before the war, perhaps suggesting that they received relatively poor pay. They were assisted by pupil teachers and monitors drawn from the ranks of older children. School inspectors visited regularly, and generally gave good reports of progress; among suggested improvements were a larger playground and new cloakrooms, and that infants should be taught as a separate group.

Frampton Boy Scouts *c.* 1906 (location unknown).

Back row: *Percival Hitchings, *Henry Elphinstone Guy, *Francis William Aldridge, *Ralph Hazell, *Harold Gleed, Benjamin Fredericks.

Front row: Harold Aldridge, *Frederick Gardner, *Albert Cook, Everitt, Cecil Franklin, Benjamin Herbert, Unknown.

There was a thriving Boy Scout patrol in the village. On Easter Monday 1911 *William Joseph Ernest Gleed led the Frampton patrol to a rally at Quedgeley House under the watchful eye of the Gloucester and District Commissioner, *Major Henry Francis Clifford. After a short rehearsal to practise their inspection, the scouts cooked their own dinners. At 2.30 p.m. they saluted the Inspecting Officer, and marched past in column and quarter column, being commended for their steadiness on parade. A bridge-building competition was held, and there were displays of physical drill, tent-pitching, ambulance work (with improvised stretchers) and signalling. The Frampton patrol took part in these last two. They simulated a signalling party discovering a fallen comrade and conveying the message to base, which was said to represent a realistic scene of ambulance work in the field. All this was to stand these young lads in good stead for what was to come during the war, in which many of them served.

The Reverend Lionel Ward was the incumbent at St Mary's, where Sunday services were held at 11 a.m. and 6.30 p.m. He lived at the vicarage, now the Old Vicarage Nursing Home. Among the social organisations of the church was the Girls' Friendly Society, which aimed to educate and improve the moral standards of ordinary working girls. At the chapel, the Reverend Henry Welby Florance was the minister until his retirement in 1911. It was then served by a series of supply preachers and lay ministers, an arrangement that lasted until the Reverend Dr John Hunter took up the office in 1990. The Sunday school at the chapel was well attended.

Edwin Hawker of Stockelm Cottage, The Green, was the registrar of births and deaths for the Frampton sub-district, and of marriages for the Wheatenhurst Union. He was also a blacksmith. William Wood, who lived at The Red House, was a carpenter and also the village undertaker, a role that his descendants still perform today. George Frederick Hitchings was the bridgekeeper at Splatt on the busy Gloucester & Berkeley Canal. Samuel Bradley, one of the village's builders, ran his business from Lake Cottage, Lake Lane. His accounts show that he engaged in various tasks, from constructing buildings to decorating rooms. His commissions included work at the chapel, St Mary's, the school, and on behalf of the parish council. In 1913 he built a billiard room at the back of the Institute (now the Rowles Room), complete with pine block floor, for a total cost of £101 1s.

Mrs Annie Stockham kept the Post Office and general store overlooking Roe's Pool. Letters arrived six days a week from the trains at Stonehouse; they were delivered twice daily around the village, at 10 a.m. and 6 p.m., by two postmen. Frampton also had a private letter carrier for local deliveries and in 1912 Frank Selwyn Betteridge, a general carrier, began a daily service, collecting the national newspapers in Stonehouse at 6 a.m. from the London train and bringing them to the local shops for sale. Each Friday copies of the two local weekly papers, the *Stroud Journal* and the *Stroud News & Gloucestershire Advertiser*, were available for 1d.

A popular way to visit Gloucester was to take the steam packets *Wave* or *Lapwing*. They provided a scheduled service on the canal, leaving the village three times a day in summer and twice in winter. The boats stopped when requested at each bridge to set down and pick up passengers. A journey from Fretherne Bridge

Stockham's shop, which overlooked Roe's Pool on the village green *c.* 1909

to Gloucester took a couple of hours at a cost of 1s 6d. Some of the villagers who emigrated at this time used this route as the first leg of their journey before taking the train from Gloucester to Liverpool or London. In 1904 Edward Silvey of Epney bought the first motor bus in the county which ran between Saul, Epney and Gloucester. Some Framptonians found that a brisk walk to Saul and Silvey's bus was quicker than taking the steam packet to the city on the canal.

At weekends during summer months, boat trips on the *Lapwing* were run from the village to the Pleasure Grounds at Sharpness, on the western part of the hill between the Old and New Docks. Mrs Sturge kept these from 1887 until the late 1920s, where she charged a small entry fee and served refreshments. Picnics could be taken among the trees on the clifftop above Sharpness, with its splendid views down the Severn and across to the Forest of Dean, before a return trip to Frampton in the evening. At Framilode, Captain Walter Long's Tea Gardens had an elevated deck for views over the river; he especially advertised his Sunday cream teas.

Frampton was also a popular destination. Besides the Bell Hotel and the Three Horseshoes, which were licensed to sell all alcoholic drinks, there were also three beer houses (often frequented by those working on the canals), the Heart of Oak, New Inn and True Heart, all in The Street. At the weekends members of the Gloucester Rowing Club sometimes lunched at the Bell, having rowed down the canal from their club house in Gloucester. Although villagers may have travelled to Gloucester or Stroud to see a silent film at one of the newly opened cinemas, the latest technology was also brought to Frampton. In January 1913, in celebration of the vicar's marriage, Messrs Moody Bell and Co. of Cheltenham showed a motion picture in the Institute.

The village cricket and football teams had been founded during the nineteenth century. Sir Lionel Darell, in his book *Ratcatcher Baronet*, recalled playing cricket on Frampton Green as 'the worst and most dangerous pitch in the world', not surprising as its boundaries were short and the village green was still grazed by sheep and cattle! Matches usually began about 3 p.m., and a large tea was taken at 4.30 p.m. in the Bell, with stumps drawn between 6.30 p.m. and 7 p.m. Each side was allowed only one innings and generally scored between 20 and 70 runs.

Also on the green, Frampton Feast celebrated the Assumption of the Blessed Virgin Mary to whom the church was dedicated. Fairground rides were driven by steam on the same spot outside the Bell where Frampton Feast Fun Fair is still held today. In 1907 the Football Club organised athletic sports to coincide with the Feast and *The Citizen* of 20 August reported that as well as 'all the fun of the fair' there were bicycle races, flat races and a half-mile donkey race, the winner arriving tail first! Further amusement was provided by a greasy pole and a prize for the funniest song, sung without laughing. The annual Frampton Horse Show, started in 1912, was held each summer, and all manner of horsemanship was to be seen. Prizes were awarded for Open Jumping, Pony Races, Horse Races, and the Best Light Turn-out. There was also an exhibition of sheep penning.

Local markets sold livestock and other produce, and provided another opportunity for social gatherings. Stroud Market was held each Friday. The larger Gloucester Market had a regular weekly routine of fatstock on Mondays, fruit on Mondays, Wednesdays and Fridays and store stock on Saturdays. There were also

Frampton Horse Show organisers *c.* 1912.
   Back row: Frederick Franklin, *Albert Brazington, *Geoffrey White, George Cooper Bubb, Arthur Lewis, Charles Williams, John Dennis.
   Centre: Charles Morse, Charles Walker, Frederick Walford Vick, 'Steward' Williams.
   Front: Joe McCullough, *Francis Franklin.

the stock fairs: horses and bulls in April, horses and cattle in July and November and the annual Barton Fair in September for sheep, horses and cattle.

Frampton's own seaside was greatly enjoyed by families during the summer months. This was the Cow's Drink, the sandy inlet on the green bank of the Gloucester & Berkeley Canal south of Fretherne Bridge where families picnicked, and many village children learnt to swim. When paddling, however, it was necessary to watch out for approaching ships; there was always a danger that a bow wave would engulf bathers. In 1913 the Frampton Gala had the usual swimming races and concluded with a water polo match played between nets set on either side of the canal. In the foreground of the picture on page 24, in the trilby hat and holding a walking stick, is Major Clifford. He is surrounded by many young men who, like him, were later to serve during the First World War.

On Tuesday 31 March 1914, there were great festivities in the village to mark the homecoming of the newly-wed *Henry Francis Clifford and Adelaide Hilda née Clay, who had enjoyed a lengthy honeymoon since their marriage the previous November. At about 4 p.m. they were greeted with an enthusiastic welcome by parishioners, who had not only erected an arch near the north end of the village green, with appropriate inscriptions, but also another at the entrance gates to The Grange. The whole length of the green was decorated with bunting, mottoes and flags, and a number of guns were fired upon their arrival. Flowers were presented by Mary Jane Bubb, tenant of Nastfield Farm, and the happy couple individually expressed their thanks to everyone. They were preceded down the green by

Frampton Gala *c.* 1913 at Fretherne Bridge.

the Boy Scouts amid more cheering and another firing of guns. Two days later, about 160 Frampton folk accepted the Cliffords' invitation to a dance at the Institute, which continued past midnight despite the very cramped conditions. The following evening, almost 180 other Frampton people sat down to supper, and their numbers swelled to 250 in time for the entertainment which included conjuring and shadowgraphy. During the war many must have reflected on these occasions which had brought the village together in happiness. Some of those present never returned from duty, Major Clifford among them.

The boys and men from the church choir enjoyed annual outings in either August or September to such places as Bristol Zoo, the Clifton Suspension Bridge, Scarborough, London (leaving Frampton at 4 a.m. and arriving back at 5 a.m. the following day!), Weston-super-Mare and Blackpool. In May 1914, the proposed visit was to Minchinhampton. When the choirboys found out they were outraged and went on strike, causing a stir in newspapers as far away as Birmingham and Reading. To some the notice they tacked on the board outside the church appeared ungracious and rude: 'We are all on strike – striking for a better outing. Who wants to go to Minchinhampton?' The absence of surviving records denies us the outcome of the dispute, which was apparently not intended as a slur on the local Cotswold town. By the summer, there were more serious matters to consider.

2

1914

POLITICAL SUMMARY

The Liberal government that took the country to war had been in office since 1905 with H. H. Asquith as prime minister since 1908. It had an impressive record of social legislation, introducing old age pensions, national insurance and minimum wages, sometimes seen as the foundation of the welfare state. The power of the overwhelmingly Conservative House of Lords had been reduced by the 1911 Parliament Act, which enabled the government to pass an act to give Home Rule to Ireland. However, this was controversial, as the Protestants in Ulster in the north fiercely opposed Home Rule; during 1914 they were acquiring guns (from Germany) and preparing for armed resistance. In the south there was gunrunning as well, and there was a very real threat of civil war in Ireland.

The government also faced a campaign of violence by suffragettes demanding votes for women, while increasing trade union militancy had been shown by a series of strikes, notably by railwaymen and miners.

Then came the European crisis that would spawn the First World War and as it deepened the Cabinet debated its response. Finally the German invasion of Belgium persuaded the majority of the Cabinet to support intervention. Three ministers resigned (but this did not damage the government) while the Conservative, Irish Nationalist and Labour parties in the Commons rallied to support the government in the national cause. Lord Kitchener, seen as the architect of victory in the Boer War, became Secretary of State for War and began the campaign to recruit volunteers to enlarge the Army.

Initially, government policy could be summed up by Churchill's phrase 'Business as usual' although several significant steps were taken. The Irish crisis was tackled by suspending the Home Rule Act until the war was ended. The Defence of the Realm Act was rushed through with virtually no opposition, giving the government sweeping powers to rule by decree and thus interfere with the lives of its citizens. A committee of senior managers of the railway companies took control of the railways and organised the successful mobilisation and despatch of the British Expeditionary Force to France. Other similar committees of managers and businessmen set up to organise production and operations were characteristic of the British war effort. To pay for the war David Lloyd George, Chancellor of the Exchequer, increased some direct taxes, but relied mainly on borrowing.

MILITARY OVERVIEW

The European crisis had arisen out of fear. The great powers of Europe had evolved alliances to deter attack by rivals but, although they felt safer with friends to help, this inevitably resulted in growing political suspicion and tension between the groups. These consisted of the Entente Powers (Britain, France and Russia) and the Central Powers (Germany and Austria-Hungary). The Central Powers believed that in the event of war Russia would need much longer to mobilise its troops than would the western powers, and therefore based their strategy on dealing with France as quickly as possible before turning their attention to the east; however, the chain of French fortresses on the frontier would not be easy to take and would seriously delay an advancing army.

The spark of war came with the assassination in Sarajevo of Archduke Franz Ferdinand, heir to the throne of Austria-Hungary, and Austria's ultimatum to Serbia; Russia immediately supported Serbia, while Germany backed Austria. All the continental powers started to mobilise, and despite attempts to limit the conflict, declarations of war followed rapidly in late July and early August 1914. Britain declared war on 4 August because Germany refused to guarantee the neutrality of Belgium, and others joined in; the Ottoman Empire joined the Central Powers and Japan declared for the Entente Powers or what became known as the Allied Powers.

The German Army then invaded Luxembourg and Belgium to bypass the French defences and drive towards Paris. Initially they succeeded in over-running Belgium and much of north east France, but the British Expeditionary Force, the professionals of the Regular Army, helped the French halt the German thrust on the Marne in early September, and indeed drove them back some 30 miles. Each army then tried to outflank the other, but both failed and the stalemate of trench warfare began.

On the Eastern Front, Serbia mounted a successful defence against the Austro-Hungarian armies, who were also pushed back by the Russians, but in the north two Russian armies were destroyed by the Germans under General von Hindenburg at Tannenberg and the Masurian Lakes.

In the wider world, the German colonies in China, Samoa, New Guinea, Togoland, Cameroon and South-West Africa were all quickly taken over by the Allies; however, in Tanganyika Colonel von Lettow-Vorbeck started a guerrilla campaign that would not end until two weeks after the Armistice.

At sea the German Navy had an early success off the coast of Chile, Admiral von Spee sinking two old British armoured cruisers at Coronel for the loss of only three men. The British response was to send reinforcements to the Falkland Islands where they destroyed the German squadron on 8 December.

FRAMPTON ON SEVERN

The vicar recorded the subject of his evening sermon on Sunday 2 August as 'war', and the text he took was Matthew 24, verse 4: 'And Jesus answered and said unto them, take heed that no man deceive you'. The verses that follow deal with future uncertainty, but we have no idea what the Reverend Ward actually said, nor how many were in his congregation, although the offertory of *6s 9d* was certainly no more than average.

The Berkeley Hunt Agricultural Society's annual show went ahead on the following day with increased entries, in spite of the cancellation of some excursion trains. John Dennis from Manor Farm was successful in two of the horse breeding classes; judging by the list of livestock and produce winners published in the *Western Daily Press*, the farming fraternity of the Vale of Berkeley turned out in force. The band of the Royal Gloucestershire Hussars played, but the 3rd, 7th, 15th and 19th Hussars, who were to have given a musical ride and mounted displays with sword, lance and revolver, were absent 'for obvious reasons'.

The cargo ship, SS *Sappho*, was at Hamburg during these early stages and was without wireless receivers. She had recently left Gloucester and Able Seaman Oscar Hubert Watts was among the local men on board. His wife, Ethel Minnie, and their young son were living in Frampton, unaware of the tight spot that Oscar was in. The German authorities prevented the *Sappho* from leaving Hamburg, initially citing documentary irregularities, and Oscar and his colleagues were taken off and held in a prison ship. They were then transferred, together with the crews of other Allied ships caught in the same predicament, to various temporary holding locations where they were poorly fed and housed. Eventually they ended up at Ruhleben, a prison camp between Berlin and Spandau, where a few thousand men were crammed into unheated stables and haylofts. Following negotiations by the International Committee of the Red Cross and neutral, especially American,

The SS *Sappho* leaving Gloucester on the Gloucester & Berkeley Canal.

diplomats there was some improvement in their conditions. It appears that Oscar was interned there for the duration of the war.

Lionel Edward Hamilton Marmaduke Darell, of Saul Lodge, Fretherne, the Brigade Major of the Gloucestershire, Warwickshire and Worcestershire Yeomanry, was attending a horse show at Henley-in-Arden when he received a telegram delivered by special messenger on the 3 August which read, 'Mobilise at once!' He quietly removed himself from the show and returned to Warwick Barracks to alert his troops. Many of the other Territorial regiments were also holding their annual camps and were similarly alerted. On Tuesday 4 August the United Kingdom formally declared war on Germany. Most people, and many politicians, thought that it would be over by Christmas.

On the military side, *Henry Francis Clifford and his groom, *Samuel Pitman, veterans of the Boer War and engaged with the Royal Gloucestershire Hussars Yeomanry, were embodied for service on 5 August. *Charles Alexander Weller, a recently qualified surgeon, enlisted with the Royal Army Medical Corps, while *Willoughby Thomas Eaketts, who was on the Reserve list following an earlier period of service, rejoined his regiment and arrived in France on 13 August. *Arthur David Berry followed him on 14 August – both men left behind a wife and baby.

Once the Territorials had been mobilised, and the British Expeditionary Force of one cavalry and four infantry divisions had crossed to France, the government launched a significant recruitment campaign spearheaded by Lord Kitchener. The newspapers regularly advertised for recruits, and among the first Frampton men to answer his call were *Thomas Henry Griffin who enlisted at Tewkesbury on 3 September, *Francis William Aldridge and *William George Birch. They joined together at Gloucester a few days later with consecutive service numbers,

The Three Horseshoes with Capener's tobacco shop adjoining to the north.

their names listed in the *Gloucester Journal* of 12 September printed as an encouragement to others to follow suit. All three served in the Gloucestershire Regiment, but it would be wrong to assume that all Frampton men went to the Glosters, which quickly became oversubscribed.

The Defence of the Realm Act was rushed through Parliament by 8 August, giving the government wide-ranging powers, in effect, to control the economy and regulate the lives of citizens. Central and regional committees of businessmen, politicians and civil servants were set up to control war work and agricultural production; Frampton's regional centre was in Bristol. Although nationally some businesses not serving the war effort closed, thus creating unemployment, Frampton seems not to have been directly affected beyond fundraising to help the unemployed. The Prince of Wales headed a relief fund for those out of work, and for the families of men who had joined the forces; at St Mary's the sermon on 23 August was on 'the present crisis' and the collection of £3 2s 2d was donated to the fund. Within a week, £1 million had been raised for distribution by local relief committees.

The *Gloucester Journal* retrospectively reported that the last anxious days of July had led some people to withdraw money from banks and to stockpile food. Nationally there was a rapid rise in the cost of food, and the government responded by fixing maximum prices for some key items. It seems unlikely that this had much significance for the rural parish of Frampton where many people were producing their own fruit and vegetables. They had ready access to meat and dairy products, and bread from the local bakers. The farm workers gathered in the harvest during the fine summer weather and John Dennis auctioned his potato crop at Manor Farm on 14 September in half-acre lots.

On the canal the *Lapwing* was requisitioned by the Admiralty. A German steamer which happened to be in Sharpness Dock was impounded and its cargo of fancy glass and musical instruments was sold off, local children apparently being the grateful recipients of mouth organs. More serious from a local perspective was the tragic drowning in the canal of the vicar of Falfield, the Reverend Wyndham Allan Chaplin, on Saturday 29 August. He had been cycling back after visiting the Reverend Lionel Ward at Frampton, and may have suffered an epileptic or cataleptic attack. The inquest, which was held at the vicarage, learned that the bridgekeeper's son *Frederick Robert William John Hitchings had assisted in getting the Reverend Chaplin out of 4 feet of water and on to the bank, and then attempted resuscitation (which he had apparently learnt as a boy scout) for twenty minutes until Dr Pinching arrived. The coroner commended Fred for his prompt actions which he said displayed great capability and sensibility. Fred Hitchings was a highly regarded pupil teacher at the school, but was later to lose his life in the war. The jury at the inquest gave their fees to the Prince of Wales' Relief Fund.

Families in Frampton began to adjust as their first few men enlisted. The village was used to the temporary absences of its watermen who were often away for days, or even weeks, at a time. Those whose sons and husbands had previously served or were in the Reserve were more familiar with military matters. Many of the new recruits were undergoing training at various locations in the UK. From the surviving records the impression gained is that, by and large, village life continued in much the same vein as before. *Henry Francis Clifford was served with

Pupils at the National School in 1914.

Back row: Naomi Halling, Emily Fredericks, Phyllis Aldridge, Lily Bateman, Phyllis Harris, Dorothy Hazell (pupil teacher), Harris, Tom Fredericks, Unknown, Unknown, Stella Wastonage (teacher), Baker, Bill Barge, Nelly Cook, Bert Davies, Harry Tainton.

Second row: Mary Pitman, Fred Longney, Dorothy McCullough, Will Purnell, Ruby Bateman, Joe Herbert, William 'Sonny' Harris.

Front row: Bill Fredericks, Allen, Arthur Barge, George Travell, Harry Herbert, Bill Guy.

compulsory requisition documents by the government in respect of land required for the extraction of gravels and sands, but there was no immediate action. The harvest collection at the chapel went to the Gloucester Royal Infirmary as usual, and at the beginning of the autumn term school life appears to have settled into its normal routine.

The school's logbook for September does not reflect the war, although the children later raised 10s for Christmas presents for the troops. There was a serious outbreak of scarlet fever which had started at the beginning of April, and the medical officer suggested disinfecting the school and limewashing its walls during the summer holidays. The beginning of the autumn term brought no let-up in the spread of the disease. Three cottages were disinfected by the authorities during the first fortnight of September, and four during the following two weeks. This pattern continued, and the school was disinfected again in early December.

The individual involvement of Frampton's servicemen during the war remains largely undiscovered, but *Arthur Harry Sutton, whose wife Bessie returned to Frampton with their children to live with her parents, William James Hart Brinkworth and Patience Elizabeth née Williams, in Hart's Cottages, was awarded the Distinguished Conduct Medal in the field in September. Later Arthur received it from the king, George V, on one of his visits to the troops in France. The citation for Corporal Sutton, who served with the Royal Field Artillery and was later promoted to Battery-Sergeant-Major, read: 'For gallantry and good work

The Eaketts family lived in one of these cottages on The Green.

throughout the campaign. On two occasions he repaired the telephone under heavy shell and rifle fire.'

*Willoughby Thomas Eaketts was taken prisoner at Ypres on 29 October while serving with the Gloucestershire Regiment. His parents lived at or near Nastfield Cottage on the village green, although his wife and child were in Gloucester during this part of the war. The Red Cross had established the International Prisoners of War Agency in Geneva in late August, and this kept lists of prisoners' names and records of their capture, as well as transfers between camps and deaths in detention. The agency received thousands of requests for information submitted by relatives of missing men, and it endeavoured to restore contact between internees and their loved ones at home. The Eaketts must have been able to stay in touch, for a photograph of Willoughby, apparently taken on 29 August 1915, appeared in the *Gloucester Journal* on 27 January 1917.

The weather turned very wet during the autumn which, while not good for Frampton, was disastrous for the growing lines of trenches on the Western Front which quickly accumulated water. The muddy conditions caused trench foot and sufferers added to the increasing numbers of casualties from the battlefields. In anticipation of gunshot wounds soldiers carried a basic field dressing, two gauze dressings, cotton wool, and a bandage in a waterproof bag, although this would not have been large enough to cover a shrapnel wound. Larger dressings were carried in a haversack by stretcher bearers such as *Peter Gandy. There were sixteen to a battalion, of whom one was trained in basic first aid.

Almost from the outset women volunteered to supplement the Army's medical services, which were under-resourced, under-equipped and quickly overwhelmed by the huge numbers of casualties. Voluntary organisations such as the British Red Cross Society, the Order of St John of Jerusalem and Voluntary Aid Detachments stepped in, providing hospitals, equipment and staff in France and at home. Lord Kitchener appealed for funds to purchase motor ambulances (of which the Army had none), and by December 250 had been bought.

The Red Cross and Order of St John nurses operated from casualty clearing stations, based a few miles behind the Front, out of artillery range. For the most part they were situated at road junctions or railway sidings, so that the seriously injured could be transported back to the base hospitals. At the casualty clearing station the battalion's medical officer divided the wounded into one of three categories. First were those with injuries that could be treated and the soldier quickly returned to the Front. (Army policy was to return even more seriously wounded to their units as soon as possible.) Second were those requiring treatment at base hospitals, and third, those considered to be beyond hope, for which no treatment was provided. Two Clifford sisters, Edith Katherine and Mabel Constance, went to France where they presumably experienced many of the horrors and frustrations later described in Vera Brittain's memoir *Testament of Youth*.

Edith was forty-six when war broke out and, in addition to being a trained nurse, had the notable advantage of speaking fluent French. Her nursing career had given her experience in a London hospital and also as a district nurse. She left for France in September receiving no salary, but her expenses were to be paid. She served at a Red Cross hospital installed in a chateau owned by an American lady at Longueil-Annel, north of Compiègne, on the Western Front. Edith wore a badge bearing the Red Cross together with the name of the chateau and the

Edith Katherine Clifford.

American flag in recognition of its owner. No specific details of her work are known, but she would have been caring for a continuous stream of wounded soldiers, something that required an unstinting devotion to duty. At the end of the war Edith was awarded the highest class of the Medal of French Gratitude by the French government, having 'rendered splendid services at the front and on the lines of communication from October 1914 to January 1919'.

Her forty-year-old sister Mabel also nursed at a Red Cross hospital, possibly with Edith at Longueil-Annel, although she had no previous nursing experience. Also fluent in French, she was awarded the Croix de Guerre. It is thought that this recognised the heroic contribution that she made during the evacuation of the hospital in which she was serving when the German invasion swept through. She was also awarded the Victory Medal. Mabel's devout and kindly disposition would no doubt have been welcomed by the soldiers and her fellow nurses, away from home, and amid the battlefields of the Western Front.

The Gloucestershire newspapers of the final four months of 1914 contain many references to shorter opening hours for shops, which had traditionally stayed open well into the evening. There had previously been a national movement to reduce the hours, and the war gave this impetus, at first citing the need for men to have time to train with the Territorials. As men enlisted and women took their places within the local economy, the natural progression was to reduce opening hours so that they could return home to provide for their families at suppertime. Shorter opening hours were eventually reinforced by a Home Office order in 1918, and so the war achieved for workers what years of trade union pressure and agitation had failed to secure. All this was particularly relevant in towns and cities, although in Frampton no doubt the close-knit community found ways of coping and helping each other out. Most traders lived at their premises, and so customers calling out of hours would have proved to be little more than an inconvenience.

Mabel Constance Clifford.

3

1915

POLITICAL SUMMARY

As the autumn of 1914 passed it became clear that the war would not be over by Christmas and the Western Front stabilised. The only way the generals envisaged breaking the deadlock was to get more men. Volunteers continued to enlist, but this was creating many problems. Men with vital skills essential to industrial production were enlisting and output suffered. Training and apprenticeship in skilled trades like engineering were controlled by the trades unions who were extremely reluctant to allow 'dilution'; that is to allow semi-skilled or unskilled men (or women) to take on jobs previously reserved for skilled men. Growing talk of shell shortages brought some local agreements between employers and unions, and in March 1915 Lloyd George convened a meeting with union leaders at which they agreed to give up the right to strike, accept arbitration in any dispute with employers and, most importantly, to accept dilution on condition that the process was controlled by them and was entirely voluntary. The resulting Treasury Agreement showed the government's recognition that the war could only be won with labour cooperation, a characteristic of Lloyd George's approach.

Criticisms of munitions shortages continued in the press and among backbench MPs. This led Asquith to reconstruct the government in May 1915. He formed a coalition with the Conservatives and Labour based on a five-man War Committee of two Liberals, two Conservatives and the Labour party leader, Arthur Henderson. Lloyd George became the Minister of Munitions.

The new government had no more success than the old. Military setbacks in the summer at Gallipoli and on the Western Front brought growing pressure for conscription, particularly in the Conservative press and from back benchers, and finally the War Committee agreed to conscription being enacted in January 1916.

1915 also brought deeper social change as increasing numbers of women took jobs to fill the gaps left by men, famously on the land, but also in munitions factories and as bus conductresses, and in many other jobs too; far fewer women were employed as domestic servants.

MILITARY OVERVIEW

With the German Army occupied on two major fronts and British volunteer recruitment progressing well, British forces started to take over additional stretches of the Western Front from the French. It was decided to mount an offensive in March to capture Neuve-Chapelle. Extensive aerial photo-reconnaissance and an intensive artillery barrage allowed British and Indian troops, supported by the first Canadian units to see action, to break through the German trenches. However, communication difficulties, ammunition shortages and delays in bringing up reinforcements allowed the Germans to recover and plug the gap: this would provide a pattern for too many such initiatives.

Meanwhile, an attempt by the French and British navies to open a southern sea route to Russia from the Mediterranean, through the narrow strait of the Dardanelles to the Black Sea, was defeated by the loss of capital ships to Turkish mines and German submarines. The Allied landings at Gallipoli in April, which saw the Australian and New Zealand Army Corps (ANZAC) in their first major campaign, were intended both to threaten Constantinople (then the Turkish capital) and to allow ships to pass. However, the brave and determined Turkish defence, combined with Allied failures to quickly press home their advantage, resulted in another stalemate, this time with only a few miles of indefensible barren ground to show for it. On the other hand, the withdrawal of Allied forces was planned and executed impeccably, with no losses to enemy action.

In May the Italians declared war on Austria-Hungary, with a view to seizing territory in the Tyrol and Slovenia, but made no progress despite bitter fighting in the high Alps, including the use of shells to bring down avalanches on opponents. On the Eastern Front, Russia was compelled to retreat from Poland. Late in the year Bulgaria joined in the attacks on Serbia which resulted in the occupation of the country by the Central Powers, despite the landing at Salonika in Greece of a Franco-British Expeditionary Force in (somewhat belated) support.

The second Battle of Ypres in April and May was a German offensive opened by the first use of poison gas, chlorine, against French and Canadian positions, but was only partially successful; the British offensive at Loos in September was the first to use aircraft to bomb ground targets, and was a total failure.

FRAMPTON ON SEVERN

It was a bitterly cold winter. A special service for the National Day of Intercessions was held on 3 January at St Mary's and most of the collection was given to the Red Cross. This was the year of Frampton's first war casualties. *Walter Henry Tainton was killed at Sanctuary Wood during the Second Battle of Ypres on 12 May, *Alfred Staplehurst on 23 July while serving in Gallipoli, and *Joseph Charles Cottle on 9 August when his battalion successfully restored the line around Hooge. *Samuel Pitman died in November following a period of poor health after contracting pneumonia and pleurisy during Army training the previous year.

St Mary's church, *c.* 1909.

According to the *Gloucester Journal*, by the end of 1914 between 750 and 1,000 Belgian refugees seeking asylum had come to Gloucestershire. The need to house them touched Frampton; on 4 January the headmaster noted the admission of eight Belgian refugee children. He recorded that he could not formally include them on the register as he had not received instructions regarding their registration. The refugees almost certainly represented one single unit, for often their families were large and it was difficult for find homes that kept members together. Nevertheless, some or all of them were accommodated at The Lake, in a cottage belonging to Miss Hobbs; the Inspector of Nuisances paid a routine visit on 11 January and found that all was well.

Voluntary Aid Detachment hospitals were established in Stroud, Nailsworth and Gloucester, as well as at Standish House, which had been empty in 1914. An open day there on Easter Monday 1915 attracted over 700 local residents and they were, of course, asked for contributions towards its conversion and upkeep. Standish VAD Hospital opened on 13 May 1915 and the first thirty-one wounded soldiers came by train from a hospital in Bristol. The three ground-floor wards, Berkeley, Painswick and Dursley, accommodated the most seriously wounded, including amputees. The second floor had wards for convalescing patients and the third floor housed the operating theatres. Eight professional nursing sisters and one residential medical officer were supported by no fewer than seventy VAD volunteers including, from Frampton, Elaine Annie Clifford and Dr Pinching.

Elaine (a younger sister of Edith and Mabel) was twenty-eight when she began her part-time service at Standish in June 1915. Having had no previous experience, she initially received basic nursing training. Volunteer duties at Standish were varied, and may have also included helping patients to write letters home. By February 1919 Elaine had given 2,075 unpaid hours and was later awarded the British Red Cross war medal. Among those men cared for at Standish

Elaine Annie Clifford.

was *Charles Henry Phipps, a Frampton man who served primarily with the Machine Gun Corps (Cavalry) in Mesopotamia. It must have aided his recovery tremendously to be near his home and among medical and nursing staff that he knew. During these last stages of his convalescence his wife, Edith, was able to visit him regularly, often staying in nearby bed and breakfast accommodation so that she could see him on the following day as well.

By the end of the war 2,292 soldiers had been treated at Standish, and many were then transferred to Newark Park to convalesce. Voluntary organisations also cared for men invalided out of service, for whom the Army had no provision for continuing treatment or rehabilitation. VAD homes were set up providing support and workshops where a trade could be learnt.

In April, the parish council considered a letter from the police requesting that a parish notice board be erected in a prominent position for the purpose of displaying government notices. The board was duly made by Dennis Barrett, who was paid £1 5s 6d. He also received a ground rent of 1s per annum for the board to stand on premises in his occupation; the family rented Severnthorpe on The Green. The parish council accounts show several entries for the purchase of paste for the notices. There would have been plenty of these, no doubt covering recruitment, food saving and patriotic government propaganda.

In July, pupil teacher *Frederick Robert William John Hitchings volunteered for service, a huge blow to the school where he was considered a great asset by the teaching staff. He was, of course, not the only Frampton man to enlist during 1915; four days earlier, in Brisbane, Australia, *Thomas Hart Brinkworth had answered the call to serve in support of his homeland. *Archibald Edward Cook and *Raymond Cook (not believed to be closely related) signed up to the Royal Naval Reserve within days of each other at the end of August, while *William James George Daw and *William Joseph Ernest Gleed had made their way to

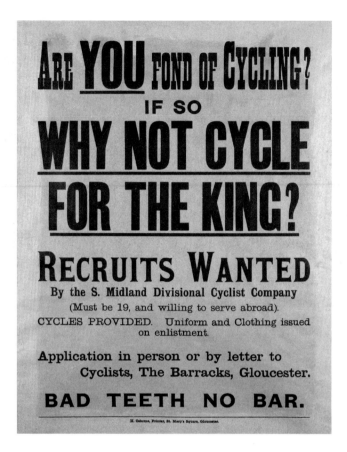

Gloucester on the same day in June (presumably together) and found themselves respectively in the Royal Flying Corps and Army Service Corps. These were by no means the only men to leave Frampton in 1915; a sense of duty propelled plenty of others into life in the Armed Forces.

The war had another significant effect on village life when work on the new Cadbury Brothers' factory began. Cadbury's required large quantities of raw milk to support its successful range of products. By 1914 these numbered over 700, and it seems likely that the decision to build the new factory in Frampton may have been taken before the war. Frampton was relatively central and accessible to the dairy farms of the Berkeley Vale where the milk was rich and plentiful. The village's proximity to the canal could facilitate easy transport of processed milk to Cadbury's main factory at Bournville, Birmingham. Although it is not specifically recorded, the building of the Frampton factory must have involved an influx of skilled and unskilled labour into the village.

Under the Defence of the Realm Act, land was purchased to the north of Fretherne Bridge and building work began in February 1915. The site included a small grain warehouse and some ten acres of orchards. A new wharf and covered causeway were built beside the warehouse, with a milk dock to accept canal barges. The milk processing plant had a large storage basement to help keep the milk cool. Coal-fired boilers provided steam for heating vats for the milk-processing and for

Looking north towards the site for the new Cadbury's factory *c.* 1912.

electric generators, the coal coming up the canal from Sharpness. The existing small warehouse, which had previously been used to store corn destined for Fromebridge Mill, was used by the builders as a machine workshop, and when the factory opened in 1916 this became the works mess room with a cook to prepare meals. Cadbury's also bought Kimberley House from *David George Herbert's father, James, for the factory foreman, John Wellings. Perhaps a less well-known fact concerned the proposed toilet facilities. According to the journal of the local Inspector of Nuisances, the architect for Cadbury's advised that the factory did not intend to have any drainage and that the lavatories, consisting of earth closets, would be some distance away.

Demand had grown for the production of munitions, and by mid-September a site in Naas Lane, Quedgeley, just west of the railway, had been chosen for a new shell-filling factory. Wet weather and labour shortages delayed some of the construction work that employed 1,100 men at its peak. It is not certain whether any of these came from Frampton, but it is entirely possible.

In parallel there was a national requirement to increase facilities for the storage of explosives and propellants and, at first, this had been met through the use of quarries, mines, caves and disused forts. A site was chosen south of Shepherd's Patch, Slimbridge, being relatively isolated and considered beyond the reach of air raids. Good communication with filling stations could be achieved by canal and rail links; it would be particularly convenient to support the Quedgeley filling factory. The sitting tenants were evicted in December (causing them much subsequent financial hardship), to allow work on the store to begin. A rail link was established to the main line at Gossington Bridge, and to the canal at Shepherd's Patch. At least three contractors were used in the construction of the site, placing an even greater demand on the local labour force.

On Tuesday 12 January a fire broke out in a two-storey builder's workshop in Frampton belonging to Frederick Walford Vick, a plumber and house repairer, causing about £80 worth of damage. The Gloucester City Fire Brigade was called to the scene at about 2 a.m., to find that villagers were already trying to extinguish the flames with buckets of water. The firemen pumped water from one of the ponds on the village green to bring the fire under control and were able to return to Gloucester a couple of hours later.

Meanwhile more cases of scarlet fever were reported and some of diphtheria too. Given the state and size of some of the cottages in the village, this had become a serious problem. On 26 February Wheatenhurst Rural District Council made closing orders on several cottages at Ward's Court, in the ownership or trusteeship of Richard Ward, as being unfit for habitation. These were situated along the lane behind Ward's shop. One of them was the home of *Frederick Hill whose children were temporarily taken into the workhouse at Eastington during March. Hill later explained his hope that the house would be finished by the end of April. He withdrew his children shortly afterwards, presumably to return home, but his youngest child was admitted back to the workhouse for medical treatment in June. In April the Inspector of Nuisances was concerned about the squalid conditions of four of the five cottages now known as School Row, The Street, and then owned by Thomas Turner of Slowwe Farm, Arlingham, which he thought were unfit for habitation. One was empty, but the rest were lived in. On 7 May the rural district council ordered notices to be served, but almost two years later, in January 1917, it was still discussing one of the cottages, a two-roomed dwelling housing two adults and eight children which was supposed to have been extended. However, finding a contractor to undertake building work was not straightforward; businesses such as Samuel Bradley's were running on a reducing labour force as men left to serve their country.

THE GREEN. LOWER FRAMPTON N° 54

Advowsons farmhouse (left), Ward's shop and Gleed's bakery (right).

During April the Inspector of Nuisances carried out routine visits to the four village bakeries and noted that one needed limewashing. The slaughterhouses of both Arthur Ernest Lewis and *William Thomas Hodder were not considered clean and were also in need of a coat of limewash. The following month it was the tailor's shop of parish council chairman, Frederick Alexander Franklin, that did not pass muster and attracted a limewash notice. All the business premises in Frampton and the surrounding villages appear to have been visited in turn and many of the tenanted properties: at the end of July all the cottages at Fromebridge successfully came through inspection. The inspector was also responsible for issuing notices regarding foul privies and uncovered cesspits, and for ensuring that the Buckholdt and Narles ditches were properly maintained.

In March, Herbert Stephens, the tenant of the Bell Hotel, auctioned his live and dead farming stock, including thirteen head of Shorthorn cattle, four young and promising mares and geldings, three sows, thirty pigs and thirteen store pigs, together with various utensils and implements. He was moving on, and all the requisites of his posting establishment such as carriages and harness were also for sale, as well as the contents of the billiard room, four upright clocks and his household furniture. George Frederick Holloway took his place and advertised as 'Ye Olde Bell'. He offered good stabling and a motor car for hire, with parties catered for and luncheons, dinners and teas. In August, as part of the war effort, licensing hours were greatly reduced; public houses could only open from noon until 2.30 p.m., and from 6 p.m. to 9 p.m., and beer strength was weakened. No doubt this had a financial impact on those owning and working in Frampton's pubs and beer houses. Although the licensees at the Three Horseshoes, Heart of Oak and True Heart remained the same, there was a change at the New Inn, but it has not been possible to say whether this was due to the economics of the shorter opening hours.

The Bell Hotel Frampton.

The Bishop of Gloucester paid a visit to the school and to St Mary's on 3 June, calling attention to the church's prayer book, which had become old and out of date. The vicar, writing in the magazine which at that time jointly served the parishes of Coaley, Fretherne, Frampton and Lower Cam, asked for donations towards a replacement but, perhaps with more pressing demands on spare funds, the parishioners of Frampton did not respond, and on 30 January 1916 he devoted the collection to paying for the replacement. The Reverend Ward also drew attention to the 600th anniversary of the consecration of St Mary's by Bishop Walter Maidstone of Worcester in July 1315. He rued the fact that, in view of the war, it was not possible to mark the occasion as parishioners would have liked, but nevertheless said that they would have an opportunity to reflect on this milestone during their dedication festival in August.

On 26 July, an inquest was held at the Institute following the death of Emma, the sixty-five-year-old mother of *William Thomas Hodder, who had died unexpectedly. Dr Pinching attributed her death to natural causes for she had gone to bed as usual and had a peaceful night's sleep before waking with a peculiarity in her breathing. The Deputy-Coroner returned the verdict accordingly.

On 2 August, the Berkeley Hunt Agricultural Society's annual show was held as usual with the committee deciding to devote all the profits to the Allies' Agricultural Relief Fund. In the event, the wet bank holiday weather proved disastrous financially, although competition entries for both livestock and produce 'lost nothing of their keenness through the year of strife and anxiety'. Entries were generally only marginally down, despite a 50 per cent drop in the number of young farmer entries as men took up their duties elsewhere. There was an advance from eighteen to sixty-six in the milking competition due to the inclusion of dairymaids. Cider exhibits were also more numerous; the reporter in the *Gloucester Journal* put this down to the war tax on beer awakening the makers

MANOR FARM, FRAMPTON F20.

of pure, unadulterated cider to greater possibilities. Once again, John Dennis of Manor Farm proved successful showing his mare and foal.

One month later, John Dennis was auctioning nine valuable Shire mares, geldings and foals, six Hackney fillies and geldings and the well-known Shire stallion, 'Lockinge Norbury'. Its seems as though the requisitioning of horses for the Army was not particularly affecting his business, although several other Frampton farmers, and the carrier Frank Selwyn Betteridge, are understood to have taken to hiding their best animals when they knew that the requisitioning officers were in the district. Such horses were, of course, desperately needed at home for farm work and transport. When the officers called at Denfurlong Farm they did not take any horses, but they did requisition a new hayrick. The Cooles' hay was labelled so that it would be properly paid for and later, when *Richard William Rowles was serving in France, he came across hay labelled 'Edgar Coole – Frampton on Severn'. (*Robert Edgar Coole later became one of the village's youngest servicemen having been born in April 1900.)

The Board of Agriculture initiated the establishment of county War Agricultural Committees with a view to increasing the output of wheat and other food products. On 24 September the rural district council was charged with setting up a sub-committee comprising four of its own members and eight farmers resident in the area. One of those was Charles Edward Williams of Church Farm, Frampton.

The number of volunteer recruits was dwindling. On 15 July the government passed the National Registration Act which required all men between the ages of fifteen and sixty-five not already in the military to register and provide details of their employment. The results became available by mid-September and a month

William Wood's workshop and yard.

later Lord Derby introduced a new recruitment programme, the Group Scheme. It appears that a mobile attestation unit visited Frampton on 15 November where *Francis Henry Franklin was among those attesting. *Thomas George Halling, *Frank Weaver and *Walter Gymer also volunteered during November and December although their attestation records have not survived.

The year drew to its close with one of the coldest Novembers in local records, during which the vicar's wife, Joan Jessie Ward, placed an advertisement for domestic help: 'Wanted, general, superior, middle-aged preferred; two in family, country vicarage; man for boots, etc'. In 1911, when the Reverend Ward had still been single, his household was completed by a housekeeper and female domestic servant. He had married Jessie in 1913, at the age of forty-eight.

On 13 December Gloucester County Court heard the case of the Gloucester Railway Carriage & Wagon Co. Ltd, which had made an application for a review of the compensation they were paying to William David Daw of Beehive Cottage, The Street, in respect of the loss of his eye while he had been working for them in March. His former employer's suspicions were aroused when his wife started collecting the weekly payments, and their enquiries found that he was working for William Wood, the Frampton carpenter and undertaker. There were five children at home under the age of ten at this time, so it was important to be able to continue work and bring in sufficient earnings. The Wagon Works challenged his degree of incapacity, and the court ordered a reduction in his weekly payments from 19s 1d to 5s, stating that although Daw (who wore a glass eye) was clearly 'a damaged lot', he could, nevertheless, still carry out a certain degree of work with his new employer.

4

1916

POLITICAL SUMMARY

1916 brought a series of problems: the Dublin Easter Rising, the inconclusive Battle of Jutland (31 May–1 June), the death of Lord Kitchener on 5 June (he was replaced as Secretary for War by Lloyd George) and the Battle of the Somme, which achieved nothing at immense cost. This failure provoked further criticism of the government in the autumn, especially from the right, which considered that Asquith was not capable of the rapid and imaginative decision making and leadership needed, a view that Lloyd George came to share. The complex discussions and meetings which followed are still the subject of controversy among historians, but the result was that Lloyd George replaced Asquith as prime minister on 7 December. He was backed by the Conservatives and about half the Liberals, causing a division and bitterness in that party which was never effectively healed.

While Asquith's War Committee had referred major decisions to the full Cabinet, Lloyd George's War Cabinet of five had full executive power, meeting every day and with secretarial support. New ministries for agriculture, shipping, propaganda and food headed by businessmen were generally successful. Guaranteed prices encouraged grain production, and food prices were controlled. The ministries of labour and pensions went to Labour MPs, highlighting the vital role of the working class in the economy and the war effort.

MILITARY OVERVIEW

The year opened with the effective stabilisation of the Allied positions on the Suez Canal and the Balkan Front, and major Russian gains from Turkey in the Caucasus, but British and Indian forces were besieged at Kut al-Amara, near Baghdad, and eventually had to surrender. Later, relief forces started a push up the Tigris and Euphrates rivers which would end in the taking of Babylon. British troops also took the offensive in Palestine, and T. E. Lawrence raised the Arab tribes to revolt against the Turks.

On the Eastern Front, a Russian offensive against Austria-Hungary made considerable gains, but civil unrest in Russia prevented any follow-up. Meanwhile, Romania entered the war on the side of the Allies. However, their initial success soon turned sour, and Bucharest fell before the end of the year.

1916 saw the one major naval encounter of the war, when at Jutland the Royal Navy retained control of the seas, despite losing more ships than the Germans and not delivering a knockout blow. The failure of the German Fleet to break out resulted in much more emphasis on submarine warfare, leading to the torpedoing of the RMS *Lusitania* and the eventual entry of the United States into the war.

On the Western Front, the German Army launched an assault on the French fortress of Verdun in February that was intended to 'bleed France white', although in fact both sides suffered similar losses. One effect was that the French could not join British and Empire troops in the Somme offensive, but both campaigns dragged on, causing huge numbers of casualties with no significant gain to either side. The aerial war was much more dynamic, with technological advances, such as the ability to fire machine guns through the propeller arc, giving each side the advantage in turn.

FRAMPTON ON SEVERN

Through his regular writings in the parish magazine, Reverend Ward encouraged everyone to do as much as they could for the war effort; many war-related

The Street looking north *c.* 1915 with the Institute in the background.

fundraising activities and meetings were held in the church Institute. Among his recommendations were rigid economy, and investment of savings in the Government's War Loan. He had called for people to unite in prayer on New Year's Eve, New Year's Day and the first Sunday in January, which had been set apart for prayer, humility and self-denial. An additional service of evensong with intercessions was held on 2 January, and the collections from all three days were given to the Joint Committee of the Order of St John and the British Red Cross Society.

With mounting casualties and Allied setbacks at Gallipoli, Loos and Verdun, the government finally introduced conscription in January 1916, initially just for single men between the ages of eighteen and forty-one, but extended to married men in June. By the end of the war the upper age limit had been increased to fifty-one. Firms like Fielding & Platt Ltd in Gloucester, who manufactured their first extrusion presses to make shell cases for the munitions industry in 1916, had already lost employees, such as *Wilfred Harris Gabb, who had volunteered in 1914. The government needed to ensure that such businesses could retain key workers and maintain the level of supply demanded. There was no definitive list of reserved occupations; it was often necessary to attend local tribunals to obtain exemption certificates for key workers.

Conscription caused problems on the local farms. Notes relating to the exemption application for nineteen-year-old Robert Chandler Eric Dowdeswell, a carter of Netherhills Farm, Fromebridge, are a rare survival from which we learn that his fifty-nine-year-old father, also named Robert, was farming 214 acres, of which fifty-one were arable. They kept twenty-two cows for cheese and butter and a further thirty cattle for meat. Before war broke out, four men had been employed; they had all enlisted, and there was now only one man left (who was not able-bodied) and one attested man (who was expecting to be called up). The tribunal heard that Robert Dowdeswell senior's eldest daughter could only work in the house, and that two of his other daughters were agricultural labourers (presumably on war work elsewhere), while the youngest was still at school. His son was looking after the fourteen horses. Robert Dowdeswell junior's exemption certificate ran from 21 March and expired on 29 September as the tribunal did not consider him entirely indispensable. Coincidentally, John James Broad of Advowsons Farm sold his livestock on the same day as the tribunal, and it appears that the Dowdeswell family may have been the purchasers. When September came round the attested man was on active service, forty-two more acres of pasture had been taken on, farming operations included a further forty cattle and forty to fifty sheep, and two daughters were helping to milk and feed the calves. Robert's exemption was renewed again. The tenant at Advowsons by this time was A. Dowdeswell, presumably a relative.

At Denfurlong, William Coole's eldest son, also William, was evidently also granted exemption, although his two younger sons, *Frederick and *Robert Edgar had to enlist, the latter only attaining the necessary age in April 1918. Their farm of at least 176 acres was predominantly pasture with just twenty acres of arable and would also have required a considerable amount of manual labour.

Conscription tested the beliefs of some, and conscientious objectors began to file applications for exemption. Only the scant tribunal notes for *William Henry

William and Lydia Coole with their children William, May, Doris and *Robert Edgar.

Stone of The Lake survive. His case was heard on 31 March when he advised that he had started to have objections to war from about November 1914, but that he did not belong to the Society of Friends (Quakers) or any similar denomination. His case was not considered genuine, his application was dismissed and he was given no right to appeal. The British Army had no precedents or guidelines for conscription prior to the First World War, so men like William Stone had to be considered. Many conscientious objectors were conscripted into the Non-Combatant Corps and served in roles which required physical labour, but not the movement of munitions. There were others who refused to serve altogether; they were court-martialled and imprisoned.

Albert Edward Travell of Vicarage Lane worked at Sharpness for a firm engaged in ship repairs and marine engineering, the Cardiff Channel Dry Docks & Pontoon Co. Ltd. He was attested at Berkeley where the officer objected to his request for exemption. However, the Thornbury tribunal found that Albert was already in a starred occupation. As he kept the tool store and was the only man left in that job, he was given conditional exemption.

Conscription caused many from Frampton to enlist, including *Frederick William Phillips Hazell, *William Thomas Hodder and *George Pragnell, who at four inches below the minimum military height, and with defective hearing and asthma, was nevertheless sent for training until a medical examination ruled him out and he was discharged, although it seems that he was later re-conscripted.

On 24 February, a meeting was held in the Institute at 8 p.m. to encourage women to work on the land and follow the example of their counterparts in France. Those present were told that the shortage of men at home was increasing,

BOARD OF TRADE.   BOARD OF AGRICULTURE.

AN APPEAL TO ALL WOMEN

ALL Englishwomen want to help their Country. The Country needs the help of every woman.

HOW ARE YOU HELPING TO WIN THE WAR? WHAT MORE CAN YOU DO? READ THIS AND THINK IT OVER.

England MUST keep up and Increase her Food Supply

It is the Farmers of England to whom we look to do this. But at the same time Farm Labourers have been called away in their thousands to serve their King and Country elsewhere. What are the Farmers to do? How can they answer their Country's call, if they have not enough men to work their Farms? They can only do it with your help. Your Country needs **your** help. Give it willingly and prove that the Women of England can help their Country with as good heart as can those of any other nation.

THESE ARE SOME OF THE WAYS IN WHICH EVERY WOMAN LIVING IN OUR VILLAGES CAN HELP.

1. — You can see to it that your own **gardens and allotments** are better worked and better managed than ever before, and help a neighbour whose husband has gone to the War if she cannot manage her garden by herself.
2. — You can see to it that there is no **waste of fruit**, wild or garden, or of **vegetables** that you can prevent.
3. — Some of you can keep pigs and **poultry** and so increase our **home made food** supplies.
4. — You can help on the farms if needed. If you cannot work all day you may be able to work part of every day. Some of you can milk once or twice a day. Some of you can give your time to be trained to take a man's place.
5. — If you cannot work yourselves, you may be able to mind the children of someone who can.

All can do something. See to it that your name is entered on the Register, which is to be kept in every village, of the Women willing to do their bit of War Service.

French Women are doing all the work of their Farms even where shells are bursting close to them.

It must not be laid to the door of Englishwomen that, because the men have left to fight for them and for their children, fewer cows are kept, fewer chickens reared, fewer potatoes grown and less land ploughed and sown so that in consequence food becomes dearer.

COME FORWARD AND DO YOUR BIT.

Printed for H.M. Stationery Office by Waterlow Bros. & Layton, Limited, Birchin Lane, London, E.C.   (71843) 50000 1-16

and that it was soon going to be necessary for women to offer themselves as replacements. All women in the district were to be canvassed and asked to volunteer for work of some kind. Under the chairmanship of Mr Granville Lloyd-Baker, this meeting took place almost a year before the establishment of Women's County War Agricultural Committees.

Government lighting regulations forced a change in the time of evensong which, from 20 February, was held at 3 p.m. instead of 6.30 p.m. British Summer Time, with a one-hour change, was introduced between 21 May and 1 October to make the most of daylight. The opinions of headmasters were later sought as to whether this had adversely affected schoolchildren. The Frampton school logbook is silent on the matter, so it is safe to assume that the pupils were not among those few in the county who had apparently appeared somewhat tired and restless during school on account of the change in their sleeping hours.

The education authorities took the question of health seriously, and references to head lice (pediculosis) feature often in the school's logbook. A particularly bad case involved the children of *George Harris, who returned to school on 15 March after a four month exclusion. The family's problems continued the following year, as Clara Harris was fined 30s at Whitminster Petty Sessions on 8 November 1917 for allowing her three children to be in a 'verminous condition', their heads being infected once again.

Communication to and from the village was boosted when the first telephones arrived around this time. Four Frampton numbers were listed at the Saul Exchange: Cadbury 12, Cliffords 11, W. Cook (carrier) 5 and the Post Office 10.

On 24 March Cadbury's application for a petroleum licence was considered by the rural district council and adjourned on the grounds that their factory had not yet been finished. Cadbury's did, in fact, begin milk processing on 1 April, employing local people who were initially supported by existing staff from Bournville. Milk came into the factory every day. Farmers near the factory brought theirs in by horse and cart, and one individual carried two bucketfuls a day by push-bike. Others left their milk in churns at agreed locations along the canal, from where they were collected by boats and replaced by clean, empty ones. Elsewhere, Cadbury's lorries collected and returned churns. In place of the conscripted men, women cleaned and washed the churns and stirred the milk in heated vats.

Churns arriving at Cadbury's by boat in 1916.

The factory's purpose was to pasteurise the milk to kill germs, so that it would keep longer and could be safely transported to Bournville. Milk was moved quickly from the dock to the storage basement beneath the milk processing plant. Without refrigeration, a cool basement was the best way to store the milk. From here it was filtered and moved to open vats in the processing plant. The vats had pipes coiled around them through which steam from the power plant circulated and heated the milk to just below boiling point in order to avoid curdling. The foaming milk was gently stirred during the heating until it was pasteurised. Another benefit of heating was that, since 80 per cent of raw milk is water, the evaporation of one third of the water significantly reduced the cost of transport to Bournville.

The official opening of Cadbury's factory took place on 22 June in persistent rain. From a report in the July copy of the *Bournville Works Magazine*, we learn that thirty-eight officials and members of staff travelled by train from Bournville and London. At Cheltenham station, chocolate was distributed to some soldiers who were on their way to Egypt. On reaching Gloucester, the party boarded the steam boat *River Queen*, which had been specially chartered. The inclement weather made the eating of lunch 'a rather strenuous business'. The magazine's account delightfully records how the wind played havoc with the straw hats, serviettes and umbrellas of the dignitaries. In particular, sudden gusts of wind caused their hats to knock over glasses of lemonade, and some even ended up in the salad and jelly, or were blown overboard. Only a few members of the party were fortunate enough to lunch below deck.

This bad weather seems to have been a feature of 1916 and resulted in many of the absences noted in the school's logbook. Gale force winds and heavy snow disrupted transport and telegraphs in late March and, later in the year, heavy rain caused disease in the potato crop resulting in shortages which drove up prices.

The number of Frampton men and women who were employed at The National Filling Factory No. 5 Quedgeley is unknown, although *John Millard, *George Pragnell and George Dark (father of *George Edward and *Stephen John) were all munitions workers at various times. Production started in early March and 2,113 women and 307 men were employed by June. The workforce increased steadily over the next three months, but a scare regarding TNT poisoning led to a temporary reduction. The work was unpleasant and this, together with shortages of raw materials due to enemy submarine action, meant that numbers fluctuated throughout the war. Initially workers were recruited from Gloucester and the villages nearby. The pay of £1 per week was comparatively low, and immediately disputed. A penny increase to the hourly rate brought it up to about £1 5s 6d, and the effect of this was discussed at the rural district council on 7 April. The council reported to the Board of Trade that the increase had precipitated an upward trend in wages, though at the time of their meeting the effects were only just being felt. The factory at Quedgeley made no allowance in respect of travelling, although permitted to do so.

The Slimbridge munitions depot, known officially as 'His Majesty's Magazine No. 23, Gloucester', was operational by July, with the first consignment of cordite being received on 5 September. Staffing levels are unclear, but the

Dursley Gazette of 30 November 1918 refers to 'a large number of hands'. More accessible to Frampton than the Quedgeley factory, villagers had certainly been involved during the construction phase; Francis Charles Gardner, who lived close to Fretherne Bridge, had mixed concrete there. He claimed, however, that the work had exacerbated an injury he had received previously while working for Messrs Ashbee, Sons & Co., timber merchants on the Bristol Road at Gloucester, and he gave up the job at Slimbridge. In the county court on 10 April he asked for an award under the Workmen's Compensation Act following the stoppage of his original compensation from Messrs Ashbee, who felt he was shamming. To ascertain the extent of the injury to his wrist and arm, fifty-one-year-old Gardner had been put under anaesthetic and given an X-ray. There was some discussion about whether he was left- or right-handed, and if indeed he was fit to work. Dr Pinching was among the five doctors who gave evidence. The judge decided that Gardner was not malingering, although he considered that light work was possible, and reduced the weekly compensation from Messrs Ashbee by 3s to 9s 6d.

On 3 May a labourer from Vicarage Lane, Glenville Charles Longney (known as Charles), was crushed by the buffers of a railway wagon during shunting operations at Shepherd's Patch and severely injured. He was working for one of the main contractors building the Slimbridge magazine, Messrs Hobrough & Co., and had been a fit and healthy twenty-eight-year-old. Following the accident Charles was conscious and brought home, but said that he hurt inside. Dr Pinching examined him and after a night's sleep, Charles was taken to the infirmary at Gloucester where he underwent an operation but did not survive. The cause of death was considered to be peritonitis caused by a rupture of the small intestine, and at the inquest the coroner gave a verdict of accidental death. Glenville Charles Longney was buried in St Mary's churchyard and his widow brought up their children alone until she married *Frederick Alexander Jones.

The death of the local MP, Captain Michael Hugh Hicks-Beach, Viscount Quenington, as a result of wounds received in action at Qatia, Egypt, on Easter Sunday, 23 April, while serving with the Royal Gloucestershire Hussars Yeomanry, triggered a by-election. The Independent candidate, William Boosey, was scheduled to address a meeting at Frampton on 9 May starting at 8.30 p.m. In line with normal practice, he was also advertised to speak at three other meetings that evening: Hartpury (7 p.m.), Hardwicke (7.30 p.m.) and Saul (8 p.m.). Mr Boosey was campaigning for more vigorous prosecution of the war effort and managed to achieve 16 per cent of the vote in this ultra-safe Conservative seat.

From April 1916, national war savings committees promoted the formation of local associations to encourage savings activities within their community. By the end of June, the Frampton association had a membership of thirty-five and savings of £12 8s. Some local employers, organisations, schools and churches also set up associations; the engineering firm R. A. Lister & Co. at Dursley boasted a membership of 644 among its employees, which may have included some from Frampton. While the focus was on raising money for the

Steam packet *Wave* on the canal near Saul Lodge *c.* 1905.

war, the government had the longer-term ambition of encouraging savings among sections of the population who, thanks to rising wages and an increase in the number of working women, had a disposable income for the first time in their lives.

Sarah, the wife of dairyman Harry Miller, who lived at Lake House, died tragically. When Harry was conscripted he initially filed for an exemption, but this was withdrawn and he joined the Army in the summer. Sarah continued the business. About midday on 16 August she was doing the milk round and driving near the canal towpath on a private road, presumably the one to Saul Lodge. When her horse started to back, pushing the float towards the canal, Sarah became frightened, jumped out and accidentally fell into the water. Despite the prompt assistance of passing watermen, the use of the drags and artificial respiration, they were unable to save her. Harry Miller obtained immediate leave for the inquest, after which arrangements were made to sell the business. It was bought by Harry Fletcher, the father of *Gilbert John and *Thomas Charles, on 11 September, who made the move to Lake House from Cirencester. On 12 October he was summoned before magistrates at Whitminster Petty Sessions for having sold adulterated milk on 14 September, just three days after taking over. Harry Fletcher was found to be an innocent party and the charge against him was dismissed. The milk was traced back to Church's farm in Saul which was already under suspicion. Miss Church tried to explain away the extraneous water in the milk by saying that she normally stood the milk pails in a tub of water to keep them cool, and that some of the water must have 'slopped over' into the milk. Her defence failed as she could not account for four distinct samples of milk, taken on three different dates, being adulterated with water to a similar degree of 10 per cent. A fine of 50s was imposed for each case.

Boy Scouts from Frampton travelled to Gloucester on Easter Monday, where 1,200 county scouts attended a simple, patriotic service at the cathedral. Afterwards they marched to Kingsholm Football Ground, watched by dense crowds lining the streets, for an inspection by Lieutenant-General Sir Robert Baden-Powell. The Chief Scout reflected on the difficulties under which the movement was working. With so many of its scoutmasters and patrol leaders called away to serve at home and abroad, (among them *William Joseph Ernest Gleed), he said that it was a great credit to all concerned that the quality and quantity of its membership was being maintained. Many had become scouts after the war had started, eager to do their bit for their country, but Baden-Powell hoped they would never have to see active service. He thanked each scout for donating the proceeds of a day's work, the money having been used to provide and equip four regulation huts at the Front for rest and refreshment for tired men when they left the trenches. Those present at the rally were treated to displays which included ambulance work, signalling and tent-pitching.

In August the traditional feast and funfair were held as usual on the village green outside the Bell Hotel. The Berkeley Hunt Agricultural Society's annual show, however, did not go ahead. The decision to cancel had been made in January, but much of the Society's educational work continued. Cadbury's requirement to increase milk production appears to have had an effect on local traditions, as the Society decided to encourage cheese-making at a time when farmers were being tempted to sell raw milk. The Society's aim was to help maintain the Vale's reputation as a cheese-making district, and an exhibition of

Note the predominance of women and children at the funfair.

cheese took place on Tuesday 8 August at the Berkeley Arms Hotel, Berkeley, with forty-five entries. The classes were for Single and Double Gloucester, Cheddar and Stilton.

Enemy submarine action was causing heavy shipping losses, and the government envisaged the mass production of standard cargo ships under a National Shipbuilding scheme. From 30 December, 110 tons of gravel were supplied from Frampton to the new shipyard construction site being built at Chepstow, later known as National Shipyard No. 1. Dug by hand, the gravel was transported by horse and cart down Perryway and loaded at Frampton wharf, north of Fretherne Bridge, into the Gloucester trow *Derby*, whose master, Mr Clutterbuck, had an exclusive contract. With Cadbury's also operating there, this became a very busy industrial area for the next twelve months. The gravel workings resulted in the loss of valuable agricultural land at Townfield Farm which the widowed Sarah Hobbs and her son Brian rented from the Estate.

Nationally there was increasing regulation. Non-essential imports were restricted and newspapers reduced in size. As military equipment became more motorised, the government needed to increase petrol supplies for the Armed Services. From the summer, petrol for civilian vehicles was restricted. Dr Pinching continued to be supplied, but found that the cost of a gallon had doubled to 1*s* due to the introduction of a tax on fuel. There were shortages of bread in the autumn, and regulations ordered reduced flour and increased husk content which resulted in so-called 'government bread'. Farmers in Gloucestershire and Somerset petitioned for a 4*d* rise in the controlled price of milk in December; this was initially refused, although the price did eventually rise.

The president of the Navy League wrote to the county council's Education Committee suggesting that all elementary and secondary schools should include teaching on British sea power and naval history. While there was general approval for the idea, the committee decided that, in the absence of a satisfactory text book on the subject, it would be difficult to carry this through. The chairman's suggestion that the secretary of the Navy League should write one himself was applauded by members.

Before the war the leaving age for schoolchildren was nominally fourteen, but a child who had gained a certificate of 'proficiency' or regular attendance could leave at thirteen, and children over twelve could work up to thirty-three hours a week if they also attended school half-time. Employers frequently put pressure on school managers to grant leaving certificates, and the Board of Education's concerns about the large numbers of boys and girls that had been exempted were discussed by the Education Committee. Its prime concern was with those aged eleven and twelve, but it also wanted to see firmer action taken against exemptions for older children. There had, apparently, been a number of instances of local tribunals taking child labour into account, and so refusing to exempt adult farm labourers from military service.

Traditionally in Frampton there had been a slow return to school at the end of the summer holidays by pupils who were needed either to work in the fields and orchards, or to stay at home to look after younger siblings while their mothers worked. The problem seems to have become more widespread for during the third week of July, with no illness around, an average of eleven children

The National School on the corner of The Street and Vicarage Lane.

were absent each day out of 101 on the books. In fact this figure was by no means unusual, as average attendance was often under 90 per cent. The school broke up for five weeks on 4 August, the holidays intended to coincide with harvest. On 9 November the school was given a half-day holiday to enable the headmaster to enter produce from the school gardens in the annual show of the Gloucestershire Root, Fruit and Grain Society at Shire Hall; the boys' six carrots of any variety received a second class certificate. The exhibition was generally hailed a success. A special feature was the war stall, from which ladies sold a variety of produce in aid of the local Red Cross hospitals; the show's profits were directed to the same fund.

On 5 December entertainment in the Institute was provided by a party of pierrots from Bristol. Their pantomime was very well attended and raised money for Frampton's servicemen. After expenses had been paid, fifty-one postal orders for 2s 6d were sent to soldiers and sailors in France and at home, while those serving in Salonika and Egypt received socks and sweetmeats. The vicar wrote to each man on behalf of the parishioners.

Frampton folk mourned the loss of *Gerald Prout, who was killed on 14 November by an enemy shell while in the front line trenches north of Courcelette, four days before the end of the Somme offensive. He had been brought up at Parks Farm, and his wider family farmed locally too. Although Gerald had emigrated to Canada some five years previously and had enlisted with the Canadian Expeditionary Force, he was still considered very much a Frampton boy. According to the vicar, the official news from the War Office had not been accompanied by any notification from his Commanding Officer, Chaplain or any of his fellow soldiers, and for a while his mother and family clung to the hope that he had been taken a prisoner of war.

HARRY GRIFFIN'S WAR DIARY

*Thomas Henry Griffin served with the Gloucestershire Regiment and later the Royal Engineers. His war diary is reproduced here in full, following his original spelling. It provides a powerful insight into the awful conditions and boredom that many servicemen endured and begins with a poem to his wife:

> Are you thinking of me,
> Are you thinking of me often
> When from me you're far away,
> Are you wishing I were nearer
> As you miss me day by day.
>
> In my heart your memory lingers,
> Sweet, tender, fond and true,
> In my life there's not a moment
> When I do not think of you.

Joyned the Army (2) Sept. 1914 at Tewkesbury.

Left home 21 Sept. 1914, went to Horfield. Left Horfield 1 October, went to Codford Sherrington Camp. Left Sherrington 13 November, went to Cheltenham. Went servant to Capt. Read. 2 December left Cheltenham.

26 April 1915 went to Fovant. Took on Officers' Mess 11 May 1915. Left Fovant 17 July 1915, went to Longbridge Devrill. Left Longbridge Devrill 21 Sept. 1915 went to Folkstone. Shipped away same night to Boulogne, France about two hours passage. Stopped in a camp two miles. Here till the 14 October and marched about seven miles to a wood. Pitched our tents near a village, Merrycourt [Méricourt]. We had to go and repair the trenches behind the [...] line some way. We left there 21 Oct. and marched back to Touley. We stayed there till 28 October and marched eighteen miles to Montvilliers. We stayed there till 11 Nov. where we took train at Amiens in cattle vans for Marsells [Marseilles] which took three days.

We went on board the H.M.S. Mars and sailed the 12th for [...] which took seven days. Very fine passage. Arrived there 18 Nov. staied ashore three days, came on board 21st. Sailed at four at night. 25 [Nov] we arrived at Salonica at 3 o'clock we left the ship. At once marched about three miles to a big camp.

The 13 Dec. we marched 13 miles across country. Went trench digging. Water very short. Had to pay 1d. for a drop of water. We done three hours trenching and had to march back 13 miles. Nearly done up.

14 Dec. we had to move again. March 12 miles to Lembert. Pitched a camp nearer the trench diging. Staid there trenching about four milles away till 22 Dec. We struck camp and marched about four miles, quite close to the trenches. We was diging Christmas day 25, very cold and hard. Biscuits and Bully Beef for dinner. Work all day.

18 Jan [1916]. taken tents off us. Had to march in the hills and pitch bivouvac. Had to make places to put them. Food very bad, put on Bom throwing.

21 Jan. Ten days course.

Sunday 30 Jan. Washing Parade. Rifle inspection at 2 o'clock. Nothing else doing.

31 Jan. Revalley 6.30. Breakfast 7.30. Marched off to trench digging. 3.30 not on parade in afternoon being on Guard Mount guard 4.45. 2 hours on 4 off. Sharp frost.

1 Feb. Dismissed 6.30. Not on Parade in the morning, trenching in the afternoon. Rifle Inspection 5.30.

2 Feb. Revally 6.30. Breakfast 7.30. Marched off 8.30 carring Sand Bags in Wine Street.

3 Feb. Trenching in Allen trench.

4 Feb. Trenching in Allen trench. Raining very hard all night. Got nearly wet through in Bed.

5 Feb. Revally 6.30. Marched off to Allens trench. Raining all day and very foggy. Rather miserable day.

6 Feb. Revally 6.30. Washing parade 9.30. Marched down to stream and back. Pay 5 franks. 11 o'clock nothing els doing.

7 Feb. Revally 6.30. Marched off 8.30 to Holmans Street for trenching. Nocked off 4.30. Marched back then had to go and draugh rations.

8 Feb. Revally 6.30. Marched off to Holmans Street for trenching all day.

9 Feb. Nothing doing in the morning. Dinner 11.30 then marched 7 miles there 7 back to have a bath. The bath was in a half tub. Nearly done up on getting back.

10 Feb. Revally 6.30. Marched off 8.30 to Holmans Street for trenching all day.

11 Feb. Revally 6.30. Breakfast 7.30. Marched off 8.30 to Wine Street for alteriations. Having to work very hard and foot very bad. Raining very hard all the afternoon and night. Blankets wet through.

12 Feb. Revally 6.30 being very cold, little snow. Repairing the bivouacs in morning, draining in the afternoon.

13 Feb. Revally 6.30 being Mess Orderly bit warmer. Church service first for a long time. Washing change of close [clothes] in the afternoon.

14 Feb. Revally 6.30. Company Drill all day not much rest. Food very bad. Dry bread for tea four nights and very cold.

15 Feb. Revally 6.30. Route march full pack, ten miles. Fall in again 3 o'clock for Company Drill. We had extended orders and rushes nearly done us in as was very tired after route march.

16 Feb. Had to man the trenches and make a big bannet [bayonet] charge. Got in to dinner at one and fall in at half past two for a washing parade, weather warmer today.

17 Feb. Revally 6.30. Marched off 8.15 in the fire trench getting it deeper. Dry biscuits for tea.

18 Feb. Revally 6.30. Marched off to Wine Street for alterations. Lights out 9 o'clock.

19 Feb. Revally 6.30. Marched off to Wine Street for alterations.

20 Feb. Revally 6.30. Breakfast 7.30. Cold backon [bacon]. Washing Parade 9.30. Nothing els doing. Lights out 7.30 pm.

21 Feb. Revally 6.30 marched of 8.45 for Company Drill. Arms Drill in the morning and on atack in the afternoon.

22 Feb. Marched of 9 for a Batt atack. Had to atack up to mountans. Nearly done up then in the afternoon another atack in the bottom. Was mess Orderly as well.

23 Feb. Had to man the trenches from 10 to 11. Bombardment going on at 12. We had to make a charge after dinner. We had to go and cover the earth on top of the trench with bushes so we could not be seen.

24 Feb. Marched off to Wine for trenching all day. Dry bread for tea.

25 Feb. Marched off to Wine Street in the morning. After dinner we had to go down on the race course to make it levall.

26 Feb. R E Fatuge [Fatigue] putting barbe wire entanglements up all day. Dry bread for tea with one pickle walnut.

27 Feb. Revally 6.30. Breakfast 7.30. Had to report at Orderly Room 8.30 being bath orderly for the day. The troops had […] parade in the morning, sports in the afternoon.

28. Feb. went sick. Had to go to hospital so 10 o'clock a sledge came down and put me on and was drawn four or five miles by a mule to a dressing station then we had the motor 6 miles to the field […] and from there to the 25 clearing station only to drop of tin [milk?].

29 Feb. Revally 7.00. Drop of milk for breakfast. Was moved to the Canada General Hospital. Had a good bath and all clean close [clothes]. Put in MC1 Ward.

1 March. Revally half past five. Wash. Breakfast seven. Got orders to be for the boat when it's fine enuff to moove. Got acute nephritis [inflammation of the kidneys]. Still in bed.

2 March. Revally 5.30. Wash. Breakfast 7 o'clock. Porage, bread, butter, egg, cup cocoa. Then dinner half past 11, bread, cup milk pudding. Tea four. Bread butter egg, cupp cocoa, two biscuits. Half past seven lights out. Still in bed all day.

3 March. Revally 5.30. Breakfast 6.30. Porage, egg, bread, butter. Dinner 12. Bread, sup, pudding. 1 o'clock had to go to the Ship, Galika. Got there at four. Had to change in to a flannel suit and got a sleeping suit as well. Tea. Bread, butter. Supper 7. Bread, jam, cocoa. Lights out 9.

4 March. Revally five. Wash, make bed. Breakfast 7. Porage, bread, butter. Ordered back to bed. Doctor came round, was to have a few days in bed. Light food. Dinner 12. Little rice pudding. Tea. Bread, butter. Lights out 9.30.

5 March. Sunday. Revally 4.30. Breakfast 7. Bread, butter, porage. Doctor came round 10. Said as I could get up a bit, being in bed 5 days. Dinner, beef tea […]. General inspection after dinner. Tea 4. Left Salonica 5.30. […] having fine [crossing …] where we are sailing for. Lights out 9.30.

6 March. Revally 4.30. Wash. Got back in bed till breakfast 7.30. Porage, bread, butter. Went on deck. Weather fine now crossing the Agean Sea. Packet of cigerretts isue. Doctor round 10 o'clock. Dinner 12.30. Beef tea. Tea, bread, butter. Lights out 9.30. Weather fine.

7 March. Revally 4.30. Wash. Breakfast 7.30. Still of [on] light food. Strong wind S.E. rather rough sea running out port hole being left open, a sea came in and made alfull mess, 6 or 7 beds being wet through. We are now crossing the Atlantic [Harry must mean the Mediterranean Sea]. Tea, supper same as usel.

8 March. Revally 4.30. Wash. Breakfast 7.30. Wind very strong. High sea running good many sea sick. Dinner 12.30. 4 o'clock we sited Malta. Going in for

orders. Got long side of quay. Tea 4.30. Had to stay on board for to night to waite orders in the morning. Hoping to have to come on to England.

9 March. Revally 4.30. Breakfast 7. Soft food. No orders yet, still waiting. Orders came at night to go off ship in morning.

10 March. Revally. Breakfast. Bread and butter. 9.30 went off the ship. Motor to St. Andrews Hospital, getting there 11 o'clock. Wash change in clean close, got into bed. Doctor came around. Staid in bed rest of the day. Put me on nothing but milk. Lights out 9 o'clock.

11 March. Revally 4.30. Wash. Bed made. Milk for breakfast. Still on milk and kept in bed.

12 March. Being Sunday. Revally 4.30. Wash. Bed made. Milk all day. Not allowed up. Lights out 9 o'clock.

13 March. Revally 4.30. Wash. Same as usel. Milk all day. Lights out 9 o'clock.

14 March. Revally 4.30, Wash. Milk as usel. Doctor round 2.30. Lights out 9.

15 March. Revally 5. Wash. Milk for breakfast. Doctor round 10.30. Put me on pudding and porage. Had today a shaving brush, tooth b[rush] som[eo]ne gave us from the Red Cross.

16 March. Revally 5. Wash. Make b[eds]. Breakfast. Bread, butter, porage. Doctor round 11.30. Dinner, rice milk, tea bread, butter, eggs. Supper 7. Bread, butter, cocoa. Lights out 9 o'clock.

17 March. Same as usuel.

18 March. Revally 5. Wash. Make beds. Breakfast 7. Doctor round 11.30. Told me to get up for one hour, first time again for eight days. Lights out 9 o'clock.

19 March. Sunday, same as usual.

20 March. Same as usulel.

21 March. Still on milk diet.

22 March. Milk diet. Lord Methuen [Governor and Commander-in-Chief of Malta] came in the afternoon to see us. Only allowed up one hour da[i]ly.

23 March. Revally 4.30. Wash. Make beds. Breakfast 7. Porage, bread, butter. Doctor came round 9.30. Said as I could get up for two hours. Cocoa 10. Dinner 1. Just a little rice pudding. Tea 3.30. Two eggs, bread, butter. Cocoa at seven. Lights out 9 o'clock.

24 March. Same as ussell.

25 March. Same as ussell.

26 March. Same as ussell.

27 March. Getting up three hours.

28 March. Batch leaving for England.

29 March. Same as usul.

30 March. Being put on ordinary minsed dinner. Getting up a little longer. Chocilate issue from Red Cross. Lights out 9 o'clock.

31 March. 1, 2, 3 April. As usuel.

4 April. Ordered to bed again.

5 April. Still in bed. Not aloud out at all.

6 April. As usuel.

7 April. Revally 5. Wash. Have bed made. Breakfast porage. Doctor came round 10.30. Cocoa 11. Dinner 1. Minsed meat. Wash 2 o'clock. Make bed. Tea 3.30.

Bread, butter, egg. Supper 6.30 cocoa. One poor chapps named Chapman passed away just after dinner, only 23 years.

8 April. As usuel.

9, 10, 11, 12, 13, 14 April. As usel. Still in bed.

15, 16, 17, 18, 19, 20, 21 April. Being Good Friday. Had a nice cross gave us by Sister [Hasket?]. Still in bed.

22, 23 April. Easter Sunday. An Easter Egg put buy our bed buy the Night Sister and cake for tea. All else same as usulel.

24, 25 April. Still in bed. Revally 5 am. Just a drop of milk mash. Make beds. Take temperature. Breakfast 7. Porage, bread, butter. Med. clean ward, them is up. Tidy beds. Doctor round 10. Cocoa 11, Biscuits. Dinner. Beef mince for me. Med. wash. Make bed. Tea 3.30. Bread, butter eggs or custard. Med. take temperature. Cocoa 6.30 pm. Tidy bed and want to move if you are all right for the night [L]ily the sister in charge. Lights out at nine. That finish the night.

26, 27, 28 April. Rather a[n] excitement hear this morning. The H.M.S. Russel[l] torped[oed] – hearing the guns.

29, 30 April. Being Sunday, everything as usul. Guns going off just after tea out at sea. Still in bed.

1 May. As usuel.

2 May. Aloude to get up for one hour after tea. Matron brought Cholate [Chocolate] round. Tobacco issued.

3 May. Same as usuel. Major and two ladies came round after tea. Gave us Box of Cholate and two boxes of matches. Up for one hour. All the boys [...] all but four of us gone to a consort [concert] at the Austrain Hall at seven o'clock. Lights out at nine.

4, 5, 6, 7 May. Being Sunday. Batch leaving for England. Other things as usul only aloud up one hour.

8 May. Tobacco issued. Doctor marked me up for three hours. Getting very hot hear.

9, 10, 11 May. Another batch leaving for England. Marked up six hours today.

12, 13 May. Put back to bed again.

14 May. Sunday. Doctor aloud me up on hour today.

15 May. Still only one hour. Cholate gave us today from Red Cross and tobacco.

16 May. Fire alarm went at 1.30 this morning. St Davids Officers Mess burned down.

17 May. Fired alarm again 11 o'clock but found only the grass fire, so soon put out. Bedding counted by Quarter Master. Getting up about three hours in the afternoon.

18 May. As usuel only sports on football ground buy RAMC.

19 May. Sports again buy RAMC but final Monday.

20 May. Batch gone to camp today. Sports again, running off the [heats?] final Monday.

21 May. Sunday. Put back to bed. Sister Hasket gave us a photo as she taking of us, very good, weather being very hot.

22, 23, 24, 25, 26 May. Nothing to report.

27 May till 1 June. Nothing to report.

2 June. Batch left for England. Had to tra[ns]fer to A Block, closing C Block.

3 June. Batch left for camp.

4, 5, 6 June. No Doctor come hear to see us yet getting up all day on our own.

7 June. Doctor came and put us on light duty. Not seeing if we was fit. We do from half past eight to half past eleven, from two till three.

8 June. Doctor came round after coming of duty. Did not say much to us. Not a very good doctor. Work don't go very well being week.

9, 10 June. Went boating down at St Georges Bay. Came back. Went to a Boxing contest.

11 June. Being Whit Sunday went to Church at night.

12, 13, 14, 15 June. Went to concerts after comming just a little rush. Fire alarm went. We had to stand to our cots.

16 June. I went to a boxing contest with the Navy and Soilders, Navy being best.

17 June. Band concert.

18 June. Sunday. Went to church in morning. Being [warned?] after dinner to get our close [clothes] for the boat tomorrow.

19 June. Had to parade 8 o'clock for the boat. Got in motor 8.30. Got on the boat Oxfordshire about ten. Sailed 2 o'clock after being in Malta 14 weeks, 5 days. Glad to leave as its very hot hear.

20 June. Rather breeze, but fine. A seaplane went buy us just before breakfast. Sea some land on the left of us, the coast of Morocco, North Africa. 8.30pm quite close to Mount Atlas. Lights out 9pm. Passed Algires in the night.

21 June. The [...] coast of Spain on our right. Weather very fine. Went in Gibraltar eleven in the morning, three days all but three hours from Malta. Droped anchor for a bit. Came out of Gib 1 o'clock to proceed on after getting Orders where to go. Good many Greeks' boats there being detained. After leaving Gib no land to see.

22 June. Still no land. Getting colder. Crossing the Atlantic. 10pm sighted the coast of Portugal. Strong wind.

23 June. Just sighted the north coast of Spain. We are in the Bay of Biskay. Smart swell on. No land the rest of the day. Saw some large whales. Looking dirty. The last thing raining.

24 June. Still no land in sight, but fine. Still in the Bay. About six at night came into a dense fog. Now being near the Isle of White had to go very slow, about 8 o'clock.

25 June. Being Sunday. Passed a schooner, thought it was the [Nitha?]. [Concert on deck?] Just mad[e] the Isle of White and being very close to it. Still fog. Droped anchor outside Southampton about twelve midnight.

26 June. Got anchor up about 9. Got longside of quay about 10. Got into train and got to Eastleigh to a clearing station for four days to get sent on. Seems a very nice place. Went to a concert at night at the YMCA being very good. Four in a hut. Food brought round to us. To be in at nine.

27 June. Another concert at night. Cakes and coffee gave us. Aloud out after half past one till eight at night.

28 June. Another concert. Cakes and coffee again.

29 June. Another concert. Fags gave us. Raining very hard.

30 June. Had to go draw Karke [Khaki] again to leave at eleven. Train for Epsom, near London, change at Waterlooue. Motor to hospital. Get there half past three. Change into hospital close [clothes] again. Put in huts. 28 in a hut.

1 July. Being Mess Orderly in the Dining Hall.

2 July. Had to parade for church but was late getting there so was dismissed. Nothing else done.

3 July. Doctor came round and put us in classes. Put me in No. 2. Nos. 1 and 2 don't do anything. 3 and 4 do drill. No. 5 is the fit class to go on furlo. Had to Parade all for a leture. They got paid out 4 shillings, the first for a long time.

4 July. Just parade at half past eight each morning. Nos. 1 and 2 fall out, the rest carry on till twelve.

5 July. The same. Had a pass for London. Do there and back for a shilling. Get in half past ten. Had a fine time.

6 July. Doctor came round again. Still left us in No. 2 Class.

7 July. No parade. Raining nearly all day. Went to pictures at night, 1*d.* to go in.

8 July. Had to change from H Division to C Division. Sent to Hut 25.

9 July. Sunday. Being Mess Orderly.

10 July. Went to concert, the London Concert Party, penny to go in.

11 July. Doctor seen us again. Still in No. 2 Sect[i]on. Got paid 4 shillings.

12 July. Had to scrub our lockers and under our beds – every man does his own.

13, 14 July. Doctor came round again.

15 July. Went to concert. It was Raffles being very good.

16 July. Sunday. Church Parade. Raining nearly all day. Went to Ashtead Church at night.

17 July. Had to get a new suit of Blue.

18 July. Being bussey. Parading as King and Queen coming to see us at half past two. They walked up through the lines and came back in their motor.

19 July. Being paid another 4 shillings.

20, 21 July. Doctor came round. Put me to a light exersize.

22, 23 July. Being Sunday got clean close issue. Sunday morning Church Parade.

24 July. Doctor came round again, leaving me still in No. 2 Sect[i]on.

25 July. Being Mess Orderly.

26 July. Same as usuel.

27, 28 July. Doctor came round. Still in No. 2 Sect[i]on.

29, 30 July. Being Sunday Church Parade and clean close.

31 July. As usuel.

1 August. Doctor came round – put me in No. 3 Sect[i]on. Went to tea at the Savoy Hotel in London. Motor there and back being a good outing.

2 August. On Rations fatud [fatigue].

3, 4, 5, 6 August. Being Sunday. Quarter Master […] in morning. Tea Rooms afternoon.

7, 8, 9, 10, 11, 12, 13 August. Sunday Church Parade.

14 August. Put in charge of No. 25 Mess.

15 16 August. Doctor came round. Marked me for Hospital again.

17 August. Draw Karky [Khaki] out again. Parade two o'clock for London County Hospital, Horton. Got there. Had to bath, change into Blue, hand in Karky. Had to stay in bed till Doctor seen me. Aloud to get up again.

18 August. Marked as unfit for overseas. Food very nice hear.

19, 20 August. Being Sunday go to church if you like.

21 August. Tobacco isued. Got to be in bed every afternoon for massage. Special nurse come.

23 August. Tobacco. Major came round.

26 August. Had a pass to go home. Left here eight, came back 29 nine o'clock. September

30, 31. Same as usuel.

4 October. We had to get our Karky and shift to another Hospital called the Manor County London War Hospital. A new place, we being the first lot there, having everything new. Very nice place.

21 October. Put back on fish, no potoes.

30 October. Put back to bed this being the Opening of this Hospital. Princess Christain came to open it.

17 January 1917. Left Manor County of London 17 January 1917. Went to Kingston Infirmary. Left there on 9 March, came back to Horton. Left County of London War Hospital [Horton] 16 April 1917 for ten days leave. Left home after leave. Went to Glo'r at four. I had to stay there till one in the morning. Came on down to Haverfordwest. Got there half past six.

27 April. Had to stop there till nine then came to Fishguard. Got there at ten. Had to stay there till midni[ght]. Fine night. Got to Ross[lare] four in the morning.

28 April. Came across in a steam boat called the Great Southern. Got into a train at Rosslear for Buttevant Barricks at five. Got there about mid day.

Sunday 29. Had to see a doctor in the morning. Major in the afternoon. I was classed as Z2. That is light fagties [fatigues] and a hour P training. We are weeding nearly all day.

4 May. Had two teeth out. Got to go in a fortnight to be fitted for some new ones.

5 May. Kit Inspection. Put on the picket for 24 hours. Put on Officers Mess.

26 May. No drills [...] only PT once a day. Monday being Whit Monday Hollowday, Sports at the Camp.

30 May. Reclassification. Put in Z1.

31 May. We had to parade. All emploied men to be changed. All Cl[ass]. 2 men to take their places, but I had to carry on. Had to have our food in tents. Had to fall in and be marched up there every meal. Food very rough, not enuff of it. Left Buttevant Barracks 6 June for Ballevanaire Camp. Five miles. Living in Huts. Had my extra pay on the 29 June, 5 shillings. Put on to TMB. On the 23 July went to Buttevant Barricks. On the 26 had the TMB and marked o1.

2 August. We left Buttevant at 6 o'clock for England. Left station at 7. Got to Mallow 7.30. Left there at night. Got to Rosslear at 12.30. Got on the Boat. Left there at 1. Got to Fishguard at five. Got on train, left there at six. Got to London at 12.30 pm. Left there at 8 [on] 3 August for Milstead Kent. Got there at six. Raining.

[several pages missing]

[…] of France and Italy. The tunnel went under the Alps. Lot of snow on them.

1 November. Still in train. Got to Taranto [Southern Italy].

4 November. After being on the train 8 days, then we went in Huts at Taranto.

6 November. Marched to the Warf. Put on lighters. No. 13 Lighter was mine. Had to take them off to steamboats with cargo and the ELC [?] had to do the work.

28 November. Still carrying on with Lighters.

5

1917

POLITICAL SUMMARY

Rising prices and food shortages through 1917, continued stalemate in France and casualties began to produce war weariness and talk of negotiated peace, particularly on the left; and Henderson's wish to attend a Socialist peace conference in August led to his departure from the War Cabinet. He was replaced by another Labour MP who was not, however, the leader of the party.

The new War Cabinet and Lloyd George's dynamic leadership produced positive results, most notably in April when, faced by catastrophic shipping losses and a real prospect of Britain being starved into surrender, the War Cabinet forced the Admiralty to adopt the convoy system. The German unrestricted submarine warfare which had caused this crisis had also brought the United States of America into the war on the Allied side. The immediate effect was to facilitate the supply of US munitions, but to train and transport US troops to Europe took time, and the summer offensives of 1917 relied on French and British forces. Lloyd George's attempts to strengthen the military command by agreeing to a single supreme commander (inevitably French) worsened his relations with the British generals. The unsuccessful Ypres offensive from July to November reinforced his low opinion of their capacity, and he made further efforts to exert political control on military decisions through the autumn and winter of 1917.

1917 was probably the worst year for industrial unrest, with discontent caused by rising prices, food shortages and attempts by the military to conscript previously exempt skilled workers. Men and women moving to work in the munitions industries caused rent rises, and also highlighted the inadequacy of the national housing stock. The government responded with more price and rent controls and set up a new Ministry of Reconstruction to plan a range of social reforms to show people what they were fighting for. It was headed, not by a businessman, but by one of Lloyd George's more progressive Liberal supporters.

MILITARY OVERVIEW

The appalling struggles of 1916 on the Somme were followed by a period of sheer survival in the rain, snow, fog, mud and flooded trenches of the winter. The

British were then first to move, forcing the Germans back over 11 miles on the Ancre but onto the prepared defences of the Hindenburg Line. The offensive then switched focus to Arras, where huge efforts went into underground warfare in the old quarries, mines and tunnels. While the first phase succeeded in the capture of Vimy Ridge (the first major action by the Canadian Corps as a single formation) and other high ground, the stalemate then returned, persisting throughout the Passchendaele campaign, the main benefit of which was to give the French time to recover from the defeat of the Nivelle offensive and the army mutinies which followed. At the end of the year, tanks (which had first been used on the Somme in 1916, but were then unreliable and vulnerable) made their first major contribution at Cambrai, where they cleared a passage through barbed wire ahead of the advancing infantry.

The Italians suffered a disastrous defeat at Caporetto, which led to military support from Britain that diverted resources from the Western Front. Greece joined the Allied cause, but there was no real development in the Balkans; further east the Revolution led to Russia's exit from the war. The Czechoslovak Legion, in order to win Allied support for their independence, defected from Austria-Hungary, defeating both them and a German army, and fought their way across Siberia to Vladivostok.

British and Indian forces made headway against Turkish and German troops in both Mesopotamia, with the capture of Baghdad, and in Palestine, which led to the capture of Jerusalem in December.

FRAMPTON ON SEVERN

The year 1917 was, perhaps, the most desperate for Frampton during the war. It began badly when *Henry Francis Clifford was killed during the Cavalry raid at Rafa, Egypt, on 9 January. In *Ratcatcher Baronet*, Sir Lionel Darell described him as 'a very gallant officer, shot through the head as he had his field glasses up

*Major Clifford (left) at Rafa.

watching the effect of the fire of his squadron'. It took some days for the news to reach Frampton, the headmaster noting it in the school's logbook on Monday 15 January. A few days later the *Gloucester Journal* wrote of:

A popular squire and keen sportsman – he was a good shot and a hard rider to hounds – Major Clifford (who was an active magistrate when at home) was greatly loved in the neighbourhood, and his death will be keenly deplored by his many friends.

The school closed on Monday 19 February so that pupils and teachers could attend his memorial service at St Mary's. The whole village felt his loss, and the church and churchyard were packed with mourners whose numbers were swollen by many of the county gentry. These close-knit families had experienced their own tragedies, particularly at Qatia the previous year, when Henry had lost several of his dearest friends.

*Edward Augustus Capener died of wounds in Mesopotamia on 11 March and, on 12 May, *Frederick Robert William John Hitchings was killed during the Second Battle of Arras. *George Henry Purnell also lost his life during the Arras offensive, on 3 June. The 'Memorial Service for the Fallen' at St Mary's on 17 June must have been a very sombre affair, when these men, together with those who had perished earlier, were remembered. The life of Horatio Allison Brinkworth was also commemorated that day; he had been electrocuted while working on some wires in Australia. Although his death on 28 February was not associated with the war, it would have been just as keenly felt by his family still in the village, and also by his brother *Thomas Hart Brinkworth.

On 3 August, *Albert Edward Townsend died of wounds. *Christopher Charles Fryer lost his life on 3 November, two days after being wounded on the front line near Sanctuary Wood, close to Ypres. This horrible year closed with the death of *Richard Sidney Winter on 30 December, killed on the last day of the Battle of Cambrai.

On 14 November 1916, *Herbert Charles Drayton had been joined in HMS *Centurion* by *Sidney Charles Mills who remained on board until 9 August. Although she sailed with a complement of 782 officers and men, it seems almost inevitable that they would have met. This postcard, which was passed by the ship's censors, was sent by Sidney Mills to his friend, *Ralph Theodore Hazell, who was working at Richard Ward's shop.

In Frampton, William Henry Goodman whose shop was at the top of the green, was fined £1 on 25 January at Stonehouse Police Court for selling underweight bread. Each of the three loaves purchased by the inspector had been about one

ounce under, something that may have harmed his reputation since there were three other bakeries in the village. Regulations also got the better of Sarah Hobbs of Townfield Farm (then known as Home Farm) who was fined £1 at Berkeley Petty Sessions on 11 April for moving two hundredweight of wheat straw without a permit.

An unfortunate accident occurred on 29 January involving Ellen, the mother of *George Harris. She had spent the day at Frampton with George, who was home on leave during his service with the Devonshire Regiment ahead of his departure for France. Ellen left George and his family at the end of the afternoon to walk home to Whitminster along the road she called Frampton Lane (Whitminster Lane). After being overtaken at close quarters by a bicycle ridden with lights, she was then hit by an unlit float driven on the wrong side of the road by Arthur Ernest Lewis, a butcher from Frampton, who was transporting cement and other heavy goods. She was twisted round, almost thrown into the ditch and the horse stood on her left thigh. Ellen lost consciousness and was taken home. The doctors considered that sixty-nine-year-old Ellen would suffer from her injuries for the rest of her life, and a county court case followed later in the year when she sued for £100 compensation for loss and damage. She had been used to working on the land during the summer and doing sewing in the winter. While there was a dispute about the exact time of the occurrence, the judge nevertheless found it was after lighting up time had passed. The road was said to be only 9 feet wide where the accident happened, and the defendant was found to have been driving too fast and in a negligent manner. Ellen Harris was awarded £33 10s 6d with costs.

The desperate conditions endured by Thomas Turner's tenant in School Row, Thomas Allen, continued and eventually, on 23 February, the rural district councillors lost their patience and resolved that proceedings should be taken under the Public Health Act. (This appears to have been an effective threat as the nuisance was abated within a month.) At the same meeting it was noted, not for the first time, that traffic associated with the National Filling Factory at Quedgeley and Cadbury's milk collections was causing damage to certain roads. Both organisations were expected to make good the damage at their own expense which, in respect of the Filling Station, amounted to more than £938. Cadbury's demanded evidence by way of a plan, something the council clearly considered a burden to produce, and it hoped for an amicable settlement. An offer of £24 5s 6d followed, which the council considered inadequate, and although Cadbury's suggested arbitration, the council opted for telling them when the necessary repairs were being effected. This protracted dispute did not end until January 1919, when Cadbury's increased offer of £50 was accepted. The district council also discussed Cadbury's milk stands which had been placed beside the highways without permission: early in 1918 it was agreed to accept them in principle so long as care was exercised regarding their positioning and construction.

Continuing food shortages brought further changes to Frampton. The Birmingham food controller had ordered that milk chocolate production cease by the end of 1916 to enable milk processing plants to move over to making butter and condensed milk. In April 1917 Cadbury's sent the necessary equipment by canal from Bournville for installation at the Frampton factory to enable the production of condensed milk. Several Bournville girls, under the charge of Miss Griffin, arrived and took up their quarters in the village. With an equal number

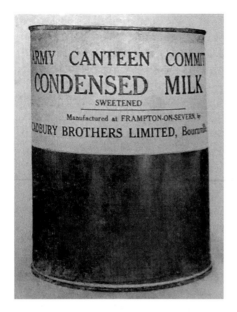

A tin of condensed milk manufactured for the
Army by Cadbury's at Frampton.

of local girls they started to work filling and soldering the tins, and labelling and
packing the new product. In spite of initial delays and difficulties they all adapted
themselves to the work and the first batches were sent out at the end of April.
Output steadily increased and large quantities were despatched to army canteens
in all parts of the country. The chairman, George Cadbury, with George Cadbury
junior, visited the factory to congratulate the girls, later writing that:

> It was interesting to see how in three weeks a new business had been started ...
> From what we gather the girls are happy and comfortable, though it is quite a new
> experience for them to be so much out of the world; they had seen no newspaper
> for several days.

The next phase in developing the Frampton factory was the construction of a
building for the manufacture of cheese.

In January 1917 the farming industry was in crisis with insufficient labour to
plant the crops. To address this shortage, enrolment into the Women's Land Army
began in conjunction with the Board of Agriculture and newly formed Women's
County War Agricultural Committees. Under the chairmanship of the Duchess
of Beaufort and with Miss Teesdale of Whitminster House as its first honorary
secretary and Mrs Clifford a member for a while, the Gloucestershire committee's
main task was to recruit and train women for farm work (for which they were
given a uniform and paid) and then to find them jobs. A system of district
representatives and village registrars was intended to ensure that every woman and
girl was canvassed, although the number of Frampton women volunteering has not
been established. It also arranged lectures for women on cooking and crafts.

It was around this time that Evelyn Lucy Hart took over as the district nurse and
midwife. She may have lived at Wonkey Cottage from the outset, certainly when
living there later she is said to have operated a small dispensary in an outbuilding

which now forms part of the adjoining Old Coffee House. Nurse Hart's service to the village, which ended in 1943, is remembered on the font cover in St Mary's.

From April onwards, 'necessaries' for soldiers were made in the Institute on Wednesday and Friday afternoons by the Work Party for War Needs, with material and patterns supplied by the county depot in Cheltenham. Within a month 100 sun shields and 13 anti-vermin shirts had been despatched to Cheltenham. The materials had to be purchased, and donations came in from several villagers to cover these. Other items that were produced included mosquito nets, pyjamas, shirts, collars and anti-vermin vests. This was considered important war work and suited those who perhaps were not fit enough to undertake more strenuous manual labour.

On 14 July the annual outing for employees of J. Reynolds & Co. Ltd, flour millers, took place in Frampton. After chartering the *River Queen* from Gloucester, they stopped during the morning to play a cricket match on the village green which, accompanied by perfect weather, was keenly contested and thoroughly enjoyed by all. Lunch was taken aboard as they made their way to the busy docks at Sharpness, where employees and their wives were particularly interested in a steamer with a powerful gun mounted on her afterdeck, a repellent against submarine attacks. Some of the party had not travelled along the canal before, and were apparently surprised at the verdure and beauty of the wild flowers displayed along its banks.

Throughout the war period, and indeed generally during the early part of the twentieth century, the parish council met fewer than four times a year, including the annual parish meeting, and sometimes planned meetings were abandoned as not being quorate. The reason for this is not entirely clear: on 20 August 1918 only the chairman turned up for the meeting. However, parish councillors seem to have made a special effort on 15 January 1917 when Frederick Alexander Franklin (tailor), William Hazell (mariner), William Henry Goodman (grocer and baker), Sydney Thomas Osborn (headmaster) and George William Hart (shopkeeper) all put in an appearance. The reason for their meeting was to act on correspondence from the county's War Agricultural Committee which had

The cricket pitch on the village green.

requested confirmation of the quantity of seed potatoes required by the village for the forthcoming season's crop. Two tons were requested and notices placed around the parish advising villagers to apply to the parish council's chairman, Frederick Franklin, for their quota.

Lord Rhondda became Minister of Food in the summer. The Corn Production Act, passed in August, guaranteed prices for farmers and established the Agricultural Wages Board to set minimum wages for farm workers on the advice of county boards with farmer and union representation. The minimum was initially set at 25s per week and no doubt affected Frampton as elsewhere. To control the distribution of sugar, Wheatenhurst Rural District Council was required to set up a committee, which had to include at least one labour representative and one woman. Miss Teesdale fulfilled the latter role. It was the committee's responsibility to ensure that sugar retailers were registered and that sugar cards were issued to the public. By January 1918 it was clear to Lord Rhondda that previous efforts of propaganda and advice were not working and he brought in formal rationing and subsidies to control prices.

To satisfy the growing demand for munitions, many new factories and other facilities were planned, including a new explosives factory at Henbury, north of Bristol. Frampton gravel was to be used in its construction and concrete blocks were to be made on a site beside Perryway. The contract negotiated with Mrs Clifford agreed the extraction of 100,000 tons of gravel from two four-acre plots. The project appears to have been urgent, for the decision to proceed was taken in January, and by 19 April, Royal Engineers had constructed a standard gauge rail link to the Midland Railway at Frocester (including a level crossing on the main Bristol Road), and the block-making plant on Perryway.

However, all this work was in vain. With the entry of the US into the war, more reliance was placed on the import of American munitions and the Henbury project was cancelled on 16 May along with the gravel contract. The *Gloucester Journal* unleashed its views once the topic was no longer under censorship. After treating the news with a degree of scepticism, it went as far as to suggest that, had the proposed works been located in a position closer to the supply of water and raw materials (i.e. near Frampton), it may have been undertaken in full. The block-making plant and railway were offered to Mrs Clifford, but she refused them, and dismantling began at the end of May. From October the capacity of the Slimbridge munitions depot was increased by the construction of another magazine at Tumpy Green which appears to have used materials from Frampton. One can only imagine Mrs Clifford's fortitude during this particularly difficult phase of her life. Although she had been overseeing Estate matters from the start of the war, she was newly widowed and heavily pregnant. Her daughter, Henrietta, was born on 8 April.

In June Frederick Walford Vick's application for exemption against conscription as a house repairer was dismissed, but three months later he appealed the decision. This time his solicitor, Mr Frank Treasure, successfully argued that he was the only plumber in the district (the next nearest was in Eastington, said to be 5 miles away). Three quarters of his work was apparently in the plumbing trade, and letters were produced from local residents confirming their appreciation of his services. His appeal was granted for six months, after which he was given an exemption card to make the arrangement permanent.

Mr and Mrs Osborn with the cookery class *c.* 1916.
    Left to right: Jessie Godwin, Daisy Betteridge, Nancy Gardner, Edith Griffin, Lisa Dath, Eva Organ, Lily Bateman, Marion Herbert, Lydia Herbert.

A whooping cough epidemic closed the school in early July. Mrs Osborn resigned from teaching at the end of the summer term, and her post was filled on 4 September by Miss L. Strange, formerly of a school in Enfield. Finding the work too difficult, she gave notice a week later, although she agreed to stay on until a replacement was found. In early October the headmaster noted that, as no fuel had been provided, the temperature in the school had dropped to ten degrees below that ordered by the Board of Education. The coldness was having a depressing effect on both teachers and pupils, especially those children who were thinly clad. On 12 October the school closed to allow staff to attend an address at Shire Hall given by the President of the Board of Education, H. A. L. Fisher, regarding the new Education Bill.

Gloucestershire was one of six counties specially requested by the Food Production Department (on behalf of the Admiralty and War Office) to collect blackberries for the jam factories supplying the Army and Navy. The schools were paid a rate of 2*d* per pound. Frampton schoolchildren were given a half-day's holiday to gather the fruit, but the headmaster recorded that, as few of the children interested themselves in the matter, only about 23 lbs were picked. County-wide, almost 82 tons were collected by 223 schools. The harvesting of blackberries at Frampton was taken far more seriously the following year, when pupils were granted six half-days for picking, although several of those were unfortunately very wet and therefore unsuitable for the work.

The weather in 1917 was bad. February was particularly cold and the canal froze. The summer was a disaster, with heavy falls of rain in June ruining much of the hay crop and badly damaging potatoes. However, the August bank

MEET of LORD FITZHARDINGE'S HOUNDS. FRAMPTON GREEN

holiday week proved to be a welcome break for many, as large manufacturers and shopkeepers closed for either the whole period or a greater part of it. In the Berkeley Vale, people took the train to the seaside, with local railway employees witnessing animated scenes as holidaymakers and soldiers vied for places.

The *Gloucester Journal* advertised the sale of farm stock on 7 September at The Gables (Advowsons Farm) by Mr A. Dowdeswell. In addition to his Shorthorn cattle and dairy cows, he also sold sheep, pigs and nine acres of fruit together with 103 head of poultry (Rhode Island Reds), eighty chickens and twenty-five ducks.

The Berkeley hounds continued to meet during the war, always providing a spectacle when in the village. It was important to keep the losses of lambs and poultry to an absolute minimum. Nationally, eggs were collected for wounded soldiers, and Frampton sent six dozen each fortnight. On 21 March the box was short, but as the eggs were so urgently needed it was thought better to send them anyway, and to make up the deficit another time.

On 17 November, *Frederick Hill's case against conscription was dismissed when he made no appearance at the military tribunal. He was a thirty-seven-year-old cowman, a single parent with a young family. This was not the first time that he had had to apply. In early January, his employer had requested an exemption from service which had been granted until 31 March. Frederick eventually enlisted at Stroud on 26 October and had, presumably, once again filed an application in the hope of some leniency. From the surviving records of the posting that he was given to 608 Agricultural Company of the Labour Corps, it appears that he may have been deployed close to home, and hence decided not to appeal his conscription.

Fundraising efforts were a feature of village life throughout the war. While the normal practices of the church and chapel to donate harvest produce, including bread, fruit, vegetables and flowers, to the infirmary at Gloucester continued, the VAD hospital at Standish was the beneficiary of financial donations from such activities as whist drives and dances; one held in January 1916 attracted 150 villagers and raised £13. The local collector for the Gloucestershire Farmers'

War Relief fund was Robert Dowdeswell of Netherhills Farm who, as reported in the *Gloucester Journal* of 10 February 1917, handed over £41 12s. Edith, the wife of *Charles Henry Phipps, donated her periodicals to the infirmary and Mrs Charles Walker, living at Buckholdt, sent along surgical appliances following the death of her husband, a former Paymaster-in-Chief of the Royal Navy. Led by the Duchess of Beaufort, everyone in the county was asked to provide warm items of clothing such as mittens, helmets and socks for the troops during the County Comforts Day on 14 December. Mrs Clifford was the collector for Frampton, while Mrs Darell undertook the same role from Saul Lodge. At Cadbury's the factory girls made their comforts in the newly opened clubroom.

Some aspects of village life were more routine. The hymn books used by the chapel's Sunday school were in a very bad condition and John Wellings (foreman at Cadbury's factory) paid for a large-type hymn roll to take their place, with the school funding a music edition and six small hymnbooks for the use of teachers and visitors. At St Mary's the time of the evening service was moved from 6 p.m. to 3 p.m. from 7 October for the winter. The chapel continued its normal practice of giving money to the London Missionary Society but, by the end of the year, was also supporting the work of the Young Men's Christian Association, in particular their Soldiers' Hut Fund. (These huts were used as refreshment and recreation centres for troops in the UK and in France and Flanders.) Wartime food restrictions, however, took their toll on the idea of giving the normal Christmas tea for pupils of the Sunday school. The children were given a book instead, 'to vary in quality etc. according to attendance'.

6

1918

POLITICAL SUMMARY

At home, setbacks in the spring, allegedly caused by a shortage of troops, brought a serious challenge in the Commons in the Maurice debate which was the only occasion on which Asquith spoke against the government. Using figures which were afterwards found to be misleading, Lloyd George survived. Major reform legislation demonstrated the government's intention to justify the war and to reward service. Thus the 1918 Reform Act trebled the electorate by giving a parliamentary vote to most women over thirty and men over twenty-one, with minimal political controversy. In July an Education Act raised the school leaving age to fourteen and made provision for school leavers between the ages of 14 and 18 to attend day continuation schools for vocational training. Central government grants permitted substantial increases in teachers' pay. On other problems much planning and talking was done, but no legislation emerged until 1919.

The end of the war in November brought a decision by the Coalition to continue in office, with the argument that national unity would now be needed to negotiate peace terms and a new international order, and to organise demobilisation both of the services and of the wartime controls at home. Lloyd George did a deal with the Conservative leader, Bonar Law, by which they provided a letter, quickly christened 'the coupon', endorsing the Coalition candidate in most constituencies. Most Conservatives, a few Labour and Lloyd George's Liberals got a coupon. Asquith's Liberals did not, nor did the Irish parties or the Labour party which formally went into opposition. A rather nasty campaign began with some emphasis on 'Homes for Heroes', smallholdings for ex-servicemen and other social reforms, but rapidly descended into anti-German hysteria. The result was a crushing Coalition victory, which could be seen as a vote for social reform as well as for punishing Germany; seventy-three Irish MPs, who refused to come to London, formed their own parliament in Dublin.

MILITARY OVERVIEW

Spring 1918 opened with Operation Michael, a highly successful German offensive on the Western Front that used new tactics, especially infiltrating troops at weak points in the Allied lines, advancing 37 miles and shelling Paris with three long-range railway guns. However, the Germans had few tanks to help consolidate their gains, and by July the Allies had halted their progress at the Marne, as in 1914. The Allied counter-offensive, the 'Hundred Days', was much more intelligently managed than previous efforts; when an attack ran into strong resistance it was stopped, and a new thrust was quickly mounted at a different place, tactics which proved extremely successful. In Germany, morale was low, industrial output had collapsed, and American troops (arriving at 10,000 per day) were helping to drive an unstoppable Allied advance.

In the south, a combined British, French, Serbian and Greek army drove up through the Balkans, forcing the surrender of Bulgaria and threatening the border of Hungary. Meanwhile, the Italians had recovered well from their defeat; along with British, French and Czech support they had won a major victory at Vittorio Veneto, and also pushed the Austro-Hungarian armies back to their own borders. In the Middle East, the British and Indian forces from Palestine and Mesopotamia had reached the borders of Turkey proper, which saw much civil turmoil.

Armistices were agreed by the Allied Powers on 30 October with the Ottoman Empire, on 3 November with Austria-Hungary and on 11 November with Germany.

FRAMPTON ON SEVERN

The year began with another National Day of Intercessions, and the morning service at St Mary's on 6 January appears to have been attended by a greater number of people than was usual. More Frampton men fell: *William Henry Morgan was killed by a bomb on 21 March while serving in Belgium and *Percival Leonard Hitchings, younger brother of the late *Frederick, was killed in action on 25 April during the Battles of the Lys. With two of their older sons also serving, bridgekeeper George Hitchings and his wife Annie must have felt the effects of the war particularly acutely. *Thomas Charles Fletcher was killed

The Street looking north.

in action on 29 June on the Western Front. The final servicemen lost their lives when back at home. *Alfred Folkes on 29 October, and *William Thomas Niblett on 29 November both succumbed to the influenza pandemic which had been exacerbated by the movement of troops worldwide.

On 25 January the rural district council discussed a letter from Superintendent Biggs of Stroud police station, who sought its views on the desirability of a public warning in the event of an air raid. Councillors decided that it would be impossible to operate a system in their 'thinly populated and widely scattered district'.

News reached Frampton during February that *Arthur Harry Sutton, by now a Battery Sergeant-Major, had once again been decorated, this time with the Belgian Croix de Guerre. His service with the Royal Field Artillery had also earned him a Certificate of Bravery in August 1917.

At the end of 1917 more gravel from Frampton's fifty-five-acre site was being demanded for the National Shipyards Nos 1 and 2 at Chepstow and Beachley, and by January work intensified following the arrival of an estimated 100 to 150 Inland Waterways & Docks Royal Engineers. Officer Commanding, Captain William Harold Mackenzie Brown, billeted his men around the village and used the Institute as a Mess room. A piledriver and cranes were hired to reconstruct the timber jetty south of Splatt Bridge so as to accept side-tipping railway wagons. Timber and rails were obtained and the railway line was rebuilt on the old track bed laid down previously by Messrs Aird & Co.

Until the railway and jetty were completed, a traction engine and wagons were hired to move gravel from the pits down Perryway to Frampton wharf. This heavy and frequent traffic pushed the wharf wall eighteen inches into the canal (a displacement which can still be seen) and there was concern of an imminent collapse. Fortunately, by early June the railway track and the jetty at Splatt were complete, and a steam dredger running on standard gauge railway tracks loaded the wagons at the gravel pits. During 1918 Captain Mackenzie Brown and his men achieved, on average, more than five sailings per week, each of between 110 and 190 tons. In all, just over 400 shipments were made.

Growing munitions production demanded more storage space for finished shells, and early in 1918 it was decided to use Frampton gravel and blocks for the Bramley Army Ordnance Depot in Hampshire. On 23 March Frampton's population was increased by the arrival of 500 German prisoners of war and 60 members of the Royal Defence Corps to guard them. It had become government policy to allow selected military prisoners of war to work outside their camps, mainly in forestry and agriculture, not only as a way of keeping them occupied, but also to help overcome shortages of manpower. These were from the ranks as no officers could be compelled to work. Their treatment was governed by the 1907 Hague Convention IV, and those brought to Frampton from the parent camp at Dorchester were generally maintained on the same footing as British troops in terms of board, lodging, clothing and medical attention. They were expected to maintain the same level of discipline as that in force in the British Army, and to undertake work that was not excessive, and was not in connection with the operations of war, although the latter rule was loosely interpreted in respect of the Frampton activities. They were paid at an equivalent rate for work done (which might be made in kind to improve their conditions and food among other things, subject to the balance being paid on their repatriation). Their clothes had a coloured patch sewn into the back for ease of recognition in the event of escape.

All the available accommodation in the village was being used by the Royal Engineers, so the new arrivals built a camp on the north of Perryway; the German prisoners of war had huts in the field between Perryway and Netherhills Covert, and the Royal Defence Corps in the adjoining field to the west. The rural district council discussed the proposed sanitary arrangements and instructed the clerk to write to the local Inspector of Nuisances in protest against what it considered to be an 'extensive scheme'. While the Camp Commandant, *Major Percy Strahan, lived with his wife in a property on the village green, the encampment for the men consisted of thirty Tarrant and Armstrong huts. Fifteen close cooking ranges and two large meat safes were also installed.

The rail connection with Frocester was restored and His Majesty's Office of Works recruited a number of local men as labourers, shunters, fitters and trainee locomotive drivers. A professional engineman, Edward Lilley, was also employed. He came from Salford, but settled in Frampton. The men were assisted by dependable prisoners who were signed out of the camp each day. Some prisoners worked in the pits with picks and loaded the gravel by hand into waiting wagons; others manufactured thousands of concrete blocks. There were four sentry boxes and 50 rolls of barbed wire which were presumably used to protect the perimeter of the camp. It has been written that the prisoners were continually under guard by soldiers with fixed bayonets, although this would have been largely for show in front of officials or during the march to work. This image suggests that the

Outside the locomotive shed at Frampton.
   Left to right: Ted Lilley (on footplate), Fred Coleman, Sammy (POW), Leo (POW), Unknown POW, Joe Overbury, Albert (seated, POW and locomotive driver in Germany), Unknown POW, Geoffrey Brinkworth, Sam Lawrence, George Bainbridge.

HM Office of Works employees and prisoners integrated well, enjoyed mutual respect and were relaxed in one another's company. Gifts are known to have been exchanged, including matchbox covers, fabricated and decorated by the Germans. The descendants of William David Daw of Beehive Cottage, who worked with the prisoners, remember him saying that he bore them no malice.

Rail facilities included an engine shed with capacity for up to six industrial locomotives. The repair shop was alongside, together with a rail-mounted 7-ton Priestman crane (later replaced by a 5-ton Smith crane). The locomotives drew three or four railway wagons of gravel at a time out of the pit. Trains consisting of about ten wagons, some with concrete blocks, were then taken to the exchange sidings at Frocester from where the Great Western Railway commenced a service with Bramley on 3 June. Loaded and empty wagons travelled on alternate days, Monday to Saturday. From July, trains were also leaving with materials for the construction of the National Shipyard No. 3 at Portbury.

A Ministry of National Service report dated 4 September confirmed that 100 of the prisoners had been reallocated to agricultural work during the previous month along with twenty guards. This type of transfer was crucial for without the assistance of prisoners of war, the gathering in of the 1918 harvest is unlikely to have been achieved. Of the 398 prisoners at Frampton on the day of the inspection, 300 were employed by HM Office of Works and twenty-one were on camp duties. The remaining seventy-seven were assisting the Royal Engineers, who had previously used a larger contingent until labour-saving equipment in the form of a 'bricket' (perhaps bucket) excavator had been introduced in June. This enabled 4-yard tip wagons to be loaded at twenty-five to thirty wagons per hour, and it was recommended that a similar machine be provided for HM Office of Works to allow the redeployment of another fifty prisoners to other work of national importance. The men worked nine hours per day except Sundays and their conduct was good with few cases of slacking. The report compares very favourably with others around the country.

Recreation was encouraged and although no specific evidence exists for Frampton it is likely that concerts and plays were put on and religious services held. The prisoners were allowed to send up to two letters each week and receive unlimited letters and parcels, all censored by both the British and German

German POW (left) and William David Daw.

authorities. With a substantial number of soldiers in Frampton, the Navy & Army Canteen Board arranged for a goods train of provisions to be sent to the village every Saturday. The consignment included Fry's chocolate, Wills's and Player's cigarettes and barrels of beer. In times of hardship, the consignment was a great temptation, and it has been reported that occasionally boxes accidentally 'broke open' and some beer was siphoned off.

In February, Major General Charles James Blomfield, CB, DSO, of Frampton Lodge, was appointed to the rural district council's Food Control Committee. His long and distinguished military career had ended in retirement when he reached the age limit in July 1917, resulting in a move to Frampton around this time. The content of 'government bread' changed, with potatoes replacing husk because the latter was needed to feed cattle, a shortage of husk in their diets having caused milk yields to fall.

On 26 February, the parish council considered a Board of Agriculture pamphlet encouraging the use of allotments. It agreed to find out who in the village needed one, and also to use the gardens of any empty properties as additional allotments. Food control posters were pasted onto the parish notice board and on 6 May the school closed for the afternoon so that a Board of Agriculture lecturer could give a talk for everyone on 'Food Preserving'. No doubt the majority of people in Frampton were already doing their very best to produce as much food as they possibly could, particularly given the size of many of their gardens, in addition to the village's other conscientious efforts to support a number of good causes associated with the war. The soil is rich and fertile. Thomas Hewlett, seen here with his wife, Emma Margaret, in their garden at Brook House, was well known after the war for taking his home-grown fruit and vegetables around the village for sale in a hand cart, and there can be little doubt that his garden was equally productive during this time too.

On 8 March, villagers attended a meeting at the school and heard an interesting address given by a member of the Agricultural Organisation Society on the formation of a fruit and vegetable growing association along cooperative lines. He promoted the government's scheme to establish pulping stations in fruit-growing areas. These, he said, would enable the whole of the crop to be used with nothing

Thomas and Emma Margaret Hewlett at Brook House *c.* 1918.

left to waste, and would help meet the demands of the Army and Navy. It was unanimously decided to form a society, and a week later Major General Blomfield chaired a meeting of local fruit-growers to take the idea forward. The same speaker attended and dealt with various questions on fruit pulping and drying, and also emphasised the urgent need not only for fruit and vegetables, but also for combining the growing of these with pig-keeping.

Frampton and District Growers Ltd had thirty-three members by the end of its first year. The growers delivered their produce to a depot in the village where it was graded, sorted and packed. Savings were made by taking it to market in bulk instead of individual consignments and £800 worth of fruit and vegetables were sold in 1918, principally apples. The plum crop, however, proved to be a complete failure.

During the spring the County Pig and Potato Production Committee promoted the formation of pig clubs to encourage pig-keeping and the production of food. Household refuse played an important role and it was shown that everyone could make a useful contribution to the enterprise. After the formation of clubs at Hardwicke, Elmore, Berkeley and Whitminster, Frampton was among several villages to host a meeting in May with a view to doing the same.

The Ministry of Food introduced a scheme under which farmers had to consign stock for slaughter either to their local market or to the distributing market for the area. In April it was ordered that Frampton farmers had to use Gloucester Market, which had been appointed a Distributing Market for Area No. 17, and no other. Stock was required urgently, and it was hoped that Gloucester would not only supply local needs, but also help provide for South Wales. Additionally, newspapers advertised that all persons not already in receipt of meat rationing cards should contact the Food Office, as many applications had been received without an address.

Gallipoli and the desert battles took their toll on Major Lionel Darell and, in the spring of 1917, he had returned home to Saul Lodge suffering from neurasthenia (a condition characterised by physical and mental exhaustion). Fond of fishing, recuperation included catching a 1 lb 7 oz trout in Frampton Lake, which had been formed through previous gravel workings. By 1918 he was taking an active role in local affairs, and on 8 June the *Gloucester Journal* reported on his initiative to encourage the parishes of Saul, Frampton, Fretherne, Arlingham, Framilode, Longney and Whitminster to hold a vegetable, fruit and poultry show on the August bank holiday. He felt that the show would be an incentive to allotment holders to cultivate their plots in the best manner possible, and at the same time funds would be raised for the Gloucester Royal Infirmary. In the event, a splendid £150 was handed over.

The following month Frampton, which was said to have become 'a very considerable centre of war work', put on a sports carnival in the grounds of Frampton Court on behalf of Standish VAD Hospital, having been challenged by the *Gloucester Journal* to equal or exceed the achievement of the Fretherne, Saul and District Fruit and Vegetable Show. It is interesting to note that the event was held on a Thursday (12 September); pupils were given a half-day's holiday at the request of the school managers in order that they could attend. Under the banner of a garden fete, a variety of races, sideshows, hat-trimming competitions, clock golf and guessing the scents attaching to twelve bags gave pleasure to a

Decorated bicycles were often paraded at local events.

large number of people. A live pig was the prize in the bowling competition, while another prizewinner walked away with a couple of rabbits. The sideshows included hoop-la, tailless donkey, Aunt Sally, butterflies and character reading, and the King's Stanley Brass Band played selections during the afternoon and evening. Tea was served in a large marquee and was deemed a great success despite wartime restrictions. The people of Frampton and District donated a quantity of provisions, vegetables and fancy articles which were sold in aid of hospital funds. Dr Pinching acted as starter for the sports races, which included 100 yards for both boys and girls. Most were of a more light-hearted nature and included the needle race, bun eating (during wartime food restrictions!), sack race, donkey race, blindfolded driving competition, tilting bucket, egg and spoon race, obstacle race, donkey driving, boot race and the apple and banana race. It was a great time for everyone: the Royal Defence Corps beat the Royal Engineers in the tug of war. The fete raised a magnificent £217 5s 9d. Later that month the Royal Engineers played the Gloucester Wagon Works at football, the game ending in a draw.

The *Cheltenham Chronicle* of 17 August addressed the question of excess produce from the Berkeley Vale's allotments: 'In peace times surpluses were sometimes left to decay. That won't do now. The food had much better not have been grown if it is to be wasted.' Suggestions of distribution to the poor and selling for profits (to be donated to the Red Cross) were made. The Berkeley Hunt Agricultural Society held a competition for the best-fenced farms in the vale in place of their show, which remained suspended 'until happier times arrive'. The newspaper also gave its views on the duplication of effort in 'that recently inaugurated industry, the milk traffic' and was critical of the lack of organisation during the collection of churns, with many motors seemingly travelling the same routes only partly laden.

Pasteurised milk from Cadbury's factory was taken daily to Stonehouse to go by train to Birmingham and other large towns. The provision of fresh milk to Birmingham, which provided for the needs of children, invalids and hospital patients, was evidently very much appreciated, for in May the Medical Officer of Health for the city expressed his warm appreciation.

Churns arrive by lorry at
Cadbury's in 1916.

People in Frampton reaped many benefits from Cadbury's presence in the village. From the outset, the ethos of the Cadbury family's Quaker traditions was experienced in the way that they tried to look after their employees with good working conditions and the works canteen. They provided a recreation ground and encouraged the works Sports and Social Club. There was education too, with a wartime purpose. In October the works magazine (another example of the way that Cadbury's promoted well-being and inclusiveness among its employees) reported that Dr Pinching had held ambulance classes for men, and that his wife had taught sewing to employees and wives of employees. The latter resulted in twenty-five flannel shirts and forty pairs of knitted socks being sent to 'the local hospital'. Boys benefited from the teaching of the foreman, John Wellings, with classes in industrial history, arithmetic and elementary science. A certain amount of the necessary equipment had been provided by the Bournville Works Committee. The presence of the factory in the village did, however, have a negative side for some people; since Cadbury's did not approve of alcohol: the village pubs and beer houses kept their shutters closed so that Mr Wellings, on his frequent walks around the village, could not see who was drinking inside.

Vera, the youngest sister of *Wells Alexander Watkins, had been a Sunday school teacher at the chapel for some years, and was also attached to the staff of Saul British School. On 8 September the Sunday school opened its doors to everyone as Vera was about to leave Frampton to enter college. In recognition of her work she was presented with a teacher's edition of the Bible by the superintendent, Lucy Hawker. 'The singing of a hymn and prayer brought a very happy occasion to a close.' The same month it was decided to make a collection in aid of the Serbian Relief Fund and 10s was raised.

Wounded soldiers from three Red Cross hospitals in Gloucester were treated to a trip down the canal by the Gloucester Branch of the Dickens Fellowship on 27 June. Attendees, who included nurses and dignitaries and numbered almost 290, had to make their way from Fretherne Bridge for tea at Framilode. The Bell Hotel was among the businesses that conveyed those who could not walk that distance.

Frampton was the scene of two tragic accidents in 1918. The first involved William Walter Harris, the nine-year-old son of *George Harris. On Wednesday 24 July, William left school as usual but did not go straight home. He wandered instead into the workshop of William Thomas Allen (of The Street) who was outside repairing his motorcycle. Once inside, William found a six-chambered revolver in a drawer loaded with a single cartridge. It is thought that he looked down the muzzle and, without realising the danger, pulled the trigger, wounding himself in the head. Mr Allen rushed into the workshop when he heard the firearm discharge and found William lying unconscious on the floor. Dr Pinching tried in vain to save the boy's life, but William Walter Harris died on the Saturday morning. He was buried in St Mary's churchyard on 1 August.

The second accident occurred on 17 October. Pioneer Arthur Wadsworth of the Royal Engineers was working as a shunter at the gravel pits while six loaded tip-wagons were being shifted from one track to another. There was a slight incline on the line and when the trucks were in position for shunting, the brake was applied. Arthur was standing beside the track and should have reached over the buffers to uncouple the wagons by hand. Something evidently went very wrong with the operation (there were no witnesses), and a shout was heard as he became crushed. After the wagons had been released, Arthur dropped to the ground. When the driver came up to him Arthur said: 'It is here I had it'. Dr Pinching was sent for and attended along with the Royal Army Medical Corps orderly. Arthur was taken to the Gloucester Red Cross Hospital in Southgate Street with serious abdominal injuries, and later transferred to the 2nd Southern General Hospital in Bristol where, after an initial period of improvement, his condition worsened. His bowel had been bruised and inflamed, and several portions of his intestine had become matted together by adhesions. An operation was performed from which Arthur Wadsworth did not recover. He was forty years old and left behind a wife and five children. His body was returned to them in Middlesbrough where he was buried in an unofficial war grave at Linthorpe Cemetery.

In addition, two German prisoners of war are said to have died in unknown circumstances and been buried in St Peter's churchyard, Frocester, in unrecorded graves. It is also understood that the carrier, Frank Selwyn Betteridge, transported the body of 'Crontie', a German prisoner of war, to St Mary's churchyard in Frampton, together with a roughly engraved concrete block in his memory, produced by one of Crontie's friends. This was refused by the vicar, but Frank kept

The memorial to Crontie, thought to have been a German prisoner of war.

it, and his descendants still have it today. The date of Crontie's death, however, pre-dates the prisoners of war camp associated with the gravel workings, leaving us with a mystery.

Throughout the war Frank Betteridge kept as many as twenty horses, employing several young lads who were too old for school and too young for active service. His governess carts and gigs were stored in a series of buildings to the north of Perryway, rented from the Estate, where the tin shed now stands. His horses were kept in nearby Barnfield and on land behind the western side of The Green and The Street. They were turned out every day onto the village green in sight of his home at present-day Kempsey House. Frank operated an important transport service for troops, prisoners of war and materials, and at the same time continued with his daily newspaper deliveries to the local villages, cheered on by his rhyme:

> Stonehouse, Frocester, Coaley, Cam,
> Frampton, Fretherne, Ar-ling-ham.

Villagers had therefore been able to follow the war, within the limits of censorship, and were well aware that hostilities were beginning to draw to a close. By early November the papers contained little else by way of news and, although it went unrecorded, one imagines that in Frampton there was an air of optimism, shared by the residents, the billeted troops and the German prisoners of war. On 11 November, news of the Armistice reached the school by lunchtime, and at the beginning of the afternoon session the headmaster spoke to the children about what it meant. In a victorious show of patriotism, the Union Jack was hoisted amid resounding cheers. The remainder of the afternoon was declared a holiday, and in the evening a Thanksgiving Service was held at St Mary's, Fretherne.

The following Sunday, Reverend Ward preached on the subject of 'Thanksgiving and Victory' taking his text from Exodus 15:

> Then sang Moses and the children of Israel this song unto the Lord, and spake, saying, I will sing unto the Lord, for he hath triumphed gloriously: the horse and his rider hath been thrown into the sea. The Lord is my strength and song, and he is become my salvation.

7

AFTER THE WAR

POLITICAL SUMMARY

Early in 1919, the government's complex and carefully thought out demobilisation plans to release first the men with key industrial skills provoked bitter resentment and what amounted to mutinies. The scheme was abandoned in favour of 'first in, first out' which proceeded rapidly. Most price controls and subsidies ended although some food rationing continued into 1921. The immediate result was a boom, with rapidly rising prices and wages. There were two pieces of social reform. The 1919 Housing Act required local authorities to assess housing needs in their areas, to plan for dealing with shortages and build the necessary houses. These were to be supported by a central government subsidy and let at a subsidised rent. This initiative was to lead to the building of Frampton's first council houses in Bridge Road and Whitminster Lane. A supplementary act gave a small subsidy to private house building. Then in 1920 the Unemployment Insurance Act extended the 1911 Act to cover most wage-earners.

However, the boom of 1919 soon came to an end, to be followed by depression and mass unemployment by the end of 1920. The government's response was to cut expenditure, so the housing subsidies were steadily reduced and part-time education for all children up to the age of eighteen, proposed by the 1918 Education Act, never really got started.

MILITARY OVERVIEW

By late 1918 the Allied armies were very organised indeed for waging a war, but in November faced a completely new challenge: with the cessation of fighting at the Armistice, and after over four years of hard and bloody warfare, the troops and their families expected everybody to return home straight away and pick up their lives. However, there were many huge high-priority tasks to accomplish which would have greatly strained even the wartime logistical systems.

Pending formal peace treaties, Allied troops occupied areas of the defeated countries for some years: British soldiers occupied Constantinople until 1923, and were in the Rhineland until 1929. British and Allied forces supported the Tsarist ('White') Russians against the ('Red') Communists until the end of 1919.

Repatriation of British and Empire prisoners of war was a priority, and as much military equipment as possible had to be recovered. British Empire and other Allied forces also had to be repatriated; this was a worldwide task. All this had to be accomplished by diminishing numbers of service personnel with the right skills, who meanwhile had to be supplied with food and fuel and allowed some leave. It was inevitable that there would be delays and disappointments during this logistical nightmare. The repatriation of German prisoners of war did not effectively start until after the Treaty of Versailles had been signed on 28 June 1919.

FRAMPTON ON SEVERN

In November 1918 the village was in the grip of the influenza pandemic which locally took several lives, including those of four German prisoners of war: Füsilier Artur Chlosta and Musketier Paul Riemer of the Prussian Army, Soldat Wilhelm Jüntgen of the Saxon Army, and Gefreiter (Lance Corporal) Johann Namislo. They were buried in St Mary's churchyard until February 1963, when their remains were removed to the German Military Cemetery at Cannock Chase, Staffordshire. Anecdotal evidence suggests that there was sadness in the village when the reburials took place, as many Frampton folk still had a fondness for the prisoners of war whom they had worked alongside and known some forty-five years earlier.

The gravel workings continued post-war, and during 1919 Frampton supplied the Gloucester Ferro-Concrete Shipbuilding Co. Ltd at Hempsted and probably

Three of the graves of German prisoners of war at St Mary's.

the construction of the Anglo–Persian oil refinery at Llandarcy, near Neath. It is not clear how long the prisoners of war remained in Frampton, nor whether their departure back to the Dorchester camp was phased, but it is known that returning servicemen were taken on at the gravel pits. In June there was a rumour that some Gloucester men were refused work in Frampton, but the Gloucester Local Employment Committee found no evidence of such discrimination. Much of the paraphernalia associated with the Royal Defence Corps and German camps was auctioned by Messrs Davis & Champion on 29 October. With the market saturated by such items Bruton, Knowles & Co. appear to have auctioned the residue from the first sale on 12 December. By the end of 1919 nearly all those working at the gravel pits were laid off as an economy measure. The furniture and fittings of the camp were offered for sale on 3 May 1922; the dismantling of the railways and disposal of plant, machinery and the jetty at Splatt was a protracted affair which took until 1923 to complete.

Following the declaration of peace, the munitions workers at Quedgeley were given three days' holiday on full pay. Stock-taking and cleaning followed during the next fortnight, after which working hours were reduced. By the end of the month 75 per cent of the workforce had been released. Over the next four years the buildings and their contents were auctioned, and in 1920 the ammunition was broken down for scrap, providing short-term employment for 150 workers (both male and female). The Slimbridge magazine continued to store propellants and high explosives, but during 1920 and 1921 became a centre for stock destruction as storage costs (which included the wages of ex-servicemen replacing the wartime military guards) outweighed the value of the goods. A red glow could be seen from Frampton as the cordite was burnt in a field near Shepherd's Patch.

Cadbury's, like many other employers, remained loyal to workers who had volunteered to serve or been conscripted during the war, such as *Arthur Edwin Lawrence. During that time replacement staff had been told that they were providing temporary cover, although with the factory's programme of expansion, and some women inevitably preferring to return to home life full time, it seems that there was plenty of opportunity to find work at Cadbury's. Many ex-servicemen spent their entire post-war careers at the Frampton factory including *Francis William Aldridge, *John Jones and *Richard William Rowles.

The demobilisation of Frampton's servicemen and their return home was a lengthy process and very few appear to have completed this transition before the end of 1918. Electoral registers were compiled for both the spring and autumn of 1919 and these, together with information from service records and the awarding of medals, indicate that the majority of those who enlisted or were conscripted came back to the village during this year. *Frederick Charles Gardner, *William Thomas Hodder and *Charles Henry Hitchings were all demobilised during February, but the families of *Timothy John Sims and *Martin Walter William Camm had to wait until November to welcome back their men permanently. Some continued in the Armed Forces, having already chosen that career path prior to the war but others, such as *Preston Dennis and *Stephen John Dark, had enlisted during the war and subsequently gave lengthy service to their country in the Army and Navy respectively.

From 1917, when men invalided out of the Armed Forces could be re-conscripted, several associations were formed to address their welfare and rights. Later, as men were demobilised, many joined; the Bradley brothers, *Francis Hugh and *Percy John, became Comrades of the Great War in June 1919. These associations were amalgamated into the British Legion on 15 May 1921 which still provides financial, social and emotional support for ex-servicemen. The Frampton and District Branch of the British Legion was one of the first in the country.

In March 1919 Harry Fletcher left Lake House after auctioning his livestock, outside effects and household furniture. He was not alone in deciding to leave the neighbourhood, for it was a time of upheaval for many villagers either seeking to rebuild their lives after the loss of a loved one, or needing to find employment after wartime contracts and service came to an end. In Harry's case, he had lost two sons and the other, *Gilbert John, had just been selected for retention for a further year. As the servicemen arrived home, some of them disabled like *Frederick William Cottle who had lost a leg, there was much adjustment and no instant return to normality. The longed-for welcome home was tempered by the reality of shell shock and other incapacities which required understanding and patience, as well as spells in hospital. For the returning men too, there were differences at home, their women having experienced greater independence, which in turn raised their expectations and aspirations.

Peace, combined with high land and house prices, brought about a flurry of activity in the property market; Greycroft (then two dwellings) and Hart's Cottages were among those auctioned at the Bell Hotel on 25 October 1919 by the trustee of Frederick Walford Vick senior. In some instances the tenants were the purchasers while in others local property owners took the opportunity to extend their portfolio. The Bell itself was for sale in 1920, the first of the Estate's properties to be put on the market after the war. It was sold to Warn & Sons,

FRAMPTON-ON-SEVERN

Particulars, Plan, and Conditions of Sale
OF THE

OLD ESTABLISHED
FULLY-LICENSED HOTEL
KNOWN AS

The Bell Hotel

Overlooking the well-known Frampton Green, with

COACH - HOUSE,   STABLING,
FARM BUILDINGS,
AND

PASTURE LAND
AND ALSO

ENCLOSURES OF SOUND OLD PASTURE
AND

VERY PRODUCTIVE ARABLE LAND
THE WHOLE BEING ABOUT
29a. 1r. 39p.
IN EXTENT

BRUTON, KNOWLES & CO.

Are instructed to Sell the above important Freehold properties by Auction
in Two Lots

AT THE BELL HOTEL, GLOUCESTER
On Saturday, June 12th, 1920
AT THREE O'CLOCK PUNCTUALLY

Further particulars may be had of R. H. PENLEY, Esq., Solicitor, Dursley, or of the
Auctioneers, Albion Chambers, Gloucester.

JOHN BELLOWS, GLOUCESTER 1894

wine and spirit merchants of Tetbury. George Frederick Holloway stayed on as proprietor and Samuel Bradley immediately began work to convert a barn at the Bell into a cinema.

The death of *Henry Francis Clifford had encumbered his estate with duties and in 1924 Church, Denfurlong and Netherhills farms were sold to the sitting tenants, Charles Edward Williams, William Coole and Charles William Morse respectively. Their descendants still own the farms today, the Williams family now living at Tanhouse Farm which includes the Church Farm land. Other properties were also sold to sitting tenants: The Denhalls (now Wisma Mulia) to Dr Charles Joseph Weller, and nearby the cottages at Tobacco Box to ex-servicemen *Arthur Edwin Lawrence, *Timothy John Sims and *William Sims, and also the Sims' father, William Henry. Church End House was sold to Rose, the wife of *Herbert Charles Drayton who was still in the Royal Navy. The Estate sold other property and land including Workhouse Orchard, Cutchy Rack and part of the Cant Leaze to Frank Selwyn Betteridge; it was a time for many to consolidate their business affairs.

Freedom from the endless war effort fundraising brought no let-up in social events in the village, although at the start of 1919 there is conflicting evidence about the availability of food. On 13 February the pupils at the chapel's Sunday school enjoyed their treat of tea and games, but the normal custom of inviting their parents and friends was still not deemed possible due to difficulties in procuring sufficient provisions. However, almost a month earlier, on 8 January, nearly 100 employees at Cadbury's attended a large social where tables were 'piled with uncouponed ham and beef' in the building normally used for the storage of condensed milk. A whist drive and games, yet more refreshments and a concert followed; this was the first of many similar events organised by the firm's Social Committee. In 1921 an ex-Army hut (of which there was a plentiful supply) was erected on the recreation field and fitted out by Cadbury's, who shared the cost of a piano with the committee. The 'Recreation Hut' hosted a wide variety of events over the coming years, just as its successor, Cadbury Hall, does today. With the war over, the firm's sports clubs flourished too and at long last the Institute was able to host its own fundraising events; a concert by Gloucester musicians and others entertained a large audience on 3 April 1919. The popular Horse Show and Sports was successfully revived on Thursday 29 July 1920 with the profits donated to the football and cricket clubs.

Parish council meetings continued sporadically, their brief minutes providing only a hint of the business that took place. On 28 November 1918 letters from the County Prisoners of War Committee were discussed but the council voted not to respond to them. There was a similar air of official reluctance to become involved on 1 July 1919. Following a circular from the Ministry of Health authorising parish councils to make payments towards peace celebrations, councillors decided to give their backing to the Peace Celebration Committee which hoped to defray the costs by means of subscription.

Very few war memorials exist for all the wars before 1914, but the enormous cost and casualties during the First World War fuelled a desire to commemorate the sacrifice that had been made. Nationally this led to the creation of the Cenotaph in Whitehall, the annual service and the two-minute silence. At St Mary's Reverend Ward preached on 'Thanksgiving for Victory' and 'Blessings of Peace' at the two services held on 17 November 1918 and part of the collection was donated to King George's Fund for Sailors. On 6 July 1919, following the signing of the peace treaty, churches throughout the country, including St Mary's, held National Thanksgiving services. The peace celebrations referred to by the parish council probably coincided with the weekend of Frampton Feast, when there was a parade service for ex-servicemen on 17 August. About fifty of them mustered on The Green and marched to St Mary's headed by the Uley Brass Band; the small number suggests that many were still not back from their duties.

The question of who was to be named on the village war memorial would have been left to the discretion of the committee that raised funds towards its erection. There were no set rules and Frampton was not alone in omitting some from the village who fell. Families had been displaced by war, and often widows asked for

The Bishop of Gloucester dedicating the war memorial in 1920.

their husband's name to be included on a memorial where they had resettled; for this reason, some men appear on more than one memorial. Frampton's was made by Arthur S. Cooke of Paganhill from Minchinhampton stone and the cost of £200 was covered by subscription.

At 6 p.m. on St George's Day, Friday 23 April 1920, the war memorial cross was dedicated by the Bishop of Gloucester. The ceremony was watched by a large congregation, which included many ex-servicemen and a contingent of Royal Gloucestershire Hussars. Anecdotal evidence suggests that the unveiling ceremony was performed by war veterans Sergeant Tom Sims (*Thomas Ernest Sims) and Private William Hunt (probably *Arthur William Hunt). Armistice Day fell on a Thursday in 1920 when a service was held at 7 p.m., a convenient time for working people. It may have retained this time the following year, but by 1922 the more familiar 11 a.m. timing had been adopted.

Despite extensive investigations, it has not been possible to identify who was responsible for erecting the plaque in the village hall that commemorates most of Frampton's servicemen. It was probably created at the same time as grateful villagers gave individual certificates of recognition to those who served. Several ex-servicemen had left the village by the end of 1922, presumably to seek work and also following marriage; the most likely date for the plaque appears to be either 1921 or 1922.

A feature of commemoration at this time was the display of captured enemy weapons, and at a meeting on 28 October 1919 the parish council accepted the War Office Trophies Committee's offer of a German machine gun. Five months later its position was still being discussed and the suggestion was made that it should be displayed in the Institute. The absence of further reference to the matter in any extant village records suggests that it may not have arrived in Frampton;

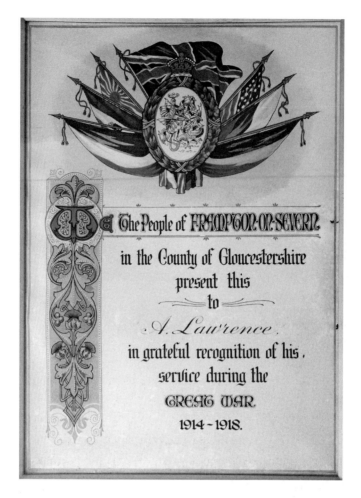

The People of FRAMPTON-ON-SEVERN in the County of Gloucestershire present this to *A. Lawrence* in grateful recognition of his service during the GREAT WAR 1914-1918.

had it come it would have almost certainly been sent for scrap in 1940 like many other similar trophies around the country. In August 1923, after Major Ardern Arthur Hulme Beaman, DSO, had come to live at Green End House (Top O' The Green), he wrote to the parish council regarding an 18-pounder gun which he was able to provide. The council arranged a public meeting outside the Old Coffee House to enable parishioners to decide how to proceed, but again the outcome is not known. Major Beaman moved into Manor Farm shortly afterwards and became very active in the Frampton and District Branch of the British Legion, which held annual parades from 1921. In 1923, under the command of Major Sir Lionel Darell, Bart, DSO, (who had succeeded his father to the baronetcy in 1919), ex-servicemen assembled on the village green and, headed by the Sharpness Silver Band, marched through Saul and then to Fretherne church for the annual service. The branch flourished, holding fundraising poppy whist drives and dances, and when the national president attended the annual dinner and smoking concert at the Institute in 1936, he found that practically 90 per cent of the ex-servicemen in the district were enrolled and that the branch was nearly 150 strong, a quite remarkable record.

The war memorial, village hall plaque and annual acts of remembrance continue to focus attention on the tragic loss of life during the First World War. The remainder of this book tells the stories of the Frampton servicemen who fought for our future. *William George Birch, seen here in the background at the war memorial with his own thoughts, served for almost the entire war. He enlisted voluntarily in early September 1914, and was demobilised during the spring or summer of 1919. Bill served alongside *Francis William Aldridge, *Christopher Charles Fryer, *Thomas Henry Griffin and *Ernest Walter Henry Tainton in the 9th (Service) Battalion of the Gloucestershire Regiment, which saw considerable action in both the Balkan and French theatres. Left at home, his wife Frances had lost two younger brothers in France, *Frederick Robert William John and *Percival Leonard Hitchings. For many, such commitment and sacrifice typified wartime life at home and abroad.

A time for reflection: the Birch family at the war memorial.

8

SERVICEMEN

FRANCIS WILLIAM ALDRIDGE, 1895–1996
Private 12513, 9th (Service) Battalion,
Gloucestershire Regiment

Remembrance Sunday 1995 was a special occasion in Frampton as First World War veteran, 'Pip' Aldridge, celebrated his 100th birthday. He sat among friends, proudly holding a certificate presented to him after the war by villagers in recognition of his service, and his telegram from Her Majesty the Queen.

Francis William Aldridge was born in Frampton on 12 November 1895 to William Aldridge, a mariner, and Rosa Kate née Wilkins. Brought up in one of the cottages at Splatt, Pip and his elder sisters and younger brother were not baptised until 20 May 1903. After leaving school he worked as a farm labourer.

In early September 1914 Pip responded to Lord Kitchener's appeal to enlist in the Army, joining at Gloucester at the same time as *William George Birch and *Frederick Gilbert Alexander Cook. Pip was posted, along with Bill Birch, to the 9th (Service) Battalion of the Gloucestershire Regiment, formed at Bristol in September 1914 as part of the Third New Army; it joined the 78th Brigade of the 26th Division, moving initially to Cheltenham and, in April 1915, to Longbridge Deverill in Wiltshire. The 9th Glosters entered France on 20 September but did not remain there long. In November they were redeployed to the Mediterranean Expeditionary Force and landed at Salonika, Greece, before moving north to strengthen Serbian resistance against Bulgarian forces. During their two and a half years in the Balkans they took part in the capture of Horseshoe Hill and the three Battles of Doiran.

In July 1918, with the weakening of the Austro-Hungarian and Bulgarian forces opposing them, the battalion was withdrawn from Greece and moved to France. Joining the 66th (2nd East Lancashire) Division at a time of being reformed after their losses in the huge German offensive of early 1918, Operation Michael, they came into the field in October for the Battle of Cambrai, followed by the Pursuit to the Selle and the offensive against the Hindenburg Line. By late September the 9th Glosters formed the Divisional Pioneers; after a week's rest they were again in action, this time to bridge the Selle, allowing the Division to cross and the South African Brigade to capture Le Cateau in a costly engagement. This river crossing was the opening stage of the Battle of the Selle, the final advance into Germany. Following the Armistice they were ordered to occupy the Rhine bridgeheads and remained there until February 1919. After demobilisation Pip was transferred to the Army Reserve.

His obituary in the *Gloucester Citizen* indicates that he was a signalman, implying that his role was in telephony and telegraphy. He was awarded the 1914–15 Star, British War Medal and Victory Medal and his service is commemorated on the plaque in the village hall.

On 5 December 1920 Pip married Ethel Florence Archer at St Mary's, Cheltenham. A couple of years later they moved to the Old Coffee House, The Green, where they brought up their two children, Eric and Doreen. Pip worked at Cadbury's for over fifty years and also looked after the churchyard grass. In 1932 he helped to found the Frampton on Severn and District Angling Club; football was another abiding passion. Villagers remember a quiet man who loved his pipe, his food and a tot of whisky. After Ethel died, their daughter Doreen helped care for Pip at home until he moved into the Old Vicarage Nursing Home when in his late nineties. Francis William Aldridge died there on 20 June 1996 aged 100 years and seven months, and was buried in St Mary's churchyard six days later.

ARTHUR DAVID BERRY, 1889–1968
Private 9251, 2nd Battalion, Oxfordshire and Buckinghamshire Light Infantry

Arthur David Berry was born in Arlingham on 11 September 1889 to Charles Vale Berry, a labourer, and Fanny Louisa née Goodfield. Home was a four-roomed cottage on the Priding Road, and Arthur was baptised at nearby St Peter's, Framilode, on 18 October the same year. The family was a large one; Arthur was a middle child of twelve. By 1911 he had enlisted in the Army and completed his basic training. At the time of the census he was a private with the 2nd Battalion of the Oxfordshire and Buckinghamshire Light Infantry at Shorncliffe Camp, near Dover. When Arthur married Elsie May Boucher at St Mary's, Fretherne, on 8 June 1913 he was stationed at Aldershot. Their first child, Arthur, was born later that year, his birth registered in Wheatenhurst which covered the Fretherne and Frampton area.

When the war came Arthur was deployed to France. His battalion arrived on 14 August and was rapidly in the thick of the heavy fighting at Mons and during the long retreat to the Marne; they suffered many casualties at the First Battle of Ypres, which almost destroyed the old Regular British Army. With reinforcements to replace the casualties, the battalion was later engaged in the major battles of

Loos and the Somme, and indeed remained on the Western Front as part of the 5th Infantry Brigade throughout the war. This would have included action to follow up the German retreat to the Hindenburg Line, the Battles of Arras and Cambrai, and the desperate fighting to stem the German Operation Michael in the spring of 1918. Arthur's family recall him briefly talking of horses and the Somme: like many of the war veterans, he did not speak much of the experiences which earned him the 1914 Star, British War Medal and Victory Medal. His war service is commemorated on the plaque in Frampton Village Hall.

There must have been brief periods of leave for Arthur as his son Charles, known as Stewart, was born in 1916 and the birth of Hubert (Frank) was registered at the beginning of 1919. The Berrys had made their home at The Lake, Frampton, with Arthur recorded as an absent voter in 1918–19. Dorothy (Joan), Ellen (Mary), Charles (Doug), Elizabeth (Betty) and Evelyn completed the family over the next few years. Arthur worked for Cadbury's, and he and Elsie later moved to 8 Bridge Road and then to 20 The Oval. Arthur David Berry died in 1968 and was cremated at Gloucester on 1 October after a service at St Mary's.

WILLIAM GEORGE BIRCH, 1894–1927
Private 12514, 9th (Service) Battalion,
Gloucestershire Regiment

William George Birch was born and baptised in Frampton in the spring of 1894, the son of George Birch, a labourer, and Susannah née Trigg. Their home was close to the end of Marsh Lane, probably in present-day Tulip Cottage. Bill, as he was known, worked as a farm labourer before the war, and on 9 January 1915 he married Frances Louise Hitchings (the sister of *Charles, *Ashley, *Frederick and *Percival) at St Mary's. Their daughter, Mary, was born in the spring of that year and the family lived in one of the cottages at Splatt.

Bill enlisted in Lord Kitchener's Army in early September 1914 at Gloucester together with *Francis William Aldridge and *Frederick Gilbert Alexander Cook. Like 'Pip' Aldridge, Bill was posted to the 9th (Service) Battalion of the Gloucestershire Regiment. They had consecutive service numbers and appear to have seen out the war together along with *Ernest Walter Henry Tainton. After training they landed in France on 20 September 1915 and were redeployed to Salonika two months later, staying in the Balkans until July 1918 when they returned to France. They were part of the final advance into Germany where they occupied the Rhine bridgeheads until February 1919. A fuller account of the actions involving the 9th Battalion is given in Pip Aldridge's biography and also, in part, in the diary of *Thomas Henry Griffin on page [57]. Bill was awarded the 1914–15 Star, British War Medal and Victory Medal and his service is commemorated on the plaque in the village hall.

After demobilisation and transfer to the Army Reserve, Bill and Frances had four more children: Frederick, Dorothy, Robert and Stanley. Frances' health was not good and Mary, being five years older than her next sibling, played a large part in bringing them up. Bill was employed as a barge worker for Cadbury's and then as a coal hobbler at Sharpness. On Sunday 20 November 1927 Bill met his brother-in-law, Daniel Tudor, for one drink at the Tudor Arms, Shepherd's Patch, and left mid-evening. It was dark, wet and windy as he cycled home along the towpath and where it narrowed to just 3 feet (including the grass margins) he either rode or fell into the canal. William George Birch's body was recovered two days later and he was buried in St Mary's churchyard on 25 November. The family remained in the village, later moving to The Green.

FRANCIS HUGH BRADLEY, 1886–1947
Acting Sergeant 149801 and WR/552171, 119th
Railway Company, Royal Engineers

Francis Hugh Bradley was born in Sutton Bridge, Lincolnshire, on 8 March 1886. Known as Hugh, he was the third child of Samuel and Elizabeth Bradley. When he was five the family moved to Lake Cottage, Lake Lane, Frampton, where Samuel set up business as a builder and decorator. By 1901 Hugh and his older brother George were working for their father as a bricklayer and carpenter respectively, but severe unemployment in the building trade encouraged the brothers to emigrate. Hugh returned in November 1915, sailing from Sierra Leone on the SS *Burutu* when he was described as a foreman of works.

No enlistment records have been found for either Hugh or his younger brother, *Percy John. Hugh was a keen footballer and enjoyed motorbikes, and family members believe that during the war he was a despatch rider. He was photographed in the uniform of a corporal in the 119th Railway Company of the Royal Engineers, and according to the medal roll he reached the rank of acting sergeant. Two service numbers are given on this record, although he remained with the Royal Engineers. Hugh received the British War Medal and Victory Medal and his service is also commemorated on the plaque in the village hall.

On 21 June 1919 Hugh became a Comrade of the Great War (one of the original four ex-service associations that amalgamated to form the British Legion in 1921). He spent many years working abroad in the building trade; in June 1923 he sailed on the SS *Morka* from Marseilles to Plymouth as part of his journey from the Malay States back to Frampton. In 1938, as a buildings overseer, he sailed from London to Singapore on the *Hakone Maru* going to the Straits Settlements. It is thought that he worked for the Singapore Harbour Board but left when the Japanese invaded. In August 1945 he returned from Australia to Oatfield Cottages, Whitminster Lane, Frampton, where he was listed as retired. Francis Hugh Bradley died on 5 November 1947 and was buried in St Mary's churchyard.

PERCY JOHN BRADLEY, 1891–1971
Private 5171, Gloucestershire Regiment; Sapper 182149, 35th Divisional Signal Company, Royal Engineers

Percy John Bradley was born on 3 June 1891 in Sutton Bridge, Lincolnshire, the fourth child of Samuel and Elizabeth Bradley. Shortly after his birth the family moved to Frampton and by 1911 Percy was employed by his father as a bricklayer.

Percy initially joined the Gloucestershire Regiment but later transferred to the Royal Engineers as a sapper, presumably to make good use of his skills, and family members understand that Percy was at Ypres. He was awarded the British War Medal and Victory Medal and his service is also commemorated on the plaque in the village hall. Percy became a Comrade of the Great War at the same time as his brother, *Francis Hugh, in 1919 and also maintained links with the Old Comrades' Association of the 35th Divisional Signal Company of the Royal Engineers.

After the war Percy continued to work for his father. He was a keen beekeeper and met his future wife, Margaret Elizabeth Cook, at Whitminster House, where he was looking after the bees and she was working as a lady's maid. They were married on 21 July 1929 at Guiting Power and had four daughters: Olive, Margaret, Rosa and Sylvia. Percy John Bradley died in Frampton on 26 July 1971 and was buried next to his father in St Mary's churchyard.

ALBERT JOSEPH BRAZINGTON, 1879–1937
Private 48392, 1st (Reserve) Garrison Battalion, Worcestershire Regiment

Albert Joseph Brazington, known as Bertie, was born in Frampton in 1879, the younger son of Edward Brazington, a waterman, and Anne (or Annie) née Bullock. The family lived in Saltwater Row (later Hart's Cottages). Bertie's mother died in 1901 and his father in 1908. By 1911 he was working as a gardener and lodging in a property belonging to the Estate.

Bertie enlisted with the 1st (Reserve) Garrison Battalion of the Worcestershire Regiment on 7 June 1917 at Stroud. He only served as a private for 152 days, for he had a long-term tubercle (an outgrowth) on his right ankle which gave him impaired movement. He was awarded the Silver War Badge to indicate his discharge from service and is remembered on the village hall plaque.

Bertie fell in love with Lilian Annie Clifford of The Grange, the elder sister of *Henry Francis and the First World War nurses, Edith Katherine, Mabel Constance and Elaine Annie. Although Lilian's mother disapproved of the liaison, the couple lived together for many years in a caravan behind The Grange. Lilian broke her hip and subsequently died of heart failure on 10 September 1937; it is said that Bertie died of a broken heart nine days later. Lilian's sister, Mabel, registered his death, giving her relationship as cousin, meant in this context as a member of his wider family. Albert Joseph Brazington was buried in St Mary's churchyard.

HAROLD WILLIAM BRINKWORTH, 1897–1983
Corporal 95718, Tank Corps

Harold William Brinkworth was born on 24 June 1897 to Joseph Henry Brinkworth and Eliza née Alder of Fromebridge. Joseph was a steam crane driver undertaking dredging on the canal and, by the age of thirteen, Harold was working in the local cloth manufacturing industry.

Perhaps it was his father's employment with heavy machinery that led Harold to serve as a corporal in the Tank Corps during the war. Tanks, or 'land battleships', were first suggested in the autumn of 1914, and an experimental machine was completed in December 1915. The first companies of tanks were raised in 1916 and some embarked for France during the summer of that year but Harold's exact role is not known. He was awarded the British War Medal and Victory Medal and his name is commemorated on the plaque in the village hall next to that of his uncle, *Thomas Hart Brinkworth.

Following demobilisation, Harold returned to Gloucestershire and married Alice Evelyn M. White, their wedding being registered in the first quarter of 1923 in the Wheatenhurst district. They lived in Alkerton, Eastington, where he worked as a fishmonger. They had one son, also called Harold. Harold William Brinkworth later moved to King's Stanley and his death was registered during the first quarter of 1983.

THOMAS HART BRINKWORTH, 1892–1949
Temporary Corporal 3169, 9th Battalion, Royal Queensland Regiment

Thomas Hart Brinkworth was baptised at St Mary's on 14 February 1892, the son of William James Hart Brinkworth, a waterman, and Patience Elizabeth née Williams. His birth was registered during the first quarter of the same year. The family lived at Hart's Cottages, The Street. Coming from a seafaring family, it is no surprise that Thomas was at sea at the age of fifteen, when he signed as a cook on the *Albion* of Poole under his older brothers, David (master) and Jabez (mate), on which he sailed to numerous British ports. Gaining experience, he later worked as an ordinary seaman, and by 1912 was working on ships not commanded by his brothers, and sailing as far as Chile. Thomas may have already emigrated by the start of the war, as on 8 July 1915 he enlisted into the Australian Army at Brisbane, perhaps an odd choice for a professional seaman. One of his next-of-kin was given as his brother Jabez, at Port Adelaide in South Australia.

After basic training Thomas embarked for Egypt. On 21 January 1916 he joined the 9th Battalion of the Royal Queensland Regiment at Tel-el-Kebir, but only five days later he suffered a septic hand and entered the first of a series of hospitals (Serapeum, Ismailia, Cairo and Heliopolis). However this did not affect his spirit as on 12 April he was in trouble for refusing to obey an order from an NCO (Non-Commissioned Officer).

Meanwhile, his battalion had been transferred to France. Thomas arrived on 9 May, but did not join them until 10 July on the Somme. Their first major action was the Battle of Pozières, which started on 23 July. On that first day Thomas suffered a gunshot wound to his left hand which led to him being sent to hospital, first in Rouen and then to Bramshott in Hampshire. After discharge he was at several depots in England where he committed further offences: twice absent without leave and again disobeying orders, compounding that with obscene language and escaping from arrest. However, he seems to have turned a corner in late 1917 after training in bayonet instruction, as at Sutton Veny he was appointed temporary corporal. By March 1918 it must have become clear that he was not going to be fit for duty within six months and, passing through the ANZAC Camp at Weymouth, he embarked for Australia on 16 May, being discharged on 19 August owing to rheumatism. He was awarded the 1914–15 Star, British War Medal and Victory Medal and his war service is remembered in Frampton with that of his nephew, *Harold William Brinkworth, on the plaque in the village hall.

Thomas married Beatrice Annie Edwards Thomson on 1 November 1918 and they had five children: Thomas Jabez William, Betty, Jean (pictured above with her father), Leslie Donald and Frederick. Thomas Hart Brinkworth died on 16 December 1949 and he and his wife are commemorated in Cheltenham Crematorium, Cheltenham, Adelaide, South Australia.

HORACE EDGAR CAMM, 1895–1961
Able Seaman 377033, Mercantile Marine

'H. Camm' on the plaque in the village hall may commemorate the war service of Horace Edgar Camm, a cousin of *Martin Walter William Camm, although his home seems to have been in Saul where he was born on 26 June 1895 to Edgar Alexander Camm, a master mariner, and Ellen Theresa (Nellie) née Harper. Horace and two of his brothers, Hedley and William, worked with their father on his trow, *Agnes*.

During the war Horace was an able seaman with the Mercantile Marine. He was awarded the British War Medal and Mercantile Marine War Medal which confirm that he sailed in coastal waters off south and east Britain, then considered dangerous zones, and possibly further afield.

In 1939, Horace and his older brother, Hedley, were living together in Saul and working as general labourers for the RAF, presumably at its No. 7 Maintenance Unit at Quedgeley. Horace Edgar Camm died at the Gloucester Royal Infirmary on 1 October 1961, and was buried in the churchyard of St James the Great, Saul.

MARTIN WALTER WILLIAM CAMM, 1894–1974
Air Mechanic 2nd Class 83988, Royal Flying Corps, later
Royal Air Force

Martin Walter William Camm was born in Saul on 25 November
1894, the son of Oliver Theodore Camm, a mariner, and
Annie Laura née Coole. By 1911 the family had moved to
present-day Fernleigh, The Green, the Frampton home in
which his mother grew up. Before the war Martin worked as
a driver and family members recall stories of him transporting
goods up Frocester Hill by horse and cart. One of his jobs was
with Cadbury's, although they only offered him a temporary
position as evidenced in a letter dated 21 March 1917, when
they confirmed his wages of 32s per week, with a 10s war
bonus. There was, however, a caveat as Cadbury's were keeping
the original job open should its employee return from the war.

Martin enlisted in the Royal Flying Corps on 7 June 1917. His work as an air
mechanic appears to have been partly at Training Depot Stations, and the absence
of his name among the surviving medal rolls may indicate that he was not working
on the front line. On 1 April 1918 the Royal Flying Corps and Royal Naval Air
Service amalgamated to form the Royal Air Force, the first air force to become
independent of army or navy control. Martin transferred to the RAF Reserve
on 16 November 1919. His war service is not remembered on the plaque in the
village hall unless 'H. Camm' is a mistake, for there are known to be a couple of
misspellings on the list of men commemorated.

On his return to Frampton, Martin continued to work at Cadbury's and lived at
The Chestnuts (now Prospect Cottage), The Green. On 23 June 1925 he married
Florence Mary Davis and they had three children: John Martin, Alec Theodore
and Betty May. The family moved to Severnthorpe in 1935 where Martin Walter
William Camm died on 16 April 1974. He was buried in St Mary's churchyard.

EDWARD AUGUSTUS CAPENER, 1876–1917
Private 20554, 7th (Service) Battalion, Gloucestershire Regiment

Edward Augustus Capener was born in 1876 and baptised on 24 December
of that year at North Nibley, the son of Thomas, a farm labourer, and
Fanny Capener. In 1891 Edward was a cowboy, living on his employer's
farm at Hawkesbury. On 7 June 1896 he married Annie Elizabeth Cooper at
St Stephen's, Cinderford, and by 1901 he was the innkeeper of the New Inn,
Painswick, living there with his wife and growing family. In 1911 Edward, Annie
and their five children, Dorothy Ivy, William Edward, Annie Christina, Charles
Richard and Helen Minnie were living in Saul, and he had once again become
a farm labourer. Their eldest daughter, Dorothy, aged thirteen, was helping at
home because Annie was an invalid. The 1913–15 electoral registers record
Edward living on Frampton Green; the Capeners' tobacco shop adjoined the
Three Horseshoes on its north side.

Details of Edward's enlistment as a private with the Gloucestershire Regiment have not been found, but on 27 October 1915 he landed in France. It is likely that Edward, whether following illness or injury, or as reinforcement, was transferred to the 7th (Service) Battalion of his regiment after their withdrawal to Egypt from Gallipoli, where they had suffered heavy losses from combat and disease. Their initial task was to defend the Suez Canal, but in February 1916 they were redeployed to Mesopotamia. The Allies then advanced up the Tigris and Euphrates rivers towards Baghdad, being involved in heavy fighting at several points.

British forces had originally taken the city of Kut al-Amara (which lies within a loop of the Tigris) in September 1915, but then in December were besieged by Turkish troops under German command and had to surrender in April 1916. It could well have been in the fierce fighting to retake Kut in February 1917 that Edward Augustus Capener suffered the wounds from which he died on 11 March; there were reports of wounded soldiers having to endure appalling conditions which led to many more deaths than would have been expected. He was buried in the Commonwealth War Graves Commission (CWGC) War Cemetery, Amara (in Iraq).

During the war Edward's wife and children appear to have moved to 11 Mercy Place, Southgate Street, Gloucester, near to Annie's family. A memorial service for Edward and other village servicemen who had lost their lives was held at St Mary's on 17 June 1917. Edward Capener was posthumously awarded the 1914–15 Star, British War Medal and Victory Medal and is commemorated on Frampton's war memorial and the plaque in the village hall.

WILLIAM HENRY CAUSON, 1896–1979?
Private S23984, 14th (Service) Battalion (West of England) and 15th (Reserve) Battalion, Gloucestershire Regiment

William Causon was born in Saul in the summer of 1896, the second child of Thomas William Ballinger Causon, a miller, and Frances Alice Mildred née Allen. He was baptised in Frampton on 20 December the same year. The family lived in present-day Shakespeare Cottage, Vicarage Lane, a property with five rooms. William caught measles in November 1910 during an epidemic which caused the death of eight children from the school that winter. He worked as a labourer before the war.

On 9 September 1915 William enlisted as a private in the 14th (Service) Battalion (West of England), Gloucestershire Regiment at Chiseldon. This regiment was known as a Bantam Battalion, the term 'bantam', in British Army usage, was used for soldiers below the minimum regulation height of 5 foot 3 inches; he was only 5 foot 1 inch tall. William sustained an injury in December 1915 during training at Tidworth, Wiltshire. He had been fallen out from drill and was running about to keep warm but fell and was kicked by another soldier running behind. His right tibia was fractured leaving him with a significant limp. William was transferred to 15th (Reserve) Battalion of the Gloucestershire Regiment in January 1916, but was later declared physically unfit and was discharged on 10 July that year. He received the Silver War Badge and his service is commemorated on the plaque in the village hall.

William returned home and appears to have lived with his parents until 1921. He has not been definitively traced after that date, although the death of a William Henry Causon born 27 June 1896 was recorded in the second quarter of 1979 in the Ogwr district of Glamorgan.

HENRY FRANCIS CLIFFORD, 1871–1917
Major 5544, Royal Gloucestershire Hussars Yeomanry

Henry Francis Clifford was born on 19 August 1871, the only son of Henry James Clifford and Annie Frances née Hilton-Green. He lived at The Grange with his sisters, three of whom became nurses during the war: Edith Katherine, Mabel Constance and Elaine Annie. Henry was educated at Haileybury College, Hertford, and Christ Church, Oxford. He enlisted in the Imperial Yeomanry (Royal Gloucestershire Hussars Company) and, while serving in South Africa, he was commissioned in the field, having been wounded during mounted operations. After the Boer War he continued with the RGH, rising to the rank of major. He married Adelaide Hilda Clay at St Peter's, Eaton Square, London, on 12 November 1913.

At the outbreak of war, his regiment were deployed in East Anglia to guard against German invasion which involved the first Zeppelin bombing raids. In 1915, to his immense disappointment, Henry was tasked with commanding the 'Stay Behind' party in Egypt which looked after the horses while the regiment served in Gallipoli on foot. He was mentioned in despatches while commanding 'B' Squadron during the tragic Battle of Qatia in the Sinai on 23 April 1916. The Cavalry raid on Rafa, near Gaza, on 9 January 1917 was to prove his final action. The detail is told here by Frank Fox (*The History of the Royal Gloucestershire Hussars Yeomanry 1898–1922*):

> In January it was decided to make an attempt to clear the enemy out of a strong post which he held at Rafa. The place was distant 29 miles from our position; it was held by over 2,000 Turkish troops, and it was the advance post of his main force based at around Beersheba. It was not our idea to capture and hold Rafa but to raid the place, inflict as much damage as possible on the Turkish force, and then retire to our base at El Arish. It was necessary that we should advance a strong force secretly across 29 miles of desert, reduce Rafa before the Turk could send reinforcements from his main body, and then get away at once.
>
> The problem was a difficult one. It was whether a force of 5,000 men could surround and cut off the retreat of a force of about 2,000 and then carry an entrenched position held by this enemy with machine guns, mountain guns in well-placed modern entrenchments, backed up by a force of unknown strength within twelve miles. The attacking force had only field guns to support the attack, had to operate 29 miles from their base, and to fight after a night march. The place had to be taken "against time", and, if it did not fall, there was some doubt if the attacking force would extricate itself without grave loss.

The task was undertaken by Lieut.-Gen. Sir Philip Chetwode, commanding a force which had been recently formed and named the Desert Column. It was wholly a mounted force. His troops consisted of the 5th Mounted Brigade (in which were the RGH), the ANZAC Mounted Division (less the 2nd Light Horse Brigade), the Imperial Camel Corps, with a battery of the HAC [Honourable Artillery Company].

Our force marched out on the night of January 8 and pushed on rapidly, so as to surround the Turkish position as far as possible before daylight. The attack opened shortly after 7am. The Turkish position was found to be of great strength, dominated by a redoubt, with field guns and machine gun posts, and surrounded by open country which gave to his entrenchments a perfect glacis. After 10 hours' fighting the attack was completely successful. Practically the whole Turkish force was destroyed. The enemy lost in killed [sic] 252, and over 1,600 unwounded prisoners were taken, and a mountain battery and six machine guns. The British force lost 71 killed, 415 were wounded, and one reported missing.

Turkish reinforcements were coming on rapidly during the later stages of the battle and it was necessary for our attacking force to detach troops to delay their advance. This was successfully done, and that night we marched back to El Arish victorious but deadly tired. The British force had marched 29 miles throughout the night of January 8, had fought for 10 hours on the day of January 9, and on the night of January 9 marched back 29 miles, an important objective fully attained. It was a cavalry operation of the first order, and an operation only possible for cavalry.

Henry Francis Clifford was among those who lost his life, shot while commanding his squadron. He was buried at Rafa and later reinterred in the CWGC Kantara War Memorial Cemetery, Suez, Egypt. His ultimate sacrifice is remembered on Frampton's war memorial and the plaque in the village hall, and also at Haileybury College and Christ Church, Oxford. Major Clifford was posthumously awarded the 1914–15 Star, British War Medal and Victory Medal. On 19 January, a memorial service was held at St Mary's, schoolchildren having been given a half-day in order to attend. His daughter, Henrietta Hilda Elizabeth Clifford, was born on 8 April 1917, three months after his death.

THOMAS HENRY COLE, 1893–?
Acting Lance Corporal 1233, K Company, 6th Battalion, and later 203511, 3/5th and 2/6th Battalions, Royal Warwickshire Regiment

Thomas Henry Cole was born in Frampton in 1893 and baptised at St Mary's on 23 July that year, the son of Albert Edward and Ruth Cole. Albert was a railway porter, and at the time of his baptism the couple's address was 5 Devon Street, Birmingham, although two years earlier Albert had been a general labourer and the family had lived at Junction Cottages, Saul. It seems that better job prospects had encouraged the move to the Midlands, for in 1901 Albert was a signalman on the railways. Thomas, though, was staying with his widowed grandmother, then named Elizabeth Payne (and formerly the widow Smith), who had been born in Frampton around 1849 but was then living in Aston, Birmingham. In 1911 Thomas was a brass worker to a bedstead-maker, living with his family at Small

Heath, Birmingham. Marriage to Ellen Carter at the registrar's office in the city followed on 6 July 1914 and their son, Thomas Edward, was born on 1 May 1916.

Meanwhile, Thomas had taken a job as gun machinist at the Birmingham Small Arms (BSA) company in Small Heath; he had also voluntarily joined the Territorial Company of the 6th Battalion of the Royal Warwickshire Regiment. He was not immediately called up (possibly because of his job), and although on 10 December 1915 he was attested at Birmingham for a Short Service engagement, he was immediately placed on the Army Reserve and was not mobilised until 22 February 1917. He then reported to the 3/5th Battalion for training, followed by embarkation for France; arriving to join the 61st Division in December. He was posted to the 2/6th Battalion on 15 February 1918 and would have had little time to wait for action as on 7 April the Germans launched the Lys Offensive (also known as the Fourth Battle of Ypres). The 2/6th Battalion was engaged in two of the main actions, at Estaires (9–11 April) and Hazebrouck (12–15 April). It was at some point in these actions, on 11 or 12 April, that Acting Lance Corporal Thomas Henry Cole was taken prisoner. He was not liberated until about 10 December 1918 when he was immediately repatriated, opting to be discharged as soon as possible, with effect from 12 February 1919.

It appears that Thomas briefly returned to Frampton for he was recorded at an address on The Green during 1920–21 and his war service is commemorated on the plaque in the village hall.

FREDERICK VICTOR COLEMAN, 1891–1956
Guardsman 14384, 1st Battalion, Grenadier Guards

Frederick Victor Coleman was born the day the census was taken, 5 April 1891. The midwife, Agnes Jackson, was recorded in the family's home at The Lake; his parents, George Coleman, a dock labourer, and Florence née Mabbett had not even had time to decide upon his name. By 1901 George was the captain of a dredger and Frederick the middle child of five. Ralph, the youngest of the Coleman children, arrived a couple of years later and the family moved to The Street around 1913.

Frederick enlisted as a private in the 2nd Battalion of the Grenadier Guards on 7 June 1909 and was stationed at the Blenheim Barracks in Aldershot at the time of the 1911 census. By the outbreak of the war Frederick had become a guardsman and had apparently transferred to the 1st Battalion. On 19 October he landed at Zeebrugge in Belgium and his battalion was immediately thrown into the First Battle of Ypres, as were his comrades of the 2nd Battalion. After this campaign each battalion retained only four officers and between 140 and 200 men from their original effective strengths of around 1,000. Although Frederick may have come safely through that trial he was later wounded, quite possibly in one of the actions of the Second Battle of Artois in May and June 1915. He was discharged on 17 July 1915 as unfit for further military service and awarded the Silver War Badge. He later received the 1914 Star, British War Medal and Victory Medal and is commemorated on the plaque in the village hall.

Frederick was not listed in the 1918 electoral register, but he was included the following year. On 19 April 1919 he married Florence Elizabeth Hitchings (the sister of *Charles, *Ashley, *Frederick and *Percival) at St Mary's. The couple moved to Parks Cottage, The Green, for a few years and were living in Newark Road, Gloucester, in 1939 when Frederick was employed as a postman. They later moved to The Glen, Corse End Road, Hartpury. Frederick Victor Coleman died on 12 April 1956.

ALBERT ERNEST COOK, 1894–1945
Rank and Service: Not known

Albert Ernest Cook was born in Pontypridd, Glamorgan, on 5 March 1894 to Thomas Cook and Thirza née Trinder. Shortly afterwards the family moved to Edgeworth, Gloucestershire, where he was baptised on 29 July the same year. Thomas was a labourer and the family moved again, probably to seek work, for by 1901 they were living in Vicarage Lane, Frampton. At the time of the 1911 census, Albert was a farm labourer but was unfortunately in Gloucester Royal Infirmary; his family had moved again, this time to The Green, to the south of Frampton Court.

Although Albert's war service is commemorated on the plaque in the village hall along with that of his older brother, *William John, no records have been found relating to it.

Following the war, Albert returned to Frampton for a few years. At the time of his mother's death in 1929 he was employed as a 'postal servant'. Albert and his wife, Emily, had two sons, Norman and Sidney. Albert Ernest Cook died in Gloucester Royal Infirmary on 29 September 1945, having lived at 62 Coney Hill Road in the city, and was buried on 3 October in St Mary's churchyard, Frampton.

ARCHIBALD EDWARD COOK, 1892–1940
Deck Hand SD 2625, Royal Naval Reserve

Archibald Edward Cook, known as Archie, was the third son of William Cook, a mariner, and his wife Elizabeth. He was born on 6 June 1892 in Saul. William's business flourished, and by 1901 he had moved his family to Elsie Villa (now Cider Press House) at the top of Frampton's village green, which he certainly owned by 1909. Archie's older brothers, *William Frederick and *Frederick Gilbert Alexander had left home by 1911 but Archie, then a postman, remained there along with his older sister, Elsie, and younger siblings, Ivy and David.

Archie enlisted into the Royal Naval Reserve on 24 August 1915 at Gloucester and reported to the Devonport training school, HMS *Vivid*, on 6 September with another local man of the same surname, *Raymond George Cook. His training being completed on 30 November, he was posted as a deck hand to the old gunboat

Sabrina; during his eighteen months on board she was converted into a diving tender and operated from Devonport. He then spent some six months in the new destroyer *Osiris* and another four aboard *Valhalla*, before starting a series of short spells in a variety of ships, including an old cruiser, *Abercrombie*, a new monitor (a fairly small warship with one or two huge guns that were fixed to fire forwards, usually for bombarding shore targets) and possibly a troopship. He completed his engagement aboard HMS *Halcyon*, an old paddle-driven minesweeper, and was demobilised on 9 September 1919. Two days after his discharge, Archie was awarded a disability pension on account of orbital cellulitis, an infection of the tissues of the eye socket which leads to inflammation and swelling; the pension continued until at least 1925. He was awarded the British War Medal and Victory Medal and his service is commemorated on the plaque in the village hall.

Archie's marriage to Mary Ann Wothers was registered during the first quarter of 1919 in the Wheatenhurst district. They lived in Bath Road, Eastington, with a growing family and Archie was recorded as a labourer in 1939. In the autumn of 1940 he was off work for seventeen weeks with stomach trouble, said to be due to old war wounds, during which time he suffered a heart attack. On his first morning back, Saturday 14 December, Archibald Edward Cook was cycling to work when he met with a fatal accident, the exact circumstances of which were not determined despite the BBC broadcasting an appeal for witnesses and information. He was found at the bottom of Whitminster Pitch on top of his badly damaged bicycle. The evidence suggested that he had been hit by a motor vehicle, probably a lorry, the driver of which was not traced and the inquest recorded an open verdict. Archie was buried in St Mary's churchyard, Fretherne, on 18 December.

FREDERICK GILBERT ALEXANDER COOK 1889–?
Rank and Service: Not known

Frederick Gilbert Alexander Cook, known as Gilbert, was the second son of William and Elizabeth Cook. Born in Saul in 1889, he was baptised on 23 July the following year at St Peter's, Framilode, with his first two names reversed. By 1901 the family had moved to Elsie Villa (now Cider Press House). Unlike his father, Gilbert did not find work in the water trade, preferring motor cars instead. By 1911 he was chauffeur to the village's general practitioner, Dr Charles Joseph Weller, and living-in with the family at Russell House.

Gilbert's role in the First World War has not been traced, although it is known that he answered Lord Kitchener's call in early September 1914 and joined at Gloucester, his name being recorded in the *Gloucester Journal* of 12 September in the same list as *Francis William Aldridge and *William George Birch. When Gilbert married Elizabeth Barton Palmer on 12 February 1918 at St John the Divine, Fairfield, Liverpool, he was a motor engineer living at Elsie Villa, from where he was listed as an absent voter in the spring of 1919. It seems that he may have been working in some motorised transport capacity for the Army in the UK. Gilbert's war service is commemorated on the plaque in the village hall alongside that of his two brothers, *William Frederick and *Archibald Edward.

RAYMOND GEORGE COOK, 1895–1940
Deck Hand SD 2674, Royal Naval Reserve

Raymond George Cook was born in Saul on 28 February 1895, the son of George White Cook and Ann Maud née Long. He was baptised with his younger sister, Thora Anne Niblett (who later married *Milton Tudor), on 11 December 1902 at St James the Great, Saul, when the family were living in Church Lane. Raymond's mother died in 1904 and his father remarried a couple of years later; by then the Cooks' home was at Priding.

By 1911 Raymond had followed his father to sea. On 31 August 1915 he volunteered for the Royal Naval Reserve, giving his address as Frampton for his father and stepmother had moved to The Street. Raymond reported to the training depot HMS *Vivid* at Devonport on 6 September, the same day as *Archibald Edward Cook (from another family of that surname). Training for sea would normally have taken about three months, but as Raymond was recorded at *Vivid* for one year, he may have been retained as an instructor. In August 1916 he was appointed to the paddle minesweeper *Halcyon* at Lowestoft and some six months later was posted to the minesweeper depot ship *Island Prince*, a trawler hired by the Navy, and based at North Shields. After two months he was again transferred, this time to the similar vessel HMS *Lord Lansdowne* at Oban, possibly for service on the Ascot-class paddle minesweeper *Doncaster*. On New Year's Day 1918 he was posted to yet another naval trawler, the *Nesmar*, again based at Oban where he was to remain until 22 June 1919; after the Armistice these vessels were kept very busy clearing both British and German mines from around the coast. During his time in the Oban area Raymond was treated at Oban Cottage Hospital for a swelling, and also appears to have been charged with being asleep on watch, but he was nevertheless awarded chevrons for his service. He also received the British War Medal and Victory Medal, but his service is not remembered on the plaque in Frampton Village Hall.

Raymond appears to have been demobilised in June 1919, although the surviving records are unclear. On 8 November 1919 he was summoned for riding a bicycle without lights in Frampton but gave the police a false name and address. After extensive efforts to find him, he appeared before the Whitminster Police Court a month later, then a seaman of the SS *John*, with an address in Bristol. Magistrates took a serious view of his actions which they considered had greatly aggravated his offence, and fined him £2 with 1s costs. An entry on his service record in June 1934 appears to be a request for a résumé of his Royal Naval Reserve service by Cardiff City Police. They were seeking information in connection with his forthcoming trial at Glamorgan Assizes 'upon several charges of housebreaking and bigamy'.

Raymond's story is next picked up through his entry on the 1939 'census' when he was living at 7 Newport Street, Cardiff, working as a deck hand on a sand boat and married to Lily. It is likely that she was formerly Lily Clark and that their wedding had taken place in 1932 in the Cardiff area.

On 11 November 1940 Raymond George Cook was the master of SS *Skarv*, a coaster working in the Bristol Channel seemingly engaged in taking sand from Nash Sands off the Glamorgan coast, when she struck a mine and the crew of five were lost. Raymond is commemorated at the Tower Hill Memorial, London, along with other men and women of the Merchant Navy and Fishing Fleets who died in both world wars and who have no known grave.

WILLIAM FREDERICK COOK 1885–?
Rank and Service: Not known

William Frederick Cook, born in 1885 in Framilode, was the eldest son of William and Elizabeth Cook. William followed his father to sea but has not been traced on the 1901 census when he may have been between ports. When he married Kate Attwood at St Cyr's, Stinchcombe, on 28 October 1907, he gave his address as Bristol, but by the time their son, William Henry, was baptised in 1909 they were living at The Lake, Frampton. Their daughter, Kate Elizabeth Sarah, was born a year later.

Details of William Frederick's war service have not been traced but, like that of his younger brothers, *Frederick Gilbert Alexander and *Archibald Edward, it is commemorated on the plaque in the village hall.

WILLIAM JOHN COOK 1890–?
Stoker Petty Officer K2854, Royal Navy

William John Cook was the eldest son of Thomas Cook and Thirza née Trinder. He was born on 25 July 1890 at Mountain Ash, Glamorgan, where Thomas was a miner. His brother, *Albert Ernest, was born in Pontypridd before the family moved to Gloucestershire, finally settling in Frampton at the turn of the century with Thomas finding work as a general labourer.

William was a coal-cutter or miner before joining the Royal Navy. He enlisted as a stoker at Devonport on 5 May 1909 for twelve years' service. After basic training he served briefly in the depot ship *Leander*, before going to sea in armoured cruisers for three years, first in HMS *Carnarvon*, then *Suffolk*. On the latter ship he was disciplined for the only two occasions of his career (serving three and five days in the cells).

From 1913 to 1914 he served in the battleship *Centurion* (along with *Herbert Charles Drayton); following further training he joined the sister battleship HMS *Ajax* in April 1914. Promotion to the rank of leading stoker came in May 1915, then his ship was one of those engaged at the Battle of Jutland, albeit not heavily (she fired at the German Fleet without identifying any hits, and received no damage herself). William gained further promotion in March 1917, his final rank being that of stoker petty officer. He left his ship in May to spend the rest of the war in HMS *Blake*, a depot ship for the 11th Destroyer Flotilla.

William was at training establishments for a year from January 1919, presumably as an instructor. His last seagoing posting was to the modern battleship *Valiant* from which he was finally discharged on 20 June 1921 having completed his term of service. He was awarded the 1914 Star, British War Medal and Victory Medal and is commemorated on the plaque in the village hall.

William and his wife Elsie had two children, Leslie and Gladys. William John Cook died in Cirencester.

FREDERICK COOLE, 1895–1976
Private 23999, Somerset Light Infantry; 30436, 13th (Reserve) and 11th (Reserve) Battalions, Worcestershire Regiment

Frederick Coole was born on 26 July 1895 and baptised a day later at St Mary's. His parents, William Coole, a castrator, and Lydia Harriet née Camm, had married in the parish of St James, Gloucester, almost four years earlier, but they soon settled at Denfurlong, one of the farms belonging to Frampton Court Estate. Before the war Fred worked on the farm as a shepherd but, unlike his eldest brother, William, he was not exempt from conscription, and he and his younger brother, *Robert Edgar, both served during the war.

Fred Coole enlisted as a private on 27 March 1916 at Bristol, and his record shows the 'fog of war' from the outset. Although Bristol was a depot of the Gloucestershire Regiment, he was posted next day to the Somerset Light Infantry, then attached two days later to the 13th (Reserve) Battalion of the Worcestershire Regiment, and formally transferred on 13 May. After training (the 13th Battalion became the 46th Training Reserve Battalion on 1 September) he was posted on 28 October to the Mediterranean Expeditionary Force based at Salonika where he joined the 11th (Reserve) Battalion of the Worcestershire Regiment as a machine gunner; much later, from April 1918, he was attached to the Machine Gun Corps. His combat operations would have been against Bulgarian, Austro-Hungarian and/or German opposition around the area where Serbia, Macedonia and Bulgaria meet.

In the Balkans field conditions were as tough as anywhere and Fred had frequent spells in hospital from June to October 1917 (illness or injury), from June to July 1918 (malaria) and again in October (dysentery). Nevertheless, he remained in theatre and his service did not end at the Armistice for he was soon attached to the 2nd Battalion of the Gloucestershire Regiment. On 3 January 1919 he sailed to Batoum on the Black Sea coast of Russia (now Batumi, Georgia) en route to Tiflis (now Tbilisi), as part of the British support for the White Russian forces in their actions against the Reds. However, while on sentry duty about 1 March, he tripped over a railway line and cut a finger which became deeply infected. By 25 March Fred was making his way home via Batoum and Salonika and on 29 May was demobilised. He was later awarded the British War Medal and Victory Medal and his service is commemorated on the plaque in the village hall.

On 20 May 1929 he married Helen Gertrude Tudor and they farmed at Alkerton, Eastington. Frederick Coole died on 20 September 1976 and was buried in St Mary's churchyard.

ROBERT EDGAR COOLE, 1900–1983
Rank unknown, Army (details unknown)

Robert Edgar Coole, then known as Edgar but in later life Joe, was the youngest son of William Coole, who farmed Denfurlong, and Lydia Harriet née Camm. Born on 27 April 1900, his childhood was barely over when war was declared. Not long afterwards the farm were supplying hay for horses abroad; Edgar's name was on the label of some hay seen by his relative, *Richard William Rowles, while serving in France.

Initially too young for conscription when it was introduced (unlike his older brother, *Frederick), Edgar's family believe that his service was in Ireland. Although the British Government had promised Home Rule for Ireland in September 1914 and very many Irish volunteered to serve in the British Army, there was continuing trouble from protests and strikes which culminated in the Easter Rising of 24 to 29 April 1916 in Dublin. About 16,000 British soldiers were stationed in Ireland during the First World War to maintain the peace, in addition to naval bases and other establishments that were purely concerned with the prosecution of the war against the Central Powers. Edgar's role is not known, but his war service is commemorated on the plaque in the village hall.

Edgar married Florence Kemp in 1929 and they brought up their children, Peggy, Leslie and Joan, at Denfurlong which the family still farm today. Robert Edgar Coole was buried on 29 January 1983 in St Mary's churchyard.

FREDERICK WILLIAM COTTLE, 1888–1966
Private 37713, 14th (Service) Battalion (West of England), Gloucestershire Regiment

Frederick William Cottle, known as Fred, was born on 16 August 1888 in Framilode, the son of Joseph Cottle, a waterman, and Rosa Anne née Hill. He was one of four children and his two brothers, *Joseph Charles and *Joseph Thomas, both served during the war. In 1901, at the age of twelve, Fred was being trained for the sea in HMS *Formidable* and stationed at Portishead, and on the night of the 1911 census he and his widowed father were recorded in their three-roomed cottage in Lake Lane, Frampton. Fred's marriage to Ethel Jones was registered in the Wheatenhurst district during the first quarter of 1915, and they subsequently had three children: Charles, Amy and Olive.

Although Fred's service records do not survive, the Silver War Badge roll states that he enlisted on 8 December 1915 into the 14th (Service) Battalion (West of England), Gloucestershire Regiment as a private. The battalion formed part of the 105th Brigade, 35th Division, which landed at Le Havre on 30 January 1916, concentrating east of St Omer. The Division was in action during the Battles of the Somme at Bazentin Ridge, Arrow Head Copse, Maltz Horn Farm and Falfemont Farm, and also in 1917, during the pursuit of the German retreat to the Hindenburg Line, at Houthulst Forest and the Second Battle of Passchendaele. It is not known where Fred fought, but at some stage he was wounded and his discharge came on 31 August 1918. It is believed that he had his leg blown off and lost a finger too. He was later awarded the British War Medal and Victory Medal and his service is commemorated on the plaque in the village hall.

Post-war Fred was aided by an artificial limb and able to work as a cobbler. He lived in Lake Lane, in the end house next to Cadbury Hall, and later at 12 Bridge Road. Frederick William Cottle was buried in St Mary's churchyard on 6 February 1966.

JOSEPH CHARLES COTTLE, 1889–1915
Private H26190, 14th Reserve Cavalry Regiment; 20573, 3rd and 2nd Battalions, York and Lancaster Regiment

Joseph Charles Cottle, known as Charles, was born on 22 October 1889, the son of Joseph Cottle and Rosa Anne née Hill. The 1891 census gives his place of birth as Framilode, but it is recorded as Frampton on the 1901 and 1911 censuses. Following the death of his mother in 1894, and with his father working on the barges, the family was split up and Charles was sent to the Jewish Synagogue Industrial School in Park Row, Bristol. In 1911 he was working for the Great Western Railway as a labourer, lodging in Swansea. His brothers, *Frederick William and *Joseph Thomas, also served during the war.

Charles enlisted at Swansea on 5 September 1914 with the 14th Reserve Cavalry Regiment giving his occupation as a collier; he appears to have previously resided, and probably worked, at Neath. He was then sent for infantry training with the 3rd Battalion of the York and Lancaster Regiment, before being posted on 14 July 1915 to join the 2nd Battalion on the Western Front. He arrived just as they were moving from a relatively quiet sector to the village of Hooge on a ridge near Ypres, which was the focus of much heavy fighting and would change hands repeatedly throughout the war. As Hooge had been subjected to heavy German attacks after the Second Battle of Ypres, the 6th Division, which included the 2nd York and Lancaster, mounted an attack on 9 August to restore the Allied front line in this most exposed part of the Ypres salient. They succeeded in capturing both the shattered chateau and the huge crater left by a mine exploded previously on 19 July; however, Private Joseph Charles Cottle was one of many killed. A measure of the significance of this action is that his battalion were awarded the Battle Honour 'Hooge 1915'.

Charles was posthumously awarded the 1914–15 Star, British War Medal and Victory Medal and is commemorated on the plaque in the village hall but not on the war memorial, despite a 'Mrs Cottel' making a contribution towards it. His effects were sent to his former landlady, Mrs Mary Ann Morgan of Swansea, on 10 January 1916.

JOSEPH THOMAS COTTLE, 1894–1968
Enlisted in Lord Kitchener's Army

The birth of Joseph Thomas Cottle was registered in the first quarter of 1894. The rector of Framilode baptised him privately on 16 January and buried his mother three days later at Saul. Tom, as he was known, was one of four children born to Joseph Cottle and Rosa Anne née Hill; his siblings were *Frederick William, *Joseph Charles and Bella Rosetta. It is not clear where Tom spent his early years, but by 1911 he was living with his aunt and uncle, Mary and William Sparrow, at Tobacco Box, Fretherne.

Tom enlisted into Lord Kitchener's Army on 25 November 1914, giving his address as Frampton. He was among the recruits obtained for the Royal Gloucestershire Hussars, 5th (Reserve) Battalion of the Gloucestershire Regiment and the Royal Field Artillery. Family sources indicate that he may have served in Gallipoli, but records do not survive to confirm this. In 1918–19, as an absent voter, his address was given as The Lake, Frampton, presumably that of his father. Tom's wartime service is not commemorated on the plaque in the village hall.

After the war Tom returned to Frampton and his marriage to Mary Anne (Polly) Hayward was registered during the first quarter of 1920. Mary already had a daughter, Mary Evelyn, known as Maisie. Their family was later completed by the births of Kathleen, Eileen, Grace and George. Tom worked at the nurseries at Fretherne and also as a boiler man on tanker ships. Joseph Thomas Cottle was buried on 28 February 1968 at St Mary's, Fretherne.

GEORGE EDWARD DARK 1889–1968
Donkeyman 916880, Mercantile Marine

George Edward Dark was born on 23 June 1889 to George Dark and Elizabeth Ann née Philp in Croydon, Surrey. His youngest brother, *Stephen John, also served during the war. George's childhood was spent moving from place to place including homes in Bristol (1891) and Abergavenny (1901), while the births of his younger siblings were variously registered in Cardiff and Newport. The family came to live in the parish of Frampton in 1904 and had settled in Fromebridge by 1911, with George Edward working as a farm labourer.

George joined the Mercantile Marine but, as the records are incomplete, his full contribution is not known, and his identity certificate only covers the latter period of his service, from 1919 to 1921. This lists (by identification number) the ships he served in during that time. As a donkeyman he was responsible for operating and maintaining the 'donkey' or secondary steam engines for powering machinery such as derricks and winches. George was awarded the British War Medal and Mercantile Marine War Medal, so he must have seen considerable wartime service. His son Bryan remembers his father telling of being torpedoed three times, encountering pirates, and running aground off Nova Scotia!

On 9 April 1924 George married Elizabeth (Bessie) Annie, the sister of *Thomas Edward Hunt, also of Fromebridge. George was still a seaman and stayed in what had become the Merchant Navy until at least 1933. They had four children: Norman, Bryan, Beryl and Shirley. Later George was employed at the RAF No. 7 Maintenance Unit at Quedgeley, while Bessie was the local post lady. George Edward Dark died at his home, 2 Whitminster Lane, on 4 March 1968 and is commemorated at Gloucester Crematorium. He is also among those listed on the plaque in the village hall in respect of his war service.

STEPHEN JOHN DARK 1898–1959
Able Seaman J34422, Royal Navy

Stephen John Dark, known as John, was the youngest child of George Dark and Elizabeth Ann née Philp. He was born on 8 December 1898 in Newport, Monmouthshire. The family moved around a great deal as George sought various types of work, but in 1904 the six youngest children were admitted to the school in Frampton. John's brother, *George Edward, was too old to attend. They settled in Fromebridge with George working as a chimney sweep. After leaving school John became a clothmill labourer.

On 2 February 1915, at the age of sixteen, he joined the Royal Navy at Devonport as a boy (essentially the equivalent of an apprenticeship for a trade) and underwent initial training at HMS *Impregnable* (the Devonport Barracks). He then joined the crew of HMS *Calliope*, a brand new light cruiser, where he spent his entire wartime service, progressing to the rank of able seaman. In March 1916 she was badly damaged by a fuel oil fire at sea, but was repaired in time to take part in the Battle of Jutland when she was hit by shells from the German battleships *Kaiser* and *Markgraf*, which killed ten of her crew. On 8 December (John's eighteenth birthday) he signed for a twelve-year engagement with the Navy. He finally left HMS *Calliope* on 1 January 1919 for an eighteen-month tour at Devonport, continuing his career until the mid-1930s. John was awarded the 1914–15 Star, British War Medal and Victory Medal and his service is commemorated on the plaque in the village hall. In 1932 he received a Long Service gratuity while serving in HMS *Resolution*.

By the mid-1940s John, who never married, was living at Maycot, The Street. Stephen John Dark was buried on 1 June 1959 in St Mary's churchyard.

WILLIAM JAMES GEORGE DAW, 1897–1967
Air Mechanic, Royal Flying Corps

William Daw was born in Frampton during the spring of 1897 and baptised at St Mary's on 18 July the same year. His parents were William David Daw, a carpenter, and Maria née Warren; the family's home was Beehive Cottage, The Street. In 1911 Bill, or Will as he was also known, was a grocer's apprentice.

There are few surviving records of Bill's service but according to the *Gloucester Journal* he enlisted at Gloucester on 18 June 1915, the same day as *William Joseph Ernest Gleed. He was an air mechanic in the Royal Flying Corps and at some stage was posted to Egypt. Bill gained four chevrons for good service and is among those commemorated on the plaque in the village hall.

Little has been traced about his life after the war, although family members recall an aircraft propeller being kept in his garage at Beehive Cottage! From 1918 to 1921, *Jacob Jonas Godwin was also registered at Beehive Cottage, probably as the Daw family's lodger, in the part now known as Falfield Cottage. In the summer of 1926 Bill married Florence Mary Brookes of West Malvern, and at some stage served as a special constable in Marlborough, Wiltshire. The death of William James George Daw was registered in the Hereford district in the spring of 1967.

PRESTON DENNIS, 1895–1972
Second Lieutenant, Army Service Corps

Preston Dennis was born on 19 October 1895, one of John Thomas Fezzy Dennis and Elizabeth Jane née Broad's nine children. His childhood home was Broadley Farm, Tamerton Foliot, near Plymouth, which his parents and maternal grandparents farmed. In 1909 the Dennis family became the tenants at Manor Farm, Frampton, while the Broads took on Advowsons Farm. On 30 March 1910 John Dennis withdrew his children from the village school and sent them to the National School in Saul because his eleven-year-old son, Holland, was not being allowed to arrive at 10 a.m. every day after completing a milk round! At this time Preston and his three older brothers were helping on the farm.

Preston enlisted into Lord Kitchener's Army on 16 November 1914 together with *Frederick Alexander Franklin. He was later recorded as a second lieutenant in the Army Service Corps. On 4 April 1918 he arrived in Salonika as part of Allied operations in support of Serbia, Romania and Greece, which led to his being awarded the British War Medal and Victory Medal. His service is commemorated on the plaque in the village hall.

The marriage of Preston Dennis to Doris May Willcock was registered in the St Germans district of Cornwall during the spring of 1921, and in late 1924 the couple had a daughter, Rosamund, whose birth was also registered in St Germans. It is clear that Preston became a Regular officer of the British Indian Army, for in September 1931 he arrived in England on the SS *Mooltan* from Bombay, and returned to Bombay in July 1932 on SS *Narkunda*, in both cases giving his address as Pillmere, Saltash, and his occupation as either captain or Army officer. Doris and Rosamund are also recorded sailing between England and India; in 1928 (to and from Karachi) and 1935 (Bombay). Doris travelled alone from Bombay to Southampton in August 1946, just one year before the independence of India and the end of the British Indian Army. The address she gave was in Cheltenham which may have been where the couple settled as the deaths of Preston Dennis and his wife occurred in that district in 1972 and 1975 respectively.

HERBERT CHARLES DRAYTON 1889–1949
Petty Officer SS2617, later J10283, Royal Navy

Herbert Charles Drayton was born in Soham, Cambridgeshire, on 12 July 1889 to Charles Drayton and Elizabeth Ann née Sheldrick. Herbert worked as a labourer in Newmarket before a brief spell as a militiaman in the 4th (Territorial) Battalion of the Suffolk Regiment between December 1906 and February 1908. After returning to civilian life as a farm labourer, he joined the Royal Navy on 29 September 1908 for a five-year engagement. Herbert served mainly in larger ships such as armoured cruisers, one of which, HMS *Aboukir*, later became very well-known early in the war as one of three sister ships to be sunk in a brief engagement by a single German U-boat; this disaster awoke all navies to a threat which had been previously underestimated. Meanwhile, Herbert extended his service by undergoing specialist training to become a torpedo operator.

In November 1913 Herbert was posted to the dreadnought battleship HMS *Centurion*, serving in her with the Home Fleet (which was based at Scapa Flow in the Orkneys) for most of the war. During this time the effective stand-off between the German and British navies meant that *Centurion* was involved in only three actions: as part of a fleet that caused German warships to withdraw from a raid on Scarborough, at the major battle of Jutland (where she fired on the German battlecruiser *Lützow*), and a distant role in the August 1916 North Sea actions against a German raid on Sunderland. During 1918 Herbert served in a minelayer, then after the war in the early aircraft carrier *Argus*, and finally in a series of training and support ships. Herbert was awarded the 1914–15 Star, British War Medal and Victory Medal and his service is commemorated on the plaque in Frampton Village Hall.

Herbert married Rose Ann Blake in Slimbridge on 24 July 1916 and three children followed: Nancy, Ronald and Leslie. The family lived in Church End House along with Rose's parents from 1918, or maybe even a couple of years earlier, renting it from Frampton Court Estate. In 1924 Rose Ann's father, Thomas Blake, bought the property in her name for £600. Herbert continued in the Navy until 1935 or 1936; his entire service seems to have been in the UK and home waters except for a brief period at a Malta shore station. He achieved the rank of petty officer and was awarded a Long Service and Good Conduct Medal in 1923. After leaving the Navy Herbert developed a significant local milk round, delivering as far as Elmore. Herbert Charles Drayton was buried in St Mary's churchyard on 21 April 1949.

JAMES EAKETTS, 1891–1968
Private M2-226541, Army Service Corps

James Eaketts (pronounced 'Ecketts') was born on 10 January 1891, the son of Thomas, a labourer, and Emily Eaketts. Jim, as he was known, spent part of his childhood in Upton St Leonards where his father was a gardener. The younger Eaketts children were admitted to the school at Frampton on 28 October 1910, and in 1911 Jim was a labourer at Henley Bank Farm, Brockworth.

Jim's enlistment papers have not been found, but we do know that he served as a private in the Army Service Corps. He married Laura Eveline (the sister of *William Henry Causon) on 28 June 1916 at All Saints, Gloucester, and gave the address of his sister-in-law, Beatrice Alice Eaketts. (Beatrice was the wife of Jim's eldest brother, *Willoughby Thomas, who was at that time a prisoner of war.) Jim was a motor driver which implies his role in the Army Service Corps. His service presumably included extensive demobilisation work for he remained an absent voter throughout 1919. He was awarded the British War Medal and Victory Medal and is commemorated on the plaque in Frampton Village Hall.

Jim and Eveline had six children: Betty, Henry, Mary, Peggy, Hilda and Lionel. The photograph shows Jim in the cab of a Cadbury's steam lorry (with its solid rubber tyres and no windscreen) and was probably taken in the 1920s. James Eaketts died at his home, 18 The Oval, on 8 April 1968 and was buried five days later in St Mary's churchyard.

WILLOUGHBY THOMAS EAKETTS, 1888–1976
Lance Corporal 8096, 1st Battalion, Gloucestershire Regiment

Willoughby Thomas Eaketts was born on 27 November 1888 in Gloucester, the oldest son of Thomas and Emily Eaketts. At the registration of his birth his Christian names were recorded in reverse order but his baptism and census returns indicate that this may have been a mistake. Indeed, Willoughby was such an unusual name that it was occasionally interchanged with William on his military records. The family, which included his next brother, *James, moved to Upton St Leonards during his childhood, and to Frampton in 1910. It is not clear when Willoughby enlisted with the 2nd Battalion of the Gloucestershire Regiment, but the 1911 census records him as a lance corporal at Verdala Barracks, Malta. However, at the time of his marriage to Beatrice Alice Smith on 27 December 1913 at All Saints, Gloucester, he was living at 12 Bishopstone Road in the city, and working as a lawyer's assistant. Their son, Willoughby James, was born during the summer of the following year.

At the onset of war Willoughby must have been called up immediately for he arrived in France on 13 August 1914 with the 1st Battalion of the Gloucestershire Regiment, just in time for the battles of Mons, Le Cateau and the Aisne. His active service was fairly brief for he was taken prisoner at Ypres on 29 October. The Red Cross and German records show that he was unwounded at capture and was then held successively in Munster (December 1914), Minden (March 1917) and Soltau (from December 1917), the largest prisoners of war camp in Germany. The Germans later transferred many of their prisoners to neutral Holland to be interned, including Willoughby who arrived there on 15 March 1918. Repatriation came after the Armistice when he arrived at Hull on 22 November 1918 on the SS *Porto*. He was awarded the 1914 Star, British War Medal and Victory Medal, but his service was not commemorated on the plaque in Frampton Village Hall.

Willoughby's prisoner of war records give his wife living at 39 Blenheim Road, Gloucester (March 1917) and Lacon Cottage, Woodchester (December 1917), although he was on the Frampton electoral register in 1918 as an absent voter so she may have come to live in the village at that time, perhaps at the Eaketts' family home at or near Nastfield Cottage, The Green. The death of Willoughby Thomas Eaketts was registered in the Gloucester district during the spring of 1976, and for completeness, his Christian names were also listed in reverse.

CECIL CHARLES JAMES ESTOP, 1890–1969
Private 27891, later 27991, 10th (Service), 8th (Service) and 1/4th (City of Bristol) Battalions, Gloucestershire Regiment

Cecil Charles James Estop was born on 16 May 1890 in Slimbridge, the fourth son of Henry Estop, a domestic gardener, and Elizabeth Emily née Powell. Home was on the Dursley Road at Cambridge and by 1911 Cecil was a builder's labourer. On 6 September 1914, just a month after the outbreak of war, he married Emily Ann Hayward Meadows at St Mary's, Frampton, his occupation then being a fireman (perhaps a stoker).

The date of Cecil's enlistment with the Gloucestershire Regiment has not been traced, but it is known that he served as a private with the 10th (Service), 8th (Service) and 1/4th (City of Bristol) Battalions and was awarded the British War Medal and Victory Medal. His war service is commemorated on the plaque in the village hall.

Cecil was recorded as an absent voter from a property in The Street, Frampton, throughout 1919, but had returned by 1920, the year that his wife, Emily, died. Four years later, during the summer of 1924, he married Louisa May Cripps. Cecil Charles James Estop later lived at 6 Chipman's Platt, Westend, Eastington, and he was buried in his parish churchyard of St Michael and All Angels on 5 November 1969.

GILBERT JOHN FLETCHER, 1897–1978
Private 7397, 5th Battalion, Norfolk Regiment; Agricultural Company,
4th (Reserve) Battalion, Gloucestershire Regiment; 172957, Works Company,
9th (Service) Battalion, Devonshire Regiment; Labour Corps

Gilbert John Fletcher was born on 7 November 1897 in Weston-super-Mare, one
of the six children of Harry Fletcher and Mary Jane née Baker, and older brother
of *Thomas Charles. Harry was employed as a dairyman and later a furniture
remover. In 1904 Gilbert's mother died, and the family moved to his father's home
town of Cirencester where both Harry and Gilbert worked as window cleaners.
In September 1916 Harry and his second wife, Sophia Bucknell, moved to Lake
House, Frampton, with Gilbert later listed as an absent voter.

Gilbert was attested for Army service on 22 May 1916 at Cirencester, but was
not mobilised until 2 October when he was posted as a private to the 5th Battalion
of the Norfolk Regiment, probably for infantry training. However, it appears
that this was not successful, as Gilbert was transferred in quick succession to the
Agricultural Company 4th (Reserve) Battalion of the Gloucestershire Regiment
and then to the Works Company 9th (Service) Battalion of the Devonshire
Regiment. Meanwhile, he began to suffer fairly early in his service from an eye
condition which he claimed had been caused by draughts when sleeping in cold
barns. Additionally a problem with his middle ears in the spring of 1917 caused
him to be medically examined several times. His final posting was in April 1917
to the recently formed Labour Corps where he spent the rest of his service in
UK-based companies. The Labour Corps was manned by officers and other ranks
who had been medically rated below the level needed for front line service.

In February 1919 he was selected for retention, which earned him a bonus
of 10s 6d per week, and he also volunteered to extend his service by one year
to September 1920. A later hospitalisation for multiple boils, together with his
worsening eye condition, seems to have led to discharge procedures being initiated
and a claim for a disability pension. However, despite a recommendation for an
operation to remove his infected tear ducts, his disability was assessed at only
10 per cent and he was transferred to the Army Reserve on 29 February 1920
without a disability pension. His war service is not commemorated on the plaque
in the village hall.

He married Lily Pawcett in the summer of 1922. Gilbert John Fletcher's death
was registered in the Cirencester district during the spring of 1978.

THOMAS CHARLES FLETCHER, 1899–1918
Private 41394, 1st Battalion, Duke of Cornwall's Light Infantry

Thomas Charles Fletcher was the third son of Harry Fletcher, a furniture removal
foreman, and Mary Jane née Baker. He was born in Weston-super-Mare in 1899.
The family moved to Cirencester, Harry's home town, probably following the
death of Mary Jane in 1904. All three of Harry's sons served during the First
World War: his eldest, also named Harry, was with the Gloucestershire Regiment
when he was listed as missing during the summer of 1916. The Fletchers moved

to Lake House, Frampton, around that time and they had a long and anxious wait for news, only learning in May 1917 that Harry (Junior) had been killed on 23 July 1916. Harry Fletcher's second son, *Gilbert John, remained in the UK during the war.

Few records have survived concerning Thomas' service, but he was posted to the 1st Battalion of the Duke of Cornwall's Light Infantry, which had been sent to Italy in December 1917 to help the Italian Army recover from its disastrous defeat at Caporetto, and returned to France in April 1918, at which time it is quite likely that Thomas arrived from England. This was a period of intense fighting on the Western Front, with the major battles of the Lys (where the Allies held firm) and Aisne (where the Germans drove forward, being stopped on the Marne by British counter-attacks). In the aftermath, on 20 June 1918, the 5th and 31st Divisions mounted an attack east of the Nieppe Forest to disrupt any enemy offensive, and to push the British lines away from the edge of the wood, where they were an easy target for German artillery.

It may well have been during those actions that Private Thomas Charles Fletcher lost his life, recorded as 'killed in action' on 29 June 1918. Thomas was interred in the CWGC Aval Wood Military Cemetery, Vieux-Berquin, France, and his ultimate sacrifice is commemorated on the Cirencester war memorial, alongside that of his oldest brother, Harry. He was posthumously awarded the British War Medal and Victory Medal, and a War Gratuity of £5 was paid to his father. The *Gloucester Journal* recorded that Thomas had been well known as a '*Citizen* boy' (another Gloucester newspaper), and had later worked as a window cleaner and chimney sweep. Despite being listed as an absent voter from Lake House in 1918, Thomas has not been remembered on Frampton's war memorial or the village hall plaque.

ALFRED FOLKES, 1887–1918
Guardsman 23203, 1st Battalion, Grenadier Guards

Alfred Folkes was born in Broadway, Worcestershire, in early 1887, the son of William Smith Folkes, a glazier's journeyman, and Alice née Parker. William later worked in his family's painting and decorating business. After leaving school Alfred first found work as a general labourer, but later joined the Gloucestershire police and moved away; however, he may have left the police before his enlistment, as he is not recorded on the Gloucestershire Police Roll of Honour.

Alfred enlisted fairly early in the war, joining the prestigious Grenadier Guards and arriving in France as part of the 3rd Guards Brigade on 23 October 1915. His battalion would have been engaged in some of the main battles of the Somme and Passchendaele campaigns, which incurred enormous numbers of casualties. It may be during the latter that Alfred was wounded, as he was honourably discharged on 11 September 1917 being no longer fit for military duties and awarded the Silver

War Badge. The regimental records confirm that he had served as a guardsman, the equivalent of a private and the rank given in some sources.

Alfred returned to Broadway and became a postman. On 3 March 1918 he married Millicent Annie Butler at St Mary's, Frampton, after which the couple lived in the village. However, Alfred Folkes contracted influenza during the 1918–19 pandemic and he died on 29 October 1918. He was given a military funeral at St Eadburgha's, Broadway, on the following Saturday. Mrs Folkes contributed 5s to Frampton's war memorial fund, and is believed to have lived in the property known as The Cottage, in The Street, for a short while afterwards. Alfred's war service is also recorded on the plaque in the village hall and on the Broadway war memorial. He was posthumously awarded the 1914–15 Star, British War Medal and Victory Medal.

FRANCIS HENRY FRANKLIN, 1893–1973
Gunner 73604, Royal Garrison Artillery

Francis Henry Franklin was born on 14 February 1893 to Frederick Alexander Franklin and Emmeline née Warren. Frederick's tailoring business was run from the family's home where clothes were made for the gentry, and Francis and his elder brother, *Frederick Alexander, worked for their father after they left school. On 8 November 1914 Francis married Muriel Evelyn Gladys Morgan at St Mary's, leaving Cecil House (now Northend House) to set up home in Passage Road, Saul.

He attested at Frampton on 15 November 1915, an unusual location as local men normally travelled to Stroud or Gloucester. This appears to reflect Lord Derby's recruitment initiative during the autumn of 1915 when it seems that mobile units were deployed to places such as Frampton. Francis was not mobilised until April 1916 when he was posted to the Royal Garrison Artillery and trained as a gunner, probably at the Siege Artillery Depot at Catterick in Yorkshire. After a few days at No. 3 (Reserve) Brigade at Prees Heath, Shropshire, he was posted to the 329th Siege Battery in France, arriving on 15 May 1917. Only two weeks later he was slightly wounded but did not require hospital treatment. The heavy guns on both sides were constant targets for the enemy and he was less lucky on 24 June; Francis received a severe gunshot wound to the right ankle which required repatriation for treatment, in his case at the Western General Hospital in Manchester. His recovery was protracted during which he was retained in the Army. Francis was reviewed by a medical board in late July 1918 who approved his discharge with a temporary pension which was effected on 20 August. His family say that his wound did not heal well and caused him to walk with a limp. He was awarded the Silver War Badge and later the British War Medal and Victory Medal. His war service is commemorated on the plaque in Frampton Village Hall.

Francis and Muriel had seven children: Francis Alan (born during the war), Gladys Muriel, Ronald Wells, Alec James, Philip Morgan, Evelyn Ruby and James

Henry. He continued to work as a tailor, possibly until his father's death in 1937, and was later employed by Cadbury's. Francis Henry Franklin died on 5 March 1973 at Cashes Green Hospital, Stroud, and was buried in the churchyard at St James the Great, Saul.

FREDERICK ALEXANDER FRANKLIN, 1890–?
Enlisted in Lord Kitchener's Army

Frederick Alexander Franklin was the eldest son of Frederick Alexander Franklin and Emmeline née Warren who registered his birth during the first quarter of 1890. He was baptised on 13 April the same year at St Mary's. Frederick (Senior) owned several properties adjoining the family's home, Cecil House (now Northend House), located on Perryway at the top of the village green. By 1911 Fred and his next brother, *Francis Henry, were working for their father's tailoring business.

Fred enlisted into Lord Kitchener's Army along with *Preston Dennis on 16 November 1914. While the plaque in the village hall confirms Fred's service during the war, it has not been possible to determine where this took place, nor in what capacity he served.

According to family members, Fred was later sent to South Africa by his father to earn a living, but he had returned by the time of his marriage to Annie Thatcher on 11 January 1928 at St Mary's, Wotton-under-Edge, when Fred gave his occupation as a farmer. They later moved to London and it is believed that they had a son.

ALBERT THOMAS FREDERICKS, 1878–?
Private 3264, 5th (Reserve) Battalion, Gloucestershire Regiment

Albert Thomas Fredericks was the son of Thomas Harding Fredericks, a ship's carpenter, and Elizabeth née Prickett. He was born in Frampton where the family lived in The Street, his birth being registered during the first quarter of 1878. Some of Albert's childhood was also spent in Fretherne but, at the time of the 1891 census, Albert's parents were recorded on their own, back in Frampton. Albert's whereabouts are unclear, and his story is next picked up when he travelled from Liverpool to Quebec in 1904 on the SS *Lake Champlain*, where he gave his occupation as a baker. It seems that he married while in Canada, although it is difficult to be certain, but when he sailed from Montreal to Avonmouth in August 1913 aboard the SS *Royal George*, he was accompanied by his wife, Mary Ann (Annie), and their two young children, Harding and George, his occupation now given as a carpenter. At the outbreak of the First World War the family were in Frampton; Albert's older brother, Harry Benjamin, was living on The Green.

On 22 September 1914, Albert attested at Gloucester and was posted to the 5th (Reserve) Battalion of the Gloucestershire Regiment. He was recorded as 'not being likely to become an efficient soldier' just eighty-nine days later and discharged, presumably on medical grounds, for his conduct was described as 'Good'. This seems to have prompted the family's journey from Liverpool on the SS *Scandinavian* on 19 March the following year, when they returned to Peterborough, Ontario, previously Albert and Annie's home for some eleven years. On the ship's manifest, they were classified as 'returning Canadians'.

CHRISTOPHER CHARLES FRYER, 1897–1917
Private 26921, 9th (Service) Battalion and 12th (Service) Battalion (Bristol), Gloucestershire Regiment

Christopher Charles Fryer, known as Charles, was born on 21 February 1897, the third child of Albert Joseph Fryer and Flora Mary née Hitchings. Albert had previously run the Coffee House on the village green, but this had closed some years earlier and he was now a haulier. The family was a large one, with only Charles, his brothers *Clevedon Wells and *Edgar John and their sister, Edith, still living at home in 1911, by which time Charles was a hall boy; family members believe that he may have found work in Slimbridge.

Charles enlisted early, joining the 9th (Service) Battalion of the Gloucestershire Regiment. He entered France on 20 September 1915 and in November moved to Salonika to support Serbia against invasion by Bulgaria and Austria-Hungary. Charles was later invalided home with dysentery. After recovery he was posted to the 12th Battalion in France as a signaller. His battalion suffered very many casualties during the first two weeks of October 1917 during the Battle of Passchendaele. On 1 November, the battalion was in the front line near Sanctuary Wood and was being relieved by the 1st Cheshires, a dangerous time as troop movements usually attracted shellfire. Private Christopher Charles Fryer was wounded in the chest, thigh and head and died on 3 November at a Casualty Clearing Station; his family report that a nurse had guided his hand to write a last letter home.

Charles was interred at the CWGC Lijssenthoek Military Cemetery at Poperinghe, near Ypres. He was posthumously awarded the British War Medal and Victory Medal, and is commemorated on both the Frampton war memorial and the plaque in the village hall. The Slimbridge war memorial also remembers a Charles Fryer but this is likely to have been Charles William Fryer of Slimbridge Street, Cambridge, who also served with the Gloucestershire Regiment.

CLEVEDON WELLS FRYER, 1892–1931
Driver L/31887, 186th Brigade, Royal Field Artillery

Clevedon Wells Fryer was born on 11 August 1892 in Frampton, one of the thirteen children of Albert Fryer and his wife Flora May née Hitchings. By 1901 the family were living in Elm Tree Cottage on the corner of The Green and Whitminster Lane. Clevedon worked as a gardener after leaving school.

On 7 June 1915 he enlisted in the 186th Brigade Royal Field Artillery as a driver. Clevedon's service records do not survive, but his nephew relates that he sustained head wounds while in the Army. He was discharged on 13 August 1918 and was awarded the Silver War Badge and later the British War Medal and Victory Medal. His service is commemorated on the plaque in the village hall.

As a result of the wounds he received, Clevedon did not work after the war and suffered frequent fits which are thought to have contributed to his early death on 8 February 1931 in Frampton. Clevedon Wells Fryer was buried in St Mary's churchyard three days later. Three of his brothers also served during the war: *Christopher Charles, *Edgar John and Walter Vimpany (whose address was Wotton-under-Edge).

EDGAR JOHN FRYER, 1898–1988
Private 13733, later 26524, 3rd (Reserve) Battalion, Royal Warwickshire Regiment

Edgar John Fryer, known as Ted, was born in Frampton on Christmas Day 1898 to Albert Joseph Fryer, a haulier, and Flora Mary née Hitchings. In 1911, at the age of twelve, Ted was still attending school despite having been recorded absent several times during September and October 1910 while employed by his father to pick walnuts. His older brothers *Christopher Charles and *Clevedon Wells, by then in employment, also served during the war. Ted later found work as a horse driver.

Although he enlisted at Gloucester on 4 December 1916, Ted was immediately placed on the Army Reserve and was not mobilised until 28 March 1917. Owing to badly faded records it is unclear to which unit he was first assigned, but on 17 August it is probable that he was transferred to the 3rd (Reserve) Battalion of the Royal Warwickshire Regiment and served in France. He also appears to have served at times with both the 5th (Reserve) and 2/7th Battalions of his regiment. Ted's family say that he was gassed while serving. In August 1918 he became ill with diarrhoea, was sent back to the UK on 31 August, and by 9 September had been transferred to the 1st Southern General Hospital in Birmingham. While in the UK he must have recovered well enough to get into a little trouble; on 7 October Private Fryer overstayed sick leave (from a tattoo!) by a few hours, and on 11 November he similarly overstayed draft leave which suggests that on the day after the Armistice he may have been about to be posted back to France. His punishments were a fine of eight days' pay and detention for twenty-one days respectively. Ted did not return to France and was discharged on 2 March 1919 after the standard twenty-eight days' leave. He was awarded the British War Medal and Victory Medal. His family still treasure the framed certificate given by the people of Frampton 'in recognition of his service during the Great War' and he is also commemorated on the plaque in the village hall.

Ted married Rosamund Mary Weare in 1921 and they had six children: Joseph Walter Pierce, Charles Edgar John, Olive Edith Mary, James Albert (Jim), Clarence Edward (Chippy) and Dawn Marie. After the war Ted worked horse-drawn barges on the canal. He was also employed at Cadbury's making Bournvita, and then at Hoffmans in Stonehouse. Edgar John Fryer died on 13 April 1988 in Cashes Green Hospital, Stroud, and was buried in St Mary's churchyard.

WILFRED HARRIS GABB, 1897–1983
Private 15774, Worcestershire Regiment; M2/164250, later DM2/164250, Army Service Corps

Wilfred Harris Gabb, usually known as Bill, was born in Fretherne on 5 August 1897 to George William Gabb, a blacksmith, and Elizabeth Ann née Harris. In 1901 Bill and his parents were living in Saul Road, Fretherne and by 1911 he was a Post Office messenger and the family were at Lion House, Saul, which still has a lion statue over the door. Soon afterwards he became a trainee mechanic for Fielding & Platt Ltd, an engineering company in Gloucester.

Bill enlisted with the Worcestershire Regiment on 4 September 1914 and he entered France on 19 July 1915. His daughter recalls that he spent time in the trenches before his mechanical skills were recognised. Private Gabb was transferred to the Army Service Corps on 29 October 1915 and he always considered that this move saved his life. As a mechanic he serviced the vehicles which went to the front. Bill apparently served alongside Australian troops and won a cup running against them. He was transferred to the Army Reserve on 29 April 1919 and awarded the 1914–15 Star, British War Medal and Victory Medal. His war service is commemorated on the plaque in Frampton Village Hall.

In October 1921 Bill married Emma Amelia (Millie) Attridge whose family lived at The Lake, Frampton. Bill and Millie set up home at The Walks, but they later moved to De Lacy Cottage, The Street. They had three children: Fred, Betty and Jean. Bill worked for the RAF No. 7 Maintenance Unit at Quedgeley delivering vehicles to local depots and Tilbury docks. Like many other First World War veterans, he was an ARP Warden during the Second World War. Wilfred

Harris Gabb died at his home in Cam in 1983 and his ashes were interred in the churchyard of his parish church of St George.

PETER GANDY, 1896–1982
Private F539, 17th (Service) Battalion (Football) and
19th (Service) Battalion (2nd Public Works Pioneers),
Middlesex Regiment

Peter Gandy, the son of Henry Gandy and Beatrice Matilda née Ireland, was born on 4 April 1896 in Fretherne. His father was a coachman at Fretherne Court. By 1911 Henry had retired and the family were living on The Green, Frampton, with Peter employed as a hall boy, perhaps also in service to the Darell family. He subsequently moved to Kensington where he worked as a footman.

Peter enlisted on 4 February 1915 at Chelsea Town Hall, being posted to the 17th (Service) Battalion (Football), Middlesex Regiment as a private. The core of the battalion was a group of professional footballers from which it derived its name. By 17 November he was serving in France as part of the 6th Brigade where he led an 'interesting' life. He was treated for short bouts of illness (scabies and trench fever), court-martialled for sleeping on sentry duty (being sentenced to eighty-four days' Field Punishment), and he received a bullet wound in the neck on 1 June 1916, for which he was treated at hospital in Rouen before rejoining his battalion on 19 June. On 31 July he was again shot, this time in the left arm, and was repatriated from 2 August to 31 December. On recovery he was posted back to France to join the 19th (Service) Battalion (2nd Public Works Pioneers) of his regiment. Peter Gandy's luck still held. He was again shot in the arm on 13 April, but it was a slight wound and he remained in the field. In September he was awarded extra pay of 6d per day, which may have rewarded his specialist military qualifications of Stretcher Bearer and 1st Class Shot. On 15 November he was transferred, probably with his battalion, to Italy, where he served until 3 March 1918.

Back in France, in mid-June, Peter came down with influenza. After convalescing at Boulogne he was sent to the UK on leave from 16 to 30 August. However, he was only a few weeks back in action before, on 9 October, he was gassed, for which he was treated in hospital at Boulogne. Peter did not rejoin his unit until 29 October, shortly before the Armistice. He returned to the UK on 30 March 1919 and was demobilised on 30 April. Peter was awarded the 1914–15 Star, British War Medal and Victory Medal and his service is commemorated on the plaque in the village hall.

After the war Peter returned to live with his parents in Frampton. He drove for Cadbury's, collecting milk from the farms and was also a special constable for a while. His later years were spent at 10 The Oval with Mervyn and Monica Davis. Peter Gandy's death was registered in the Gloucester district during the spring of 1982.

FREDERICK CHARLES GARDNER, 1894–1965
Sergeant 8071, 22 Squadron, Royal Flying Corps, later Royal Air Force

Frederick Charles Gardner was born in Gloucester on 7 February 1894 to John William Gardner, a beer-seller, and Ellen née Draper. His parents ran a public house in King's Walk and in his early years an outbreak of smallpox resulted in Fred being sent to stay with his grandparents in Frampton. By 1901 he was living with his parents and older sister, Florence, in Cardiff House, The Street, where his father was running a grocer's shop and carrying business. In March 1906 Fred was awarded third prize (a pencil, pen and case), for the highest number of marks obtained in a term's worth of weekly examinations at the school. (The recipient of the first prize was *William Sims.)

Fred left school in February 1907 and by 1911 was an apprentice tailor. On 28 August 1915 he enlisted into the Royal Flying Corps (where tailoring skills would have been very useful in repairing aircraft skinned mostly with fabric), and trained as a mechanic. Posted to No. 22 Squadron in France, he would have worked on the maintenance and repair of FE2b reconnaissance aircraft. These were slow and vulnerable to rear attack. During 1917, 22 Squadron's FE2bs were replaced by the much faster and more manoeuvrable Bristol F2b aircraft. German fighters had to treat them with great respect. Fred became one of the founder members of the Royal Air Force on its formation on 1 April 1918, and earned promotion to sergeant before being transferred to the RAF Reserve on 15 February 1919. He was awarded the British War Medal and Victory Medal and his service is commemorated on the plaque in the village hall. Fred related to his family some of his experiences from the war, including the reluctance of his men to remove a dead pilot from a crashed aircraft to effect its recovery.

After the war Fred returned to tailoring, and on 10 October 1922 he married May Nash at St Mary's. However, business dropped off with an increase in ready-made clothing, so they moved to a cottage in Fitcherbury, bought some milking cows and started a milk round. He subsequently rented the council-owned Mangrove Farm in Saul, the tenancy of which was later taken over by his son, Richard. Fred and May also had a daughter, Sheila. Frederick Charles Gardner was buried in St Mary's churchyard on 9 February 1965.

HAROLD JAMES FREDERICK GLEED, 1899–1963
Private 37691, Duke of Cornwall's Light Infantry; 043838, Army Ordnance Corps

Harold James Frederick Gleed, later known as Bam, was the second son of Ernest William Gleed, a baker, and Mary née Brown. Harold was born in Frampton on 2 August 1899 and baptised on 15 October the same year at St Mary's where

his father was parish clerk and sexton, roles previously held by his great-grandfather, Giles Frape. When the census was taken in 1911, Harold was still at school along with three of his sisters; his older brother, *William Joseph Ernest, was already at work, and his older sister, Jane, was assisting at home.

Details of Harold's enlistment into the Army have not been found although anecdotal evidence suggests that another of Frampton's servicemen, *Timothy John Sims, met Harold on his birthday at Ypres. We only know of Harold's record from the medal rolls which confirm that he served as a private in the Duke of Cornwall's Light Infantry, and later in the Army Ordnance Corps. He was transferred to the Reserve on 20 November 1919 and awarded the British War Medal and Victory Medal. His service is commemorated on the plaque in the village hall and his family still retain the certificate which the grateful people of Frampton awarded him.

After the war, Harold returned to the village and worked at Cadbury's. On 15 September 1924 he married Ruby Emeline Morgan at St Mary's and moved to Saul. Two sons followed, Eric James and Kenneth Morgan. Harold James Frederick Gleed died on 10 August 1963 at Roselea, Saul, and was buried at his parish church of St James the Great.

WILLIAM JOSEPH ERNEST GLEED, 1894–1963
Private S/4122483, Army Service Corps

William Joseph Ernest Gleed was the first of the seven children born in Frampton to Ernest William Gleed and Mary née Brown, one of whom, Ivor, died in infancy. William was baptised on Christmas Day 1894 at St Mary's. Home was the property now known as The Old Bakery (at the north end of The Street), from where Ernest ran his bakery business. By 1911 William had become a postman.

He enlisted at Gloucester on 18 June 1915 (the same day as *William James George Daw) into the Army Service Corps. A baker by trade, on 13 July he was posted to 40 Field Bakery, part of the 53rd (Welsh) Division, being deployed with them to the Mediterranean theatre and landing at Suvla Bay, Gallipoli, on 3 August. He became ill in late September and was evacuated first to hospital (probably a hospital ship), and then to the UK where he arrived on 27 October. Owing to losses in action, casualties from illness and a November blizzard, the entire Division was reduced to about 15 per cent of its effective strength and in December was withdrawn to Egypt.

Members of William's family recall that a Christmas cake was despatched to him at Gallipoli, but it missed him and in due course followed him to France, where he arrived on 20 March 1916 to serve with 9 Field Bakery. He stayed for nearly a year. In March 1917 he appears to have suffered medical problems, recorded as heart disease, and was repatriated for discharge as no longer physically fit for war service. At discharge a month later he was described as 'A good baker, honest, sober and reliable', and received a disability pension for twenty weeks, together with the Silver War Badge. He was later awarded the 1914–15 Star, British War Medal and Victory Medal and his service is commemorated on the plaque in the village hall alongside that of his brother *Harold James Frederick.

On 2 July 1917 William, then a clerk, married Constance Rose Robins at St Andrew's, Alvington. They settled into married life at Redmarley, where they may have run a Post Office, and had three children: Constance Mary, Grantley William and Robin Harold. In 1943 William bought Ward's Court in Frampton, which was then called The Nurseries. William Joseph Ernest Gleed died in Frampton and was buried in St Mary's churchyard on 18 October 1963.

JACOB JONAS GODWIN, 1874–1944
Driver 80813, Royal Engineers

Jacob Jonas Godwin was born in Minety, Wiltshire, on 16 June 1874, the son of John Godwin, a licensed victualler, and Emma Westwood née Kent. His father ran the Vale of the White Horse Inn in Minety where Jacob spent his childhood. Jacob married Myra Highnam in 1903 with whom he had three daughters: Jessie, Muriel and Joyce. On 2 April 1911 the family were living on the Channel Island of Jersey, where Jacob worked as a cowman but Myra died shortly afterwards.

Jacob served as a driver (equivalent to private) in the Royal Engineers, entering France on 29 August 1915. At the end of the war he transferred to the Army Reserve and was awarded the 1914–15 Star, British War Medal and Victory Medal.

In the 1918 electoral registers for Frampton, Jacob was listed as an absent voter at Beehive Cottage where he would have been the tenant of William David Daw. By the autumn of 1919 he was back in Frampton and thought to have been living in the present-day Falfield Cottage part of the building. On 21 October 1921 Jacob married again, to Ellen Elizabeth Jones, giving his occupation as a horse driver, perhaps an indication that during the war he may well have driven horses rather than motor vehicles. He and Ellen later lived on The Green. Jacob Jonas Godwin was buried in St Mary's churchyard on 6 January 1944. His war service is commemorated on the plaque in the village hall.

RALPH JAMES GOODMAN, 1885–1954
Private 183585, Canadian Army Service Corps

Ralph James Goodman was born in Hornsey, Middlesex, on 25 January 1885, the third son of William Henry Goodman and Ada née Gazeley. By 1901, the family were running the grocer's shop at the top of the village green in Frampton. In 1907 Ralph and his next eldest brother, William, sailed on the *Lake Erie* from Liverpool to St John, Canada, with the intention of settling in Calgary, described respectively a labourer and a baker. Two years later, having returned at some stage, both brothers made a similar journey on the *Empress of Ireland*, this time described as Canadians, and Ralph as a grocer.

On 6 November 1915 Ralph, then a baker, voluntarily attested for service with the Canadian Expeditionary Force at Calgary. Although the date of his posting to France is not known, he was one of the 1,145 Canadian soldiers who returned to Canada from Liverpool on 28 October 1917 under 'Special Authority'. His unit was the Canadian Army Service Corps, so it is very likely that Private Goodman worked at his trade to feed the troops.

On 25 September 1918 Ralph arrived in London from Montreal on the Canadian Pacific ship *Corsican*, giving his occupation as baker, his destination Seaford (Sussex), and his country of permanent residence as Canada. This journey was clearly for his marriage, registered in Eastbourne in late 1918, to Ethel Maud Carr. Ralph and Ethel lived in Frampton during the 1920s, but later moved away. Ralph James Goodman died in the Norton Radstock district of Somerset in 1954. His service during the war is commemorated on the plaque in Frampton Village Hall.

PHILIP GRAY
Rank and Service: Not known

The only details found for Philip Gray are that he was recorded as an absent military or naval voter in 1918–19 at a property on The Green, Frampton, together with Mary Jane Gray who may have been his wife. A boy named Walter Gray was admitted to the school on 10 August 1918.

THOMAS HENRY GRIFFIN, 1880–1957
Lance Corporal 12607, 9th (Service) Battalion, Gloucestershire Regiment; 334131, later WR509202, Inland Water Transport Branch, Royal Engineers

Thomas Henry Griffin, known as Harry, was born in the autumn of 1880 in Saul, one of the eight children of William Griffin and Emily Jane née Balch. His father was a waterman and the family lived close to his work on the canal, variously in Saul and Framilode. Harry was also a mariner and on 27 August 1902 he married Beatrice Eveline, the sister of *Thomas Ernest Sims, at St John's, Gloucester. By 1911, they were living on The Green in Frampton. Before the war four of their five surviving children were born: Edith Emily Rose, Evelyn Georgina Annie, Freda Dora Elsie and Georgina Kate. Henry William George arrived in 1917.

On 3 September 1914 Harry voluntarily enlisted for the Army at Tewkesbury. He was posted to the 9th (Service) Battalion of the Gloucestershire Regiment.

Harry kept a diary during his period of service which has been transcribed on page 57. It gives an interesting insight into his everyday life which is only summarised here. It was not until 19 September 1915 that Harry's battalion left the UK for France as part of the British Expeditionary Force. He spent less than two months there before being transferred to the Mediterranean Expeditionary Force on 11 November. In the Balkans he worked in the trenches until 28 February 1916 when he was hospitalised with nephritis (kidney inflammation), the initial journey of 4 or 5 miles being on a mule-drawn sledge. Harry was shipped to Malta where he was also diagnosed with neurasthenia (a form of chronic fatigue). He stayed in hospital until 19 June when he was considered strong enough to make the journey to England where he continued to be hospitalised until 16 April 1917. Harry's granddaughter recalls him saying that it was Marmite that kept him alive in Salonika!

At this point his professional capabilities seem to have been recognised. He was transferred to the Inland Water Transport Branch of the Royal Engineers to be employed as a lighterman, a move which clearly suited Harry who, by 25 October, was rated as 'skilled', awarded additional Engineer Pay, and posted to the major naval base at Taranto in Italy. On 25 April 1918 he was upgraded to 'superior' skills and a higher pay rate, followed by appointment to acting lance corporal on 1 June. Despite a fractured wrist later that month (having fallen on a slippery deck), he was soon appointed substantive lance corporal, and then further upgraded to 'very superior' skills on 1 November with a further pay rise. He was repatriated on 16 February 1919 and transferred to the Army Reserve on 17 March. He was awarded the 1914–15 Star, British War Medal and Victory Medal and his service is commemorated on the plaque in the village hall.

During the war, like so many servicemen, Harry missed his wife, Eveline, a great deal and his diary begins with a poem for her. After the war Harry returned to Frampton and resumed work as a waterman; on one occasion he survived a sinking in the river when he lost all of his possessions. Harry is pictured with Eveline and their granddaughter, Christine, outside their cottage in The Street, now the site of Bendles. Thomas Henry Griffin died on 26 July 1957 and was buried in St Mary's churchyard.

HENRY ELPHINSTONE GUY, 1892–1953
Rank and Service: Not known

Henry Elphinstone Guy, 'Elph', was born in Frampton on 15 September 1892, the only son of Henry James Guy and Jane née Davies. He was baptised on 24 June 1894 at the same time as his older sister, Elsie Jane, four days after their mother had been buried. Their home was a three-roomed cottage on the corner of the lane leading to the chapel (now part of Roe's Pool House). It could not have been easy for Henry

James as a mariner left with four young children (at the time of the 1891 census he had been on board the *Elizabeth* at Weston-super-Mare) and he married again during the late 1890s.

Elph took up work as a domestic gardener, continuing to live in the family's home with his stepmother, Mary Anne, after his father's death in 1909. Although he was listed as an absent voter in 1918–19, no record has been found of his service during the war other than recognition of it on the plaque in the village hall.

He returned to the village for a short while before moving to London where he married Ethel Rosa Turner in 1922. The couple were living at 2 Killarney Road, Wandsworth in 1939 when Elph was foreman packer for a publishing company. Henry Elphinstone Guy was still at that address when he died in January 1953. He was buried in St Anne's churchyard, Wandsworth.

WALTER GYMER, 1885–1950
Private 33459, 11th (Service) Battalion (Pioneers), Hampshire Regiment

Walter Gymer was born in either East or West Rudham, Norfolk, on 2 July 1885 to Charles Hubbard Gymer, an agricultural labourer, and Elizabeth née Cooper. The two adjoining villages are both mentioned in his records. By 1911 Walter was a groom at Greens Norton Hall Stables, Towcester, while later that year he married Mabel Mary Short. Their first child, Alan, was born in Norfolk in 1913.

Walter enlisted on 12 December 1915, joining the 11th (Service) Battalion (Pioneers) Hampshire Regiment; as they landed in Le Havre on 18 December en route to the Western Front, he can't have had much prior training. The battalion were the Pioneers for the 16th (Irish) Division, deployed near Loos, their baptism of fire coming with the German gas attacks at Hulluch in April 1916 in which each side lost over 1,000 casualties to the gas. In July they moved to the Somme and were intensively engaged in that campaign, playing an important part in the capture of the towns of Ginchy and Guillemont in September and, despite heavy losses, the Division gained a reputation as first-class shock troops. These actions were notable for the success of air observation in guiding Allied artillery to destroy many of the German guns, which in turn was made possible by almost complete air superiority. Although the Division continued to serve on the Western Front until the end of the war, Walter Gymer was discharged on 12 April 1917 owing to sickness. His service to his country was later recognised by the award of the Silver War Badge in respect of his disability, together with the British War Medal and Victory Medal.

It is unclear when the Gymers moved to Frampton, but the birth of their second son, Basil, was registered in the Wheatenhurst district during the spring of 1917. The family lived in The Street before moving to The Green where their daughter Beryl was born in 1920. Home was The Arch, and Walter worked at Cadbury's and was recorded as a storekeeper in 1939. Walter Gymer was buried in St Mary's churchyard on 28 October 1950. His war service is commemorated on the plaque in the village hall.

THOMAS GEORGE HALLING, 1888–1960
Sergeant 12588, Royal Flying Corps, later Royal Air Force

Thomas George Halling was born on 7 April 1888 in Frampton, the son of a waterman, William Halling, and his wife Georgina née Winchcombe. Like his eldest brother, *William, Thomas went to sea after leaving school. He married Beatrice Jane May Jermyn in the Cardiff area in 1913 and they subsequently had five children: George Thomas Jermyn, Mabel Doreen, Lawrence Jermyn, Beatrice J. G. and Douglas Jermyn.

As a rigger in civilian life, Thomas would have been an obvious choice for work on aircraft. He enlisted on 1 November 1915 into the Royal Flying Corps as an air mechanic second class. His surviving service records are incomplete but show that he was posted to the No. 2 (Auxiliary) School of Aerial Gunnery at Turnberry, Scotland, the military aerodrome established on Turnberry golf course in January 1917, and later to the No. 1 (Auxiliary) School of Aerial Gunnery at Hythe, Kent. From June 1918 he was stationed at an unidentified repair depot before being seconded to an American Mission a month later where he remained until after the Armistice. From 8 December he spent a couple of months at the training depot station at Gormanston (north of Dublin) before his final move in February 1919 to nearby Baldonnel airfield (today the only airfield of the Irish Air Corps). A month later he was transferred to the Reserve and 'Deemed Discharged' on 30 April 1920. He was promoted several times during his service; air mechanic first class (December 1916), corporal (July 1917) and acting sergeant (November 1917). At the formation of the Royal Air Force on 1 April 1918 Thomas was a senior mechanic in the rank of sergeant.

Thomas's address on discharge from the RAF was given as Frampton, presumably that of his parents for his wife and children appear to have remained in the Cardiff area. In 1939 the family were living in Swansea where Thomas was the master of a sand dredger. Thomas George Halling's death is believed to have been registered in the Swansea area during the first quarter of 1960. His war service is commemorated on the plaque in Frampton Village Hall.

WILLIAM HALLING, 1880–1964
Rank and Service: Not known

William Halling, known as Bill, was born in Frampton on 7 January 1880, but it was not until the following January that he was baptised at St Mary's, the eldest son of William Halling and Georgina née Winchcombe. His father was a waterman, so the river trade was in his blood. Georgina bore nine children and, somewhat disparagingly, the 1911 census records her as having 'no occupation'! A waterman's household was full of comings and goings, and as the three eldest Halling boys left school, they too took up the trade. Bill married a mariner's daughter, Ada Maria Herbert, and their wedding at St Mary's on 29 April 1902 brought together two families with kindred spirits. Good money could be earned by hard work, and Bill and Ada made their home at Chapel House, with Bill master of his father-in-law's trow, *Victory*. By 1914 five children had been born: William James, Naomi, Nellie, Tom and Jack.

Bill's service record during the war has not survived. However, his name on the plaque in the village hall acknowledges his wartime contribution alongside that of his younger brother, *Thomas George.

After the war, the family continued to live in Chapel House. William Halling died on 5 December 1964 and was buried in St Mary's churchyard four days later.

J. HARLEY
Rank and Service: Not known

The plaque in the village hall lists J. Harley among 'those who went from Frampton to serve their king and country'. Details of this serviceman have not been traced, although it is believed that a 'Jim Harley' appears on an early 1920s photograph taken outside Cadbury's Recreation Hut.

GEORGE HARRIS, 1877–?
Private, Devonshire Regiment

George Harris was born in Whitminster on 3 March 1877 to George William and Ellen Harris. His childhood home was on the Bristol Road at Whitminster from where his father variously found work on local farms or as a carpenter. Ellen supplemented the family's income as a tailoress. On 12 February 1906 George married Clara Maria Pearce at her parish church of St Michael and All Angels, Eastington. By 1911 they were living in a three-roomed property in Whittles Lane, Frampton, with their young children, Elsie Marion, Phyllis May and William Walter, and George was working for Frampton Court Estate as a carpenter.

Evidence of George's service during the war is provided through two incidents reported in the newspapers concerning members of his family. The first was an unfortunate accident that befell his mother, Ellen, who was knocked over in the road and badly injured. She was returning to Whitminster after visiting George in Frampton on 29 January 1917, just before he left for France. The second occurred while he was serving as a private in the Devonshire Regiment on 3 August 1918. Tragically, George's nine-year-old son, William Walter, found a revolver in a workshop in Frampton and accidentally shot himself. Despite the doctor's best efforts, the boy died shortly afterwards. By then the family were living on The Green. (A more detailed account of both accidents can be found on pages 69 and 84.)

The Harris family seem to have left Frampton around 1921 and in 1939 George and Clara's home was at Millend, Eastington, with George still working as a carpenter. George Harris' war service is commemorated on the plaque in Frampton Village Hall.

THOMAS HAWKER, 1867–1933
Rank and Service: Not known

Thomas Hawker was born in Frampton in 1867, the son of Thomas Hawker, a brickmaker, and Ann Maria née Goulding. When he volunteered at Woolwich for the Royal Artillery on 20 May 1884, Thomas was a well-built labourer and added two years to his age. He suffered an injury the following June for which he spent six weeks in hospital. Despite the use of a 'lead potion' he recovered well enough to be posted to India and arrived at Secunderabad on 15 November 1885. During his six years there he also served in the military cantonments of Bangalore and Mhow, earning a short-lived promotion to bombardier (corporal equivalent) and being transferred into the Royal Horse Artillery. In January 1892 he returned to Britain on the troopship HMS *Crocodile* and was discharged at the end of his engagement on 16 May 1896. Thomas became a police constable and on 9 December 1896 he married Minnie Edith Wales at St Leonard's, Shoreditch. By 1901 their home was in Hackney and their eldest son, *Thomas Miles, was four. In 1911, with the addition of Edith Annie and William, the family were living in a three-roomed property at nearby Kingsland.

Thomas' involvement in the First World War has not been established due to the loss of records, but it seems likely that his past experience would have been put to good use in the training of those sent to front line combat. For this, of course, he would have seen no award of medals and the only remaining tangible recognition of his war service comes from his inclusion in the list of Frampton men commemorated on the plaque in the village hall.

After the war Thomas returned with his family to Frampton to live at Brooklyn, The Street. Thomas Hawker was buried in St Mary's churchyard on 12 May 1933. After Thomas' death, his wife lived at The Stores in Frampton with their son William.

THOMAS MILES HAWKER, 1897–1962
Rank and Service: Not known

Thomas Miles Hawker was born in Holme-next-the-Sea, Norfolk, on 22 March 1897, the son of *Thomas Hawker, a police constable, and Minnie Edith née Wales (who also hailed from the same coastal village). From July 1905 to April 1911 Thomas attended Enfield Road School in Hackney, leaving just after his twelfth birthday.

No records of his war service have been traced, but he is commemorated on the plaque in Frampton Village Hall. After a brief spell in the village around 1920, when he lived with his parents at Brooklyn, The Street, Thomas moved to Cheltenham and worked as a police constable at the Central Police Station. On 3 April 1926 he married the widowed Elsie Hannah Burnham (née Skidmore) at St Luke's church in Cheltenham. He later returned to Frampton and lived at Ashleigh House, The Street. Thomas Miles Hawker died in 1962, his death being registered in Gloucester Rural District which included Frampton.

FREDERICK WILLIAM PHILLIPS HAZELL, 1897–1982
Acting Lance Corporal 340444, 5th Battalion, 4th Battalion and 3rd Battalion, Worcestershire Regiment

Frederick William Phillips Hazell was born in Frampton on 7 May 1897, the first of William Hazell and Susan née Phillips' three children. Home was Yew Tree House, The Street, but William, a fisherman, was often away working; the 1911 census records him in the Wye at Chepstow on board *Industry*. Meanwhile, at the age of thirteen, Fred was still at school.

Only fragments of Fred's official service record survive; his Silver War Badge card and roll, and confirmation of a period of furlough (leave). His sister, Dorothy, kept a notebook during the war period from which some additional information has been gleaned. Fred enlisted on 15 January 1916, but he may not have been called up until 16 May, the date given by Dorothy for his entry into the Army, being posted to the Worcestershire Regiment. She recorded his address (without a date) as '27 Room B Coy, 5 Batt: Worcestershire Regt, Tregantle Fort, Plymouth'. This was a training establishment; many of its rifle ranges slope steeply towards the sea and are still in use today. After training he was probably posted to the 4th Battalion during the Somme campaign, and certainly by 9 August 1917 he was in Britain for treatment when his mother wrote to him at the VAD hospital at Abbey Manor, Evesham: 'We were disappointed not to hear from you this morning, as we are anxious to know the Dr's report, hope you are feeling better.' By October he had been transferred to Croydon War Hospital. At this stage he was serving with the 4th Battalion and in the rank of acting (or temporary) lance corporal. He was given nine days' leave, no doubt a welcome relief to both him and his family. As a result of his wounds, Fred was discharged from the Army on 11 October 1918 in his substantive rank of private in the 3rd Battalion, and was given the Silver War Badge. He was later awarded the British War Medal and Victory Medal and, like his brother, *Ralph Theodore, his war service is commemorated on the plaque in the village hall.

After the war Fred ran a shop on the village green, the site of a hairdressers in recent years. Numerous villagers, many of them youngsters, worked there and helped with the deliveries. After retirement from the grocery business, Fred moved to Dorset where, well into his sixties, he married Freda Antell. Frederick William Phillips Hazell died in the Poole area in 1982.

RALPH THEODORE HAZELL, 1898–1989
Private 25891, later 395292, Army Service Corps

Ralph Theodore Hazell was born at Yew Tree House, The Street, on 30 July 1898. He was the middle child of William Hazell, a fisherman, and Susan née Phillips;

his brother, *Frederick William Phillips and sister, Dorothy Alice, completed the household. After leaving school, Ralph was apprenticed to one of the village grocers, Richard Ward.

Ralph was attested for Army service at Gloucester on 3 August 1916 and was medically examined in November, but not called for duty until 14 January 1918; his records contain reference to phthisis (pulmonary tuberculosis), although a medical review concluded that the only symptom was a shortness of breath. After basic recruit training Private Ralph Hazell was posted to the Mechanical Transport Driving School of the Army Service Corps for specialist training. By 18 May he had qualified as a heavy lorry driver with a note suggesting that he had driven American Peerless trucks. On 22 September he embarked on the *Maid of Orleans* at Southampton, arriving at Basra to join 1115 MT Company on 6 November with only five days of the war remaining, and receiving 1s per day war pay. On 5 February 1919 he was taken ill with colitis, requiring hospital treatment for about three months. He then served in Mesopotamia (transport personnel are usually the last to leave any theatre) until embarking for the UK on 8 January 1920. He arrived on 19 February and was demobilised one month later. Ralph was awarded the British War Medal and Victory Medal and his service is commemorated on the plaque in the village hall.

After his return Ralph drove a steam lorry for Cadbury's and continued to live at Yew Tree House. On 19 June 1929 he married Vera Louise Morgan and they had a daughter, Susan. He was a superb gardener and won many prizes, particularly for his sweet peas which he would give away generously to his friends. He was a staunch teetotaller, a bell-ringer at St Mary's and at Gloucester Cathedral, and he also sang in the choir in Arlingham with his sister Dorothy. Ralph played bowls and was at one time captain of Frampton Bowls Club. It is said that he was very proud of his fine head of hair and would wash it only in rainwater heated over a primus stove! During the last few months of his life Ralph was cared for by his daughter, Susan. Ralph Theodore Hazell died at her home, Ashleigh House, The Street, on 15th July 1989 and was buried in St Mary's churchyard five days later.

DAVID GEORGE HERBERT, 1894–1974
Private 19123, 10th (Prince of Wales's Own Royal) Hussars; Stoker I K29622, Royal Navy

One of the seventeen children of James Herbert, a waterman, and Emma Jemima née Aldridge, David George Herbert, known as George, was born on 27 July 1894 at Lea Court Farm, Framilode. As the family grew, and James became a master mariner and owner of boats, he had Kimberley House built near Fretherne Bridge to house his extensive family. Frampton's school records indicate that the Herbert children were often late; on 16 July 1909, for instance, they arrived at 9.20 a.m.

and were sent home. After Emma's death, James wrote on his 1911 census form that he was unable to be away on his boats; his daughter Lily was housekeeper while George was working his trow, *Reliance*. James later sold his house and its grounds to Cadbury's and it became their factory manager's home.

In George's own words to his family, 'after a drunken night out' he enlisted in the 10th (Prince of Wales's Own Royal) Hussars on 27 September 1914. However, he was set on getting out so that he could join the Navy, so while on sentry duty he would fire his rifle at cabbages in the fields and then call out the guard to pick up the 'bodies'! Eventually the Hussars gave way; on 28 December the same year he was discharged for misconduct on condition that he then joined the Royal Navy. These were *most* unusual circumstances.

A year later, George enlisted as a stoker in the Royal Navy, his date of birth being recorded as 27 July 1896, exactly two years after the actual date. This proved to be a more successful contribution to the war effort; after three months at the Navy's training establishment at Devonport, HMS *Vivid*, George was transferred to HMS *Gloucester*. When George arrived on board on 15 March 1916 she was based at Scapa Flow; he was to stay with her until the end of his service. During the Easter Rising in Ireland she landed marines in Galway Bay and later on in the year she saw action in the Battle of Jutland. From December that year *Gloucester* was transferred to the 8th Light Cruiser Squadron in the Adriatic, and later served off East Africa. George was awarded the British War Medal and Victory Medal, but his service is not commemorated on the plaque in the village hall.

After his discharge from the Navy on 17 May 1919, George resumed work on his father's boats from which he used to wave to a servant girl at Saul Lodge. This was Ivy Henrietta Willis, whom he married at St Mary's on 25 September 1922. They rented a small cottage at Church End, Frampton, next to the churchyard.

The depression hit the canal trade hard, making life very difficult for George and Ivy as their seven children arrived: Archibald George, Walter James, Lilian Ivy, Frederick William, Nancy Margaret, Eric and Rosemary Ann. In a book recording the family's history, their eldest son noted that his father was a hard worker and a strict disciplinarian, but also liked his alcohol, and was best avoided when drunk! In 1937 they were allocated a council house at 10 Whitminster Lane. David George Herbert was buried in St Mary's churchyard on 14 September 1974 after suffering gangrene poisoning following a stroke.

FREDERICK HILL, 1881–1947
Private 392111, 608 Agricultural Company, Labour Corps

Frederick Hill was born in Frampton in 1881 to John Hill, by then a mariner, and Sarah née Guy. His parents had married relatively late in life; Sarah was forty-nine by this time, having given birth to Fred's older brother, *Henry John, five years earlier. After leaving school Fred worked as a general labourer, although at the time of his marriage to Ada Jackson on 6 April 1904 he was a sailor. Their wedding took place at All Saints, Gloucester, and Fred and Ada settled into family life in Frampton with the successive arrivals of Ada Matilda, Margaret Annie, Helen and Edwin Frederick John. In 1911 they were living at Ward's Court at the south end of the village green with Fred as a grocer's assistant, perhaps at the neighbouring Ward's shop (in recent years a restaurant). On 21 October 1912, however, Ada died, leaving Fred as a single parent. Their home was in a very poor condition, and on 26 February 1915 Wheatenhurst Rural District Council issued a closing order to the landlord to make necessary repairs. The following month Fred's children were sent to the workhouse at Eastington for a few weeks while the work was done.

Fred was initially exempted from conscription on the grounds of his employment as a cowman, but on 26 October 1917 he enlisted at Stroud and was medically assessed as Cii (i.e. able to walk 5 miles, to see and hear sufficiently for ordinary purposes and therefore suitable for service in garrisons at home). He gave his next of kin as his eldest daughter, Ada Matilda; the children were under the care of their Jackson grandmother in Saul. At thirty-seven years of age, with his medical category and perhaps given his family circumstances, he was not sent overseas. Instead Fred was posted to the 608 Agricultural Company of the Labour Corps, working in the Bristol area, perhaps even closer to home. On 23 July 1918 his medical category was raised to 'A', rendering him liable to front line service, but he was not posted overseas. At that time considerable controversy had arisen about the 'optimistic' gradings awarded to soldiers and recruits by Medical Boards, and a month before his discharge Fred was regraded to Bii (suitable for lines of communication in France). He was demobilised on 22 March 1919 and transferred to the Reserve. His war service is commemorated on the plaque in the village hall.

After the war Fred returned to Ward's Court to resume family life. Frederick Hill died at The Elms, Swindon Road, Cheltenham, and was buried in St Mary's churchyard, Frampton, on 16 June 1947.

HENRY JOHN HILL, 1876–1935
Rank unknown, Army (details unknown)

Henry John Hill, known as Harry, was born in 1876 in Frampton, the eldest of the two sons of John Hill, a labourer, and Sarah née Guy. Neither of his parents could write when they had married two years earlier at St Mary's. It was an unsettling time for John and Sarah for the cottage they rented from Henry James Clifford, close to the end of Marsh Lane, was under threat of being pulled down. Harry's brother, *Frederick, was five years his junior. With a young family to support, John soon became a mariner. By 1891 Harry was working as a farm servant but was a waterman on the barges in 1901. At the time of the 1911 census, Harry was living in present-day Tudor Cottage, The Street, a labourer awaiting his marriage to Emma Townsend on 22 April at St Mary de Lode, Gloucester. Their son, Henry George, was born in 1913.

A record of Harry's war service has not been found; however, a surviving photograph shows him in Army uniform. He was an absent voter in 1918–19, and his contribution is remembered on the plaque in the village hall. Henry John Hill died on 18 January 1935.

ASHLEY VICTOR HITCHINGS, 1890–1972
Private S4/125354, Army Service Corps; 55983, Welsh Regiment

Ashley Victor Hitchings was born in Frampton on 10 December 1890 to George Frederick Hitchings, a bridgekeeper, and Mary Ann née Halling. His childhood was spent alongside many brothers and sisters, three of whom also served during the war: *Charles Henry, *Frederick Robert William John and *Percival Leonard. Before the war it is believed that Ashley may have worked at Fretherne Court and also as a baker.

Ashley was a private in the Army Service Corps and later transferred to the Welsh Regiment, his service resulting in the award of the British War Medal and Victory Medal, and recognition on the plaque in the village hall. No further details, however, have been traced.

In March 1919 Ashley married Edith (Edie) Tate in Petworth, Sussex, after their banns had been called at St Mary's. Their daughter, Una, was born in 1935. The death of Ashley Victor Hitchings was registered in the Devizes district of Wiltshire during the first quarter of 1972.

CHARLES HENRY HITCHINGS
1886–1968
Stoker I K32274, Royal Navy

Charles Henry Hitchings, known as Charlie, was born in Quedgeley on 28 July 1886. He was baptised at its parish church, St James, on 5 September. His father, George Frederick Hitchings, worked as a bridgekeeper on the Gloucester & Berkeley Canal and the family moved to Frampton during the following year. His mother, Mary Ann (Annie) née Halling, gave birth to eleven children; conditions must have been fairly cramped in the bridgekeeper's house at Splatt which only had four rooms. Among his siblings were three brothers who also served during the war: *Ashley Victor, *Frederick Robert William John and *Percival Leonard. Charlie was a farm labourer in 1911, but his occupation soon turned to that of bargeman.

Charlie had been in the Royal Naval Volunteer Reserve before he enlisted for war service as a stoker at Devonport on 17 April 1916. On completion of his training at HMS *Vivid*, Devonport, he was posted to HMS *Sutlej*, a 12,000-ton armoured cruiser, then based in the Azores. Built by John Brown on Clydeside at the turn of the century, *Sutlej* was rather out of date from a stoker's point of view: she had thirty boilers to keep fuelled with coal, and in July 1910 a boiler explosion had killed four men. In September the ship was recalled to serve in the 9th Cruiser Squadron, escorting merchant shipping convoys off the French and Iberian coasts.

Sutlej was withdrawn from active service on 4 May 1917 and Charlie was back at Devonport for three months, probably for further training. His next ship, which he joined on 4 August, and in which he saw out the rest of his service, was HMS *Cornwall*, another elderly coal-fired armoured cruiser, but one with an interesting service history. She had fought at the Battle of the Falklands in 1914, in which she was hit eighteen times by the German cruiser *Leipzig* but did not lose a single man, while *Cornwall*'s shells set *Leipzig* on fire, eventually to sink. She later patrolled off the German colonies in east and south-west Africa, supported the Allied forces in the Dardanelles, and served on the China station. By the time Charlie went on board, *Cornwall* was on Atlantic convoy escort duty. His demobilisation came on 21 February 1919 and he was awarded the British War Medal and Victory Medal. Although Charlie does not appear to be commemorated on the village hall plaque, his service may have been recorded under 'G. Hitchings'. (There are other spelling errors on the board and no person with that initial has been found who was likely to have served.)

On 27 August 1927 Charlie married Minnie, sister of *Albert Edward Townsend, at St Mary's and they lived at 6 Vicarage Lane. Charles Henry Hitchings was buried in the churchyard on 17 February 1968 after losing his battle with cancer and tuberculosis in Standish Hospital. He was described by his doctor as a very brave man who never complained.

EDGAR HITCHINGS, 1887–1939
Private 3868, 7th (The Princess Royal's) Dragoon Guards

Edgar Hitchings was born in Chelsea on 6 November 1887 to Owen Orchard Hitchings and Eliza or Elizabeth Jane née Peglar. By 1901 his father was a timber porter at the docks, presumably at Paddington where the family were living, although his eldest siblings had spent their early childhood in Frampton. Edgar was the cousin of *Charles Henry, *Ashley Victor, *Frederick Robert William John and *Percival Leonard Hitchings.

Although his service record is incomplete, we know that Edgar was a porter when he enlisted into the 7th (The Princess Royal's) Dragoon Guards on 27 September 1909, and was based at Preston Barracks near Brighton when the census was taken in 1911. By 1914 his regiment was stationed in India as part of the 9th (Secunderabad) Cavalry Brigade, along with two Indian cavalry regiments (20th Deccan Horse and 34th Poona Horse). At the outbreak of war his brigade was moved to France, arriving at Marseilles on 13 October to form part of the 1st Indian Cavalry Division. They were immediately involved in the battles of

La Bassée, Armentières and Givenchy, and although often held in reserve in case of a breakthrough, they also fought in 1916 in the Somme campaign, notably at Bazentin (14–17 July) where Edgar was wounded. This was reported in the *Western Daily Press* on 10 August, when his residence was given as Frampton (his father may have come back to live in the village around this time). Edgar does not appear to have returned to front line duties. On 14 December 1918 he was demobilised and transferred to Reserve Service with the Tank Corps from which he was discharged on 26 September 1921 having completed his twelve-year engagement with the colours and on reserve. His conduct was recorded as 'Very Good'. Edgar was awarded the 1914 Star, British War Medal and Victory Medal, but his service is not remembered on the plaque in the village hall.

Edgar became blind after the war and when he married Florence Annie Lewis on 31 October 1921 at St Michael and All Angels, Eastington, he signed his name with a mark, giving his occupation as commercial traveller. The couple settled in Cheltenham where, from 1923, Edgar found employment at the Workshop for the Blind. Florence's death was registered in the first quarter of 1932, and a year or so later Edgar married Mabel E. Yates. He made the news in the autumn of 1936 when he and three of his Cheltenham workshop colleagues marched with other West Country men to London. Once in the capital, the timing of their demonstration, which was directed to bring pressure on the government to standardise welfare and employment for blind people across the country, coincided with the famous Jarrow march, itself part of a general rally against unemployment. From a personal point of view, the day of the protest did not go to plan. With badly blistered feet he was taken to hospital, while one of his sisters, whom he had not met for twenty years, searched in vain for him among the marchers. Eventually she passed a note to the organisers asking for an announcement to be made and they were reunited at the hospital. Edgar Hitchings died in Delancey Fever Hospital, Cheltenham, on 16 June 1939.

FREDERICK ROBERT WILLIAM JOHN HITCHINGS, 1896–1917
Private 23434, 11th (Reserve) Battalion, Gloucestershire Regiment; Corporal or Lance Serjeant 30846, 10th (Service) Battalion, Lancashire Fusiliers

Frederick Robert William John Hitchings' birth was registered during the last quarter of 1896 and he was baptised at St Mary's on 20 December the same year. Home was the busy bridgekeeper's house at Splatt with his parents, George Frederick Hitchings and Mary Ann née Halling, and their large family. His brothers *Charles Henry, *Ashley Victor and *Percival Leonard also served during the war. Fred must have enjoyed his education at school and done well for in July 1910 he was appointed monitor. During the next three years he took annual Cambridge Local Examinations at the Chapter House, Gloucester. His progress earned him a £2 increase in salary to £10 per annum in February 1913 and he was finally rewarded with the appointment of pupil teacher at the school from August the same year. This photograph shows Fred at the school gardening club with the headmaster and some of the boys around 1912.

In the meantime, Fred had joined the Frampton Boy Scouts and was becoming a very useful member of the local community, as demonstrated by his efforts to save a man's life on 29 August 1914, which are told in more detail on page [29]. On 12 July 1915 the school logbook recorded: 'Frederick Hitchings P.T. whose apprenticeship expires at the end of this month has been permitted by the Education Authorities to join His Majesty's Army (11th Gloucesters) and has this morning started for London.'

Fred was first posted to the 11th (Reserve) Battalion of the Gloucestershire Regiment, serving in the attestation office at Stroud for a while before he was, quite possibly before seeing action, transferred to the 10th (Service) Battalion of the Lancashire Fusiliers. With the Fusiliers he may have been in action during the Somme campaign of 1916, but would have been at the actions on the Scarpe in early 1917, part of the major Battles of Arras. On 12 May 1917 the 10th Battalion were at Gavrelle, mounting an attack as part of a drive to take the village of Rouex, when they became involved in what was described as 'a terrible bayonet and fist fight in German-held trenches'. Their casualties amounted to thirteen officers and 226 soldiers, one of whom was Frederick Robert William John Hitchings.

The news took some time to reach Frampton and it was not until 15 June that the headmaster wrote in the school logbook, recording his personal sadness at Frederick's death and remarking that he was the best pupil teacher he had ever trained. Fred had, apparently, enlisted for purely patriotic reasons despite being so close to achieving his dream of becoming a teacher which could have exempted him from service.

Corporal Frederick Hitchings was posthumously awarded the British War Medal and Victory Medal. His ultimate sacrifice is commemorated on Frampton's war memorial and the plaque in the village hall, and also on the CWGC Memorial at Faubourg d'Amiens Cemetery, Arras, where his rank is recorded as Lance Serjeant.

PERCIVAL LEONARD HITCHINGS, 1898–1918
Private 33069, 12th (Service) Battalion (Bristol), Gloucestershire Regiment

Percival Leonard Hitchings, the youngest son of George Frederick Hitchings and Mary Ann née Halling, was born during the summer of 1898. His older brothers, *Charles Henry, *Ashley Victor and *Frederick Robert William John all served during the war in different capacities and it must have been an anxious time at home in the bridgekeeper's house at Splatt waiting for news, especially after the wounding of his cousin, *Edgar, in 1916 and Fred's death in 1917.

Few details of Percy's service have survived. He was a private with the 12th (Service) Battalion (Bristol) of the Gloucestershire Regiment and we can only presume that he is likely to have served with his battalion in the Passchendaele campaign of 1917, and possibly in the Somme for at least some of the previous year. However, it is highly probable that (unless prevented by illness or injury) he went with them to Italy in November 1917 to support the Italian Army after its heavy defeat at Caporetto. Returning to France in April 1918, they would have been engaged straight away in the desperate fighting to stop the German breakthrough on the Lys, from the Lys Canal through the Nieppe Forest. On 25 April the 12th Glosters were detailed to capture the farm at Le Vert Bois (since known as 'Gloucester Farm'); they were completely successful despite machine gun fire, consolidating their positions and capturing over thirty Germans. However, two officers and twenty-one soldiers were killed in this action, including Percival Leonard Hitchings, who was posthumously awarded the British War Medal and Victory Medal.

Percy's ultimate sacrifice is commemorated on Frampton's war memorial, on the plaque in the village hall and at the CWGC Merville Communal Cemetery in France, near where he died at 'Gloucester Farm'.

WILLIAM THOMAS HODDER, 1876–?
Private TR/7/4614, 93rd Training Reserve Battalion; 240229, 5th Battalion (Territorial), Gloucestershire Regiment; 10th Battalion, Oxfordshire and Buckinghamshire Light Infantry; 428287, Labour Corps

William Thomas Hodder, known as Thomas, was born in Sharpness in 1876 to James Hodder, a farmer, and Emma née Timbrell, the middle child of three. In 1881, James was farming at Halmore. The family were at Oldlands Farm, Hamfallow, in 1891, but had moved to Frampton by 1901. On 16 July 1903 Thomas married Florence Mabel, sister of *Frederick Charles Gardner, and five children followed: Doreen, Hilda Muriel, twins William and James, and Jack Phillip. Thomas worked as a horse breaker, dealer and butcher from the property often called Ye Olde Cruck House, The Street.

On 18 August 1916 the recruiting office at Stroud sent Thomas Hodder a standard notice requesting him to attend a medical even though it appears that he had previously been rejected for service. He was called up at Stroud on 21 November and asked for the Army Veterinary Corps or the Remounts Service; not surprising given his background in horses. He was posted as a private to the 93rd Training Reserve Battalion and three weeks later to the 5th Battalion (Territorial), Gloucestershire Regiment. At some stage he was also posted to the 10th Battalion of the Oxfordshire and Buckinghamshire Light Infantry from where, in October 1917, he was transferred to 536 Agricultural Company, Labour Corps. He was discharged on 17 February 1919.

The Hodder family continued to live in Frampton for a few years after the war and Thomas Hodder's war service is commemorated on the plaque in the village hall.

ALBERT EDWARD HOGG, 1898–1970
Rank and Service: Not known

Albert Edward Hogg was born on 16 September 1898 in Frampton, the second son of George William Hogg and Clara Elizabeth (widow of Edwin Leighton) née Hunt. At Albert's baptism, George was recorded as a waterman, but his employment was generally farm work. By 1911 the family had moved from Splatt to live on The Green, probably in one of the Estate's properties on the east side below Frampton Court. Albert and his younger siblings, Mary Ann (Annie) and Walter, were still at school, while his older brother, *William Thomas, was already at work. Between 1915 and 1918 they moved again, this time to Vicarage Lane.

Although Albert was registered as an absent voter in 1918–19, no records have been traced of his war service which is commemorated on the plaque in the village hall.

In 1939 Albert was working as a labourer for the Royal Air Force Department, presumably at No. 7 Maintenance Unit at Quedgeley, and had moved again to The Street, just to the north of Wild Goose Cottage, living with his widowed father and younger brother, Walter. (At this stage Albert's father, George, was recorded as a gravel digger – at the age of 69!) Albert's final move, with Walter, was to 18 Oatfield Road. Albert Edward Hogg was buried in St Mary's churchyard on 8 December 1970.

WILLIAM THOMAS HOGG, 1896–1960
Possibly Driver TF 1604, later 48522, Army Service Corps

William Thomas Hogg, known as Bill, was born in Frampton on 10 November 1896, the eldest child of George William Hogg and Clara Elizabeth née Hunt, the widow of Edwin Leighton. George was a farm labourer and by 1911 Bill was similarly employed, and still living with his family which included his next brother, *Albert Edward.

Bill was recorded as an absent voter from 1918 to 1922, a longer time than most. It seems possible, although not proven (as few records have survived), that he may have served with the Army Service Corps, later the Royal Army Service Corps, for a William Thomas Hogg, originally in the Territorial Force, re-enlisted with them on 7 April 1919, and this coincides with Bill's extended absence from home. (He may therefore have been awarded the British War Medal and Victory Medal.) What is certain, however, is that the plaque in the village hall commemorates Bill's service during the war.

In 1927 Bill, then a labourer, married Edith Marion, sister of *Clevedon Wells, *Christopher Charles and *Edgar John Fryer. As their family grew he became a stoker at Cadbury's factory and the couple had three daughters: May, Kathleen and Eileen. By this time the family were living at Parks Cottage on The Green. William Thomas Hogg was buried on 24 October 1960 in St Mary's churchyard.

F. HUDSON
Rank and Service: Not known

It has not been possible to positively identify F. Hudson, who is listed on the plaque in the village hall. The electoral registers of 1920–22 record a Frank Hudson living on The Green, and this may be the same man. An undated photograph from this period taken outside Cadbury's Recreation Hut is believed to include an 'F. Hudson'.

ALBERT EDWARD HUNT, 1888–1973
Rank and Service: Not known

Albert Edward Hunt, born on 14 October 1888, was the eldest of the two sons of Albert Hunt, a farm labourer, and Alice Eliza née Hogg of Fromebridge. He was baptised on 11 December the same year at St Mary's, the vicar recording his date of birth alongside the entry in the register. Alice was a woollen cloth worker, like many of her neighbours. By 1901 Albert (Senior) was a carter and the family had been completed by the arrival of *Arthur William. Both boys were employed as woollen cloth workers by 1911.

Almost fifty medal roll index cards relating to men by the name of Albert E. Hunt survive and it is impossible to say whether Albert's is among them. The only tangible evidence of his service during the war is the inclusion of his name on the plaque in the village hall, and the record of him as an absent voter in 1918–20.

Albert married Alice Louisa Miles during the summer of 1920 and the couple remained in Fromebridge until at least 1936. However, by 1939 they had moved to Cress Green, Eastington, when Albert was working as a tarmacadam ganger and Alice part-time on Post Office duties. The death of Albert Edward Hunt was registered in the local area in the autumn of 1973.

ARTHUR WILLIAM HUNT, 1896–1972
Private, Service unknown

Arthur William Hunt, known as William, was born on 19 March 1896, the younger son of Albert Hunt and Alice Eliza née Hogg. Their home in the hamlet of Fromebridge had four rooms, comparatively sizeable accommodation for William and his older brother, *Albert Edward, to grow up in. By 1911 they were both woollen cloth workers.

Details of William's war service have not been found, although his contribution is commemorated on the plaque in the village hall and he was registered as an absent voter in 1918–19. Anecdotal evidence suggests that Private William Hunt was one of two Frampton servicemen to unveil the village's war memorial on 23 April 1920.

William worked in engineering after the war. On 14 October 1922 he married Sybil Mildred Hilda White at St Michael and All Angels, Eastington; one of their witnesses was *Harold William Brinkworth, William's childhood neighbour at Fromebridge. The couple moved away shortly afterwards, perhaps to Eastington, where they were living in 1939. The death of Arthur William Hunt was registered in Gloucester City during the summer of 1972.

THOMAS EDWARD HUNT, 1896–1933
Gunner 14485, Royal Marine Artillery

Thomas Edward Hunt, the eldest child of three, was born on 6 August 1896 to Thomas Arthur Hunt, a miller's carter, and Matilda née Dainty. The family lived in the hamlet of Fromebridge. Thomas had left school by the time of the 1911 census and became a wool finisher.

On 1 December 1914 he enlisted into the Royal Marine Artillery at Bristol as a private. After training Thomas became a gunner on 30 May 1915 and appears to have served on the Western Front from 27 July 1915 to 17 October 1917, followed by a transfer to an Anti-Aircraft Battery at Chatham Dockyard until June 1918. He then recrossed the English Channel to serve on anti-aircraft guns at Dunkirk for the rest of the war.

The Armistice, however, did not signal the end of Thomas Hunt's service; by April 1919 he was posted to the Aegean Garrison, serving at Constantinople until November. Only three months later he was again in the Mediterranean theatre, joining HMS *Emperor of India* in the Black Sea as part of the British intervention in the Russian Civil War. Returning home at the end of March 1921, he was again sent overseas: he appears to have spent the next two years at the Royal Navy shore station *Benbow* on the island of Trinidad. His last recorded seagoing post was in the battleship *Barham* from May to July 1923, before being transferred to Plymouth Division. Thomas was awarded the Long Service and Good Conduct Medal at Plymouth in January 1930, but was discharged on 15 June 1932 on the grounds of ill health as he had apparently been suffering from epileptic fits.

On retirement, he planned to enter into partnership with Richard Hart, a farmer in Westbury on Severn, but on 22 October 1933, about a fortnight after he had moved to Moys Hill Cottage, Westbury, Thomas Edward Hunt was found dead in his bed having suffered a fatal fit. He was buried in St Mary's churchyard in Frampton three days later. For his service during the war Thomas was awarded the 1914–15 Star, British War Medal and Victory Medal and he is commemorated on the plaque in the village hall.

WALTER EDWARD HUNT, 1878–1955
Private 2555, 1st Battalion and 2/5th Battalion, Gloucestershire Regiment

Walter Edward Hunt was the youngest child of Charles Moses Hunt (known as Moses) and Elizabeth née Woodward. He was born in the parish of Eastington on 19 January 1878; the family's home was on Bristol Road, close to its junction with Perryway. By 1891 Moses, an agricultural labourer, Elizabeth and Walter had moved to The Street, near to Frampton's vicarage. Walter, like many young men of his generation, left the village to seek work, and spent a short while at

Western Colliery, Pontypridd, before moving to Norton Canon, near Weobley, Herefordshire as a labourer.

On 29 July 1895 Walter enlisted in the Militia, claiming to be a year older than he was, but with a physique to back it up. He was posted to the 4th Battalion of the King's (Shropshire Light Infantry). However, the periodic training and two-week annual camps were not enough for him, and on 27 May 1899 he joined the 'Special Service Section' of the Militia, which rendered him liable for overseas service with the Regular Army. He did not then have long to wait; with the outbreak of the Boer War on 11 October that year, he was embodied into the 2nd Battalion and embarked for South Africa. Arriving after the ignominious defeats of Magersfontein and Colenso, he might well have had a first experience of the barbed wire, machine guns and trenches (things that we associate primarily with the First World War) during the offensive which led to the relief of Ladysmith. Walter came home on 31 May 1902 and was discharged in July 1902 at the end of his engagement.

Walter married his cousin, Annie Maria Hunt, at St Michael's, Gloucester, on 18 April 1903, giving his occupation as a waterman. Their son, William Charles Edward, was born on 13 May the same year and when he was baptised at St Mary's on 22 May 1904 Reverend Ward, somewhat mistakenly, suggested in the register that his parents were unmarried. He also gave Walter's occupation as a private in the Gloucestershire Regiment. The Hunts' home by 1911 was one of the cottages, since demolished, between The Villa and Wild Goose Cottage on The Street; at the time of the census, Moses was living with them, and Walter was an able seaman on board the trow, *Industry*, near Chepstow.

With the outbreak of the First World War, Walter re-enlisted. Serving with the 1st Battalion of the Gloucestershire Regiment he was soon back in action, landing in France on 28 November 1914. Arriving during the First Battle of Ypres, he would have served with his unit throughout the Neuve-Chapelle, Second Ypres, Artois and Loos campaigns. We know that he was transferred at some point to the 2/5th Battalion, which was deployed to the Front in May 1916; he might have joined them as an experienced soldier to help show the new men the ropes, or it might have been after he suffered a wound, as reported in the *Gloucester Journal* of 28 April 1917. He is likely to have been with them on the Somme, at Cambrai, on the Lys and in the heavy fighting of the final Allied 'Hundred Days' offensive. Walter was later awarded the 1914–15 Star, British War Medal and Victory Medal and his service is commemorated on the plaque in the village hall.

After the war Walter and Annie remained in The Street for a while before moving first to The Glen (a bungalow on Perryway), and then to Alexandra Cottage, Bridge Road. He worked at Cadbury's and was a popular Father Christmas at their annual children's party for many years. Walter Edward Hunt died suddenly at home on 5 October 1955 and was buried in St Mary's churchyard three days later.

FREDERICK ALEXANDER JONES, 1879–1958
Rank and Service: Not known

The early life of Frederick Alexander Jones has not been traced, although, according to records dated 1939, he was born on 22 February 1879. Frederick's marriage to Hilda Millicent Rose Longney (née Shill) was registered during the first quarter of 1918, the year he was listed as an absent military or naval voter, living on The Green. Hilda was the widow of Glenville Charles Longney who had tragically died following an accident at the Slimbridge munitions store in 1916 (see page 52 for more details). In addition to Hilda's own children, the couple had a further child, Leonard, on 29 December 1919, who is seen here in the photograph.

Frederick and Hilda later moved to The Lake, and Frederick worked as a farm labourer. Frederick Alexander Jones was buried in St Mary's churchyard on 4 March 1958. It has not been possible to find details of Frederick's service during the war and he is not among the men remembered on the plaque in the village hall.

JOHN JONES, 1891–1940
Rank and Service: Not known

John Jones was born on 11 July 1891 and his father was Thomas Jones, a miner. Details of John's early life and war service have not been traced but it is believed that he was the 'J. Jones' commemorated on the plaque in the village hall.

John married Gertrude Emily Brown at St Mary's on 24 May 1920. The couple made their home in Vicarage Lane (in present-day Fern Cottage) and John also started work at Cadbury's around this time, where he was a boiler stoker. During his shift on the evening of Saturday 30 November 1940, John Jones left his station but was not immediately missed by his fellow workers. When they did start to search they found him drowned in the canal. His colleagues could shed no light on the circumstances for he had no reason to be at the edge of the canal, and his widow reported to the inquest at the Bell Hotel that he had been in good health and spirits apart from being concerned about his eyesight. He was buried the following day in St Mary's churchyard. In later years, Gertrude moved to Sunnyside, on the village green.

THOMAS DANIEL JONES, 1887–1953
Private WR312596, Inland Waterways & Docks, Royal Engineers; 526827, 699 Agricultural Company, Labour Corps; 27494, 389th (HS) Labour Company, Labour Corps

Thomas Daniel Jones was born in Arlingham in 1887 to Albert Paxton Jones, a dealer, and Florence Mary née Dwyer. The family were living in a three-roomed property in Arlingham's High Street in 1891, with Albert having to support his wife and four young children as a general labourer. Albert died two years later and Florence took on work as a charwoman. By 1901 Thomas was working as a plough boy; ten years later Thomas (then a farm labourer), and his mother had moved to Colthill.

According to those census records, Thomas was blind in one eye but, despite his disability, he served as a private during the war. His medical category restricted him to Home Service and on 22 August 1917, then of The Lake, Frampton, he reported to the Inland Waterways & Docks, Royal Engineers, at the White City in London. We do not know where he served at first, but he was later transferred to the 699 Agricultural Company of the Labour Corps at Canterbury and appears to have finished his service with the 389th (HS) Labour Company of the Labour Corps, working in the Canterbury depot of 'The Buffs', the Royal East Kent Regiment. Thomas was finally discharged on 12 November 1919 and his war service is commemorated on the plaque in the village hall.

Thomas stayed on briefly in Frampton after the war before moving away for some years. He later returned to the village to live, once more at The Lake. Thomas Daniel Jones was buried in St Mary's churchyard on 28 March 1953.

JOHN HENRY LANNING, 1886–1951
Private M2/035031, Army Service Corps

John Henry Lanning, the son of George Lanning and Elizabeth Way née Gibbs, was born on 18 September 1886, in Englefield Green, Egham, Surrey, where his parents were in service. In 1901 John was a grocer's clerk in Egham, but he had moved to Walk Lane (Whitminster Lane), Frampton, by 1911 when he was a domestic chauffeur, possibly for the Teesdale family of nearby Whitminster House. On 6 July the same year he married Ethel Ross Graham in Egham. Their two children, Barbara Florence and Joan Emily, were born prior to the start of the war.

Enlisting at Reading on 22 October 1914, John served in the Army Service Corps as a private, initially with the 2nd Mounted Division Supply Column, and then with 273 Company ASC of the 21st Division Supply Column. On 4 September 1915 he moved with his unit from Southampton aboard the *Viper*, arriving at Rouen, France, the next day. As part of the 21st Division Supply Column he was employed as a lorry driver, and earned a Good Conduct badge on 9 November 1916.

John was allowed home leave on three occasions during his service: 26 December 1916 to 5 January 1917, 28 January to 11 February 1918 (after which he was detained in the Christian Military Hospital at Englefield Green until 1 March) and 10–24 October 1918 (which was extended to 31 October). His Army records state that he was sober and reliable. His unit had become the 21st Division Mechanical Transport Company and although on enlistment he had given his wife's address (as next of kin) as that of her parents in Egham, his address for pay prior to discharge was Walk Lane. He was placed in Priority Group 26 for discharge; on 2 May 1919 at No. 1 Dispersal Unit, Crystal Palace, he was given twenty-eight days' paid leave, and on 30 May transferred to the Army Reserve. John was awarded the 1914–15 Star, British War and Victory Medals but his war service is not commemorated on the plaque in the village hall.

Although John was listed as an absent voter at Walk Lane in 1918–19, he appears to have left the Frampton area immediately afterwards. John Henry Lanning of Egham died on 17 August in 1951.

WILLIAM REGINALD LAW, 1893–1961
Private 18713, 10th (Service) Battalion and later, 48395, 1st (Reserve) Garrison Battalion, Worcestershire Regiment; Sapper 317478, later WR/507737, Inland Waterways & Docks, Royal Engineers

William Reginald Law was born in Eastington on 4 April 1893 to Robert Law, an agricultural labourer, and Fanny née Davies. By 1911 he was the only one of their eight surviving children to still be living at home, at that time employed as a general labourer in a timber yard. Two years later, on 19 April 1913, he married Ida Matilda, sister of *William George Birch, at the Wheatenhurst Register Office. Their first two children, Ida Beatrice and Winifred Doris, were born in Eastington, but the family had moved to School Row, The Street, Frampton, by the time their son Robert William Reginald George was born in 1916.

Volunteering early to enlist, William attested at Stroud on 2 September 1914 and was provisionally posted to the 10th (Service) Battalion of the Worcestershire Regiment. He was sent to Tidworth Camp, Wiltshire, for training but failed a medical review and was discharged on 22 September. Men such as William were reassessed after the Military Service (Review of Exceptions) Act of 1917 and on 14 June of that year, when working as a waterman, he was called up. He was sent for induction to the 1st (Reserve) Garrison Battalion of the Worcestershire Regiment on the Isle of Wight, but with his experience, and having made a specific request, he was transferred to the Inland Waterways & Docks Section of the Royal Engineers. William was posted in the rank of sapper to the Western Front on 25 August and served in France until after the end of the war, very probably transporting supplies towards the front on French canals, in which his skills won him a professional assessment of 'Very Superior'. However, a medical review on 19 May 1919 led to his repatriation three days later and discharge on 8 July. William was awarded the British War Medal and Victory Medal and his service is commemorated on the plaque in the village hall.

After the war the family continued to live in the village, moving first to Frombridge and then to 5 The Oval. William Reginald Law was buried in St Mary's churchyard on 27 December 1961.

ARTHUR EDWIN LAWRENCE, 1893–1971
Rank unknown, Volunteer Force (Regiment unknown)

Arthur Edwin Lawrence was born in Saul on 9 November 1893, one of the seven children of Edwin Charles Lawrence, a master mariner, and Jane née Walkley, and the younger brother of *Victor Charles. The family's home became one of the cottages at Tobacco Box. By 1911 Arthur was a bricklayer, but he joined Cadbury's in 1916 where he started work at 6 a.m. to light the fires in the Sentinel steam wagons.

Little is known about Arthur's service during the war but it is commemorated on the plaque in Frampton Village Hall and family recall him working on a farm in Dorset during 1918–19. The cap badge in this photograph suggests that he served in the Volunteer Force rather than in the Regular Army. From the outset of war groups of volunteers had established companies for local defence. The 1916 restatement of the Volunteer Act of 1863 passed control of these to the county Territorial Associations whereupon the units became volunteer regiments. In 1918 all county Volunteer Regiments became Volunteer Battalions of line regiments but the history of these is generally vague.

After the war Arthur returned to Cadbury's and was employed as a greaser until transferring to the churn repair shop in 1953. He retired five years later. During that time he had umpired local cricket matches and acted as a football linesman; latterly he was also a very enthusiastic member of the factory's bowls club. On 16 September 1925 Arthur married Maud Berry at St Mary's, Frampton, and they had three children: Sam, Ray and Rita. Arthur Edwin Lawrence died in Stroud Hospital in August 1971 and was cremated at Gloucester Crematorium, his commemorative plaque later being transferred to Dursley Crematorium.

VICTOR CHARLES LAWRENCE, 1890–1957
Rank unknown, US Army

Victor Charles Lawrence, known as Charles, was born in Saul on 22 February 1890 and his early years were spent in Church Lane. His father, Edwin Charles Lawrence, was often away at sea so it was left to his mother, Jane née Walkley, to look after a growing family which included his younger brother, *Arthur Edwin. By 1901 the Lawrences had moved to a cottage at Tobacco Box. Charles was then a labourer on a corrugating machine in a galvanising department, presumably at the same workplace as his cousin, Arthur Walkley, with whom he was lodging in Pontrhydyrun, Monmouthshire. Charles emigrated to the United States during the autumn of 1913, the final leg of his journey was aboard the SS *Princess Charlotte* from Vancouver, British Columbia, one of the coastal vessels of the Canadian Pacific Railway.

Following the United States' break in diplomatic relations with Germany in February 1917, there was a call for volunteers to serve in the Armed Forces. However, only 73,000 volunteered out of a target of 1 million, so the Selective Service Act was passed in May which required the registration of all males aged twenty-one to thirty for military service and prohibited all forms of the paid substitution which had occurred during the American Civil War. On 5 June Charles Lawrence completed a Draft Registration Card, claiming no exemption from service. He was not a US citizen, but had declared his intention to become one. He was an engineer working for H. E. Starrett of Stratford, California, and lived in the nearby town of Lemoore. It is clear from his naturalisation application on 9 May 1918 that he had enlisted into the US Army and was then serving at Camp Lewis, near Tacoma, in the state of Washington.

Camp Lewis was built for the lowest cost and in the shortest time of any US military cantonment; construction only began on 5 July 1917, but the first building was finished in just three days and, after ninety days, some 10,000 men had put up 1,757 buildings and 422 other structures, lighted, plumbed, and heated. Roads and railroad spurs were underway, and the camp was ready for its planned 50,000 men. The 91st Infantry Division trained at Camp Lewis from 5 September 1917 until it shipped out in late June 1918 for France, where it served with distinction. The 13th Infantry Division was organised at Camp Lewis in 1918 and was in training for trench warfare when the Armistice was signed. We do not know whether Charles served with one of these divisions, but the latter seems more likely as he did not arrive in Washington State until 1 May 1918. His service is commemorated on the plaque in Frampton Village Hall.

During the latter part of 1919, Charles was in England for his marriage to Elsie Harvey which was registered in the Rotherham district of Yorkshire. She completed an emergency passport application on 2 February 1920 to enable her to accompany him back to America where their son, Samuel, was born the following year. They subsequently returned to England for a couple of months during the late spring/early summer of 1922, sailing on the SS *Olympic* (the sister ship to *Titanic*). Another son, Edwin Harvey, was born in 1928 in the Rotherham district. The Lawrence family eventually settled in Yorkshire where Charles worked for the Gas Board, his American naturalisation being cancelled on 9 January 1935. Victor Charles Lawrence died on 1 March 1957 in the Rother Valley district.

CECIL CHARLES LEONARD, 1877–1947
Acting Sergeant M2/270334, Army Service Corps

Cecil Charles Leonard was born on 14 January 1877 in Newton Solney, Derbyshire. The eldest son, he was named for his parents, Charles Leonard and

Mary Ann née Cecil. Charles was a coachman and it is clear that from an early age, Cecil wanted to follow in his father's footsteps; he was a stable boy by 1891. When Cecil left home he went to Holly Bush Hall, Newborough, a few miles to the west, beyond Burton-on-Trent, to work for Charles John Clay as second coachman, living-in to begin with, among an extensive array of servants. It was here that he first met the Clay's daughter, Adelaide Hilda who, in November 1913, married *Henry Francis Clifford. By this time, Cecil was also married, to Julia Mumford, in 1909. It seems that Cecil and Julia moved to Frampton to work for the newly-wed Cliffords.

Knowledge of Cecil's war service, which is commemorated on the plaque in the village hall, is limited to the survival of his medal roll card. He served with the Army Service Corps in the rank of acting sergeant, and was awarded the British War Medal and Victory Medal.

After Julia died in 1923, Cecil married Louisa Dowden in the Bournemouth area in 1927. They had a daughter, Elizabeth Joan, in 1928, but Louisa died a couple of years later. Olive Diaper became Cecil's third wife in 1931. Home was The Firs (North), on the village green, in one of the Estate's houses, for Cecil had remained chauffeur to the Clifford family. However, Olive's death in 1938 left Cecil as a single parent once again and in 1939 a widow, Mary Weaver, was his housekeeper. Cecil Charles Leonard was buried in St Mary's churchyard on 13 May 1947.

EDWARD THOMAS MORSE LIGHT, 1884–1958
Sergeant 15943, 1st Life Guards; 3633, Guards Machine Gun Regiment

Edward Thomas Morse Light, known as Tom, was born in 1884 in Gloucester to John Light and Frances Emma née Morse. His childhood was spent partly in Quedgeley where his father was a coachman, and later at the Plough Inn, Sheepscombe, which John kept. Frances died in 1904 and by 1911 John had moved again, to Frampton, where he was working as a jobbing gardener but living at the Three Horseshoes. On 6 December 1918 John was the subject of a short article in the *Stroud News* celebrating the survival of all five of his sons, and also that of the husband of his only daughter, Annie. Of John's sons, only Tom and his brother, *Sidney John, have been singled out for inclusion here as they were listed as absent voters in the 1918–19 electoral registers for Frampton. Additionally, Tom's war service is commemorated on the plaque in the village hall.

In 1901 Tom worked as a house boy in Painswick, progressing to become footman by 1905. In that year he enlisted in the 1st (King's) Dragoon Guards, serving in North India (where he contracted malaria) from 1907 until his repatriation and transfer to the Reserve in March 1912. He was then mobilised on 5 August 1914, posted to the 1st Life Guards, and served in France for the rest of the war. After being out of action with a shell wound to the head (November 1914–April 1915), he progressed steadily to sergeant, and was transferred to the Guards Machine Gun Regiment. Tom was later awarded the 1914 Star, British War Medal and Victory Medal.

On 5 August 1918 Tom married Minnie Mary, sister of *Clevedon Wells, *Christopher Charles and *Edgar John Fryer, at St Lawrence's, Barnwood. At the time she was a housemaid at Barnwood House Asylum. Edward Thomas Morse Light died on 25 January 1958 having lived with Minnie in Stroud.

SIDNEY JOHN LIGHT 1882–1961
Private MR/103173, Army Service Corps

Sidney John Light was one of five sons born to John Light and Frances Emma née Morse, all of whom served during the war, although only two had direct Frampton connections, the other being *Edward Thomas Morse. Sidney was born on 15 August 1882, and his birth was registered in Gloucester. The family moved around during his childhood, his father finding work as a coachman in Quedgeley and later as the innkeeper of the Plough Inn, Sheepscombe. Sidney worked as a blacksmith before serving in the Royal Army Medical Corps from June 1900 for twelve years, which included active service during the Boer War (1899–1902), for which he was awarded the Queen's South Africa Medal, with Clasps for 1901 and 1902. Remaining in South Africa until April 1906, he also earned Good Conduct badges. Following his discharge in 1912, he became a private chauffeur and lived in Gloucester.

With the outbreak of the First World War, it is clear that Sidney rejoined the Army, this time in the Army Service Corps, where he served as a private in Mechanical Transport, almost certainly as a lorry driver. His joining date and training is not known, but by 18 July 1915 he was in Egypt. He was later reported to have served at Salonika until late 1918. Sidney was discharged on 27 June 1919 to the Army Reserve and awarded the 1914–15 Star, British War Medal and Victory Medal.

During 1918–19 he was listed as an absent voter in The Street, Frampton. However, his service during the war is not commemorated on the plaque in the village hall. In the autumn of 1919 he married Alice Green. The couple had two daughters, Frances and Marion Elizabeth, and lived in Sheepscombe. The death of Sidney John Light was registered in the Stroud district during the last quarter of 1961.

MAURICE MEADOWS, 1879–1939
Rank and Service: Not known

Maurice Meadows was born in Frampton on 31 July 1879, the son of Edwin Meadows, a farm labourer, and Lucy Silvannah née Hayward. Before the war, Maurice was a bricklayer's labourer and lived in The Street in the vicinity of Buckholdt Cottages.

Although Maurice was listed as an absent voter in 1918–19, no trace has been found of his war service other than on the plaque in the village hall.

He continued working as a bricklayer after the war, living in The Street, next door to his older brother Alfred. It was Alfred's wife, Elizabeth, who found Maurice Meadows dead in his bed on the morning of 29 December 1939. He had been well-known in the district through his sporting connections and was a regular supporter of Gloucester Rugby Football Club. His funeral service at St Mary's was attended by representatives of the Frampton and District British Legion (of which he was a member), and his coffin was covered by the Union Jack. The bearers included First World War veterans *Milton Tudor and *Cecil Charles James Estop.

JOHN MILLARD, 1899–1960
Rifleman 36171, 5th (Reserve) Battalion and 12th (Service) Battalion, Rifle Brigade; Private 39962, 1st Battalion, Gloucestershire Regiment

John Millard was born at Beanhall Lane, Fretherne, on 1 May 1899, the only son of John Millard, a bricklayer, and Rose Edith née Derrick. He had three older sisters, Florence, Elsie, and Violet, and was followed by Lucy and Elizabeth. By 1913 the family had moved to The Green, Frampton.

John enlisted for the Army at Stroud on 11 December 1916, but was not mobilised until 1 June of the following year. He was then listed as a munitions worker, classified as 'G40', which was presumably not one of those reserved occupations that were normally given higher priority than conscription into the Services. He was initially posted to the 5th (Reserve) Battalion of the Rifle Brigade but on 3 April 1918 he was transferred to the 12th (Service) Battalion in France. John served as a rifleman (equivalent to a private), and his records show two sentences of Field Punishment No. 2 which meant the wearing of handcuffs and fetters, and therefore could not have been awarded when he was on the front line: on 19 June 1918 he was given twenty-eight days for being asleep on duty (for which soldiers on the front line had been shot), and on 26 June a further fourteen days for being 'generally dirty on defaulters' parade'. Two spells in hospital were recorded later; for dysentery in July and August 1918, and again in November 1918 to January 1919. Nevertheless, on 3 February 1919, John volunteered to re-enlist for a further four years, this time into the 1st Battalion of the Gloucestershire Regiment, and was sent home on leave pending this change. During this time, however, he was examined at the Special Military Surgical Hospital at Southmead, Bristol, with swollen neck glands. After an operation, and a medical review that found he had very bad teeth, he was discharged at Bath War Hospital on 9 August 1919 as permanently unfit for military service, with a £5 gratuity. He was awarded the Silver War Badge and later the British War Medal and Victory Medal. His war service is commemorated on the plaque in the village hall.

John lived with his parents until his marriage in 1924 to Maggie Doris Knight Harris. Their first home was Oatfield Cottage, where John George and Albert Wilfred (Bill) were born, after which they moved to Ward's Court where their family was completed by the arrival of Doris Christine and Derrick Henry. In 1939 John was a builder's labourer; his son, Derrick, recalls that he cycled to Droitwich to get work for a while, coming home for weekends. John Millard was buried on 10 August 1960 in St Mary's churchyard after battling with Parkinson's disease.

SIDNEY CHARLES MILLS, 1897–?
Able Seaman J58765, Royal Navy

Sidney Charles Mills was born in Frampton on 29 September 1897 to Mark Mills, a bricklayer, and Flora Ellen née Aldridge. By 1911 the family's home was at present-day Ferndale, The Street, next to the New Inn. Sidney was the second youngest of seven children, three years older than his brother, *Walter Harold. In May 1906 the school logbook records him being one of only three children to attend every session the preceding year. It is not certain what Sidney did immediately after leaving school, but the opening of Cadbury's factory in the spring of 1916 brought him employment, for when he enlisted in the late summer, he gave his occupation as a chocolate worker.

On 15 September 1916 he joined the Royal Navy at Devonport as an ordinary seaman and was appointed to its training school, HMS *Vivid*. After two months he was posted to the battleship HMS *Centurion*, in which he was a shipmate of *Herbert Charles Drayton, until 9 August 1917. Sidney then underwent a further three months of training which resulted in promotion to able seaman, before serving in HMS *Devonshire*, a cruiser escorting Atlantic convoys, until July 1918. He was then posted back to Devonport until his demobilisation on 14 April 1919 after which he was awarded the British War Medal and Victory Medal and paid a War Gratuity.

Sidney returned to Frampton, probably to his parents' address, until at least the mid-1920s and his war service is commemorated on the plaque in the village hall.

WALTER HAROLD MILLS, 1900–1978
Rank and Service: Not known

Walter Harold Mills, known as Harold, was one of the youngest men to see service in the First World War for he was born in Frampton on 2 May 1900, the last of the children of Mark Mills, a bricklayer, and Flora Ellen née Aldridge. The family lived on The Street, adjoining the New Inn; in 1911 only Harold's immediate older siblings, *Sidney Charles and Ada Lilian were still at home.

No records have been found of Harold's work prior to his wartime service which, due to his age, would have been brief. Nevertheless, he was registered as an absent voter in 1918–19 and his service is commemorated on the plaque in the village hall.

On 7 June 1924 Harold married Dorothy Rita Eliza, sister of *Martin Walter William Camm, at St Mary's (seen here on their wedding day). At first they lived at Hart's Cottages, later moving to Springfield, both in The Street. Harold worked at Cadbury's factory and their son, Harold David, was born in 1929. Walter Harold Mills died on 12 February 1978 and was buried in St Mary's churchyard four days later.

WILLIAM HENRY MORGAN, 1876–1918
Rifleman R/34035, 16th (Service) Battalion (Church Lads' Brigade), King's Royal Rifle Corps

William Henry Morgan was born in Frampton during the spring of 1876; his parents were William Frederick Home Morgan, a bricklayer, and Jane née Evans. The family were in Slimbridge for part of William's childhood, but they returned to live on Perryway, in a house (now Perryway Cottage) with two sitting rooms and four bedrooms; an adjoining workshop was used by William's father for his building business. After leaving school William became a shop assistant in clothing and footwear, and by 1911 he had his own shop and was living in Sharpness.

William is said to have volunteered for the Army during 1915, but could not have seen active service before 1916 for he was not awarded the 1914–15 Star. He made his will on 12 September 1916, perhaps just before he joined the 16th (Service) Battalion (Church Lads' Brigade) of the King's Royal Rifle Corps on the borders of France and Belgium. He would have been active through the battles on the Somme, at Arras and Ypres. The first few weeks of 1918 may, therefore, have seemed relatively quiet. It was in the days leading up to the German offensive on the Lys that Rifleman William Henry Morgan was killed, on 21 March, reportedly by a 'bomb', which would probably have meant a mortar shell, rather than an aircraft bomb. He was interred at CWGC Ypres Reservoir Cemetery, West-Vlaanderen, Belgium.

According to the *Cheltenham Chronicle*, he was mourned by many friends at Sharpness, having seen much active service overseas. William was posthumously awarded the British War Medal and Victory Medal, and his ultimate sacrifice is commemorated on Frampton's war memorial and the plaque in the village hall.

THOMAS WILLIAM NIBLETT, 1882–1918
Private 493446, 440 Agricultural Company, Labour Corps

Thomas William Niblett, known as William, was born at Corse in 1882 to Albert Niblett, an agricultural labourer, and his wife, Alice. He followed his father into farm work. William married Edith Alice Taylor in 1905 and by 1911 they were living at Claypits with their three children: Henry Albert, James and Charles William. William was a waggoner at a grist mill, almost certainly at Fromebridge, where they moved to during the war.

William's service is largely unclear, but he was a private with the 440 Agricultural Company of the Labour Corps in 1918. The Armistice of 11 November may have meant an immediate return home, perhaps for leave or through illness. Thomas William Niblett died in Fromebridge on 29 November prior to being demobilised, a victim of the influenza pandemic, and he was buried in St Mary's churchyard. William's death and wartime service are remembered on the plaque in the village hall, but not on the war memorial. Edith remained at Fromebridge, marrying Edward Jones in 1931.

CHARLES HENRY PHIPPS, 1889–1972
Trooper 2437, Royal Gloucestershire Hussars
Yeomanry; Private 47977, Machine Gun Corps
(Cavalry)

Charles Henry Phipps was born on 3 December 1889 at the Pike House, Perryway, the son of Henry Phipps, a labourer, and Mary Ann née Cartwright. He was privately baptised by the vicar of Frampton on 16 December the same year, and then received into St Mary's church on 12 January 1890. Shortly afterwards the family briefly moved to the Bristol Road (just into Eastington parish), before returning to Frampton to live in The Street. In 1911 Charles was a confectioner in Gloucester, boarding with another confectioner, Albert Taylor.

On 22 September 1914 Charles enlisted at Gloucester, being certified as suitable for service in the Royal Gloucestershire Hussars Yeomanry. On 3 April 1915 he married Edith Emma Whiting at St Lawrence's church, Barnwood, while serving as a trooper in the RGH. He appears to have remained in the UK until 19 October 1917; unfortunately the crucial part of his service record is badly burnt, so although he was 'posted' twice, we do not know to which units. However, in October 1917 he arrived in Mesopotamia where he certainly served, and probably from the outset, as a private with the Machine Gun Corps (Cavalry). The next event on his records was his admission to 33 BG Hospital Makina Masus, near Basra, on 10 January 1918 with a thumb injury from a month before (not incurred while on duty); this was assessed as 'not affecting his future efficiency as a soldier'. Family members have related that later a shell was said to have exploded next to him, burying him in the sand with two comrades from which incident he was the only survivor. It is believed that this event may have caused what was known as shell shock and this, quite naturally, had a profound effect on him. Today the condition is known as post-traumatic stress disorder; it is recognised as occurring in both civilians and service personnel in emergencies and operations, and is sympathetically treated. During and after the First World War, however, treatment was seldom kind. The records relating to Charles' repatriation are indistinct, but he was admitted to Dykebar War Hospital in Paisley, and then discharged as not physically fit for military service on 17 June 1919. Charles was awarded the Silver War Badge and his family report that he convalesced in Standish VAD Hospital with his wife often visiting. By January 1920 he was corresponding with the Army about his British War Medal and Victory Medal. His service is commemorated on the plaque in the village hall.

Charles and Edith had three children: Leslie, Barbara (Peggy) and Raymond. For some time he worked as a gardener for Mabel Constance Clifford. The family lived in Greycroft and later in one of the cottages that were formerly on the site of Bendles, both in The Street. Charles Henry Phipps died on 3 July 1972 at his home in King's Stanley (a bungalow he named 'Frampton'), surrounded by his family, having spent the final years of his life being cared for by his son and daughter-in-law, Leslie and Edith. He was buried in St Mary's churchyard three days later.

SAMUEL PITMAN 1867–1915
Private 1276, Royal Gloucestershire Hussars Yeomanry

Samuel Pitman's birth was registered by his parents, Eli Pitman, an agricultural labourer, and Susan née Shield, during the first quarter of 1867. He was born in Tytherington, and by the age of fifteen had left home to work at Acton House Farm, Iron Acton.

Samuel enlisted in the Royal Artillery on 3 January 1889 on a seven-year engagement with five years in the Reserves. He spent all but his first year in India (where he suffered two bouts of enteric fever), completing his primary term in January 1897. Samuel was recalled in

December 1899, shortly after his marriage to Jane Hart, to serve in the Boer War with the 65th Field Battery throughout 1900 and 1901, for which he was awarded the Queen's South Africa Medal, with clasps for Cape Colony and the Orange Free State.

As a driver, his job would have been to move guns or ammunition around, and he was probably responsible for two horses and their harnesses. Afterwards, Samuel's ability with horses enabled him to secure employment as a groom to *Henry Francis Clifford at Frampton where his sister, Annie, and sister-in-law, Elizabeth Hart, worked at Frampton Court as housemaid and parlourmaid respectively. Samuel and Jane's first son, Francis Samuel, died shortly after his birth; their second son, Frederick William, was born in 1902. Jane died in 1905, and in 1908 Samuel married her sister, Elizabeth, their family being completed with the arrival of Mary Elizabeth the following year.

In the meantime, Samuel had enlisted in the Royal Gloucestershire Hussars Yeomanry and attended their annual training camps. On 5 August 1914, the day after war was declared, Samuel was embodied into the Army, and went with his unit for training in Norfolk. He became ill on 27 November and was hospitalised at Overstrand until 23 December, when he was sent home on sick leave. After a medical review concluded that he was permanently unfit for service, he was discharged on 6 May 1915, claiming a pension that was agreed for a period of one year. However, Samuel Pitman failed to recover from what had been diagnosed as pneumonia and pleurisy and he was buried in St Mary's churchyard on 24 November 1915. He is commemorated on Frampton's war memorial and the plaque in the village hall. At the age of forty-seven, he had been prepared to fight again for his country, 'a steady, sober, honest and industrious soldier'.

GEORGE PRAGNELL, 1880–1948
Private 26805, 15th (Reserve) Battalion, Gloucestershire Regiment

George Pragnell was born in the late autumn of 1880 in Overton, Hampshire, to Uriah Pragnell, a cattle farmer, and Sarah née Faddis. By the mid-1880s the family had set up home in The Street, Frampton, where Uriah engaged in a variety of occupations including gardener, butcher and newsagent and, in 1901, vermin destroyer. They later moved to Splatt Lane. George's employment record was also varied for before the war he worked successively as a confectioner and breadmaker, farm labourer and then a cowman; however, by 1916 he was a munitions worker.

On 28 March 1916 he went to Stroud to enlist, being posted to the 15th (Service) Battalion of the Gloucestershire Regiment. He was sent to Warwick for training where a medical examination revealed that he was only 4 foot 11 inches tall, poorly developed (with only a 33 1/4 inch chest), had defective hearing, and suffered from both bronchitis and asthma. As he was below military height and chest measurement, and his disabilities were considered permanent and specifically stated as not being due to intemperance or misconduct, he was discharged on 29 May as 'Not being likely to become an efficient soldier' (i.e. medically unfit). His Army conduct was formally recorded as 'Very Good'. However, George was listed as an absent military or naval voter in The Street in 1918 and the spring of 1919, which may indicate that he was re-conscripted under the Military Service (Review of Exceptions) Act of 1917; in view of his medical condition, his service would almost certainly have been limited to such light duties as sentry, storeman or clerk in the UK. It is commemorated on the plaque in the village hall.

After final demobilisation he appears to have lived with his mother, Sarah, until her death in 1922. He was recorded on the electoral registers for a few more years but local people recall that he became one of a few homeless people fed regularly at the back door of Buckholdt by a kitchenmaid. George Pragnell, of no fixed address, later found work as a night watchman for a building firm engaged in repairs on maisonettes in Stonehouse, but died suddenly on 20 March 1948. He was buried in St Nicholas' churchyard, Standish, five days later.

GERALD PROUT, 1888–1916
Private 160990, 82nd Battalion and 54th (Kootenay) Battalion, Canadian Expeditionary Force

Gerald Prout, born on 4 July 1888, was the youngest of the nine children of James Prout and Kate née Cave. Home was Parks Farm, rented from the Cliffords' Frampton Court Estate. It was probably through the influence of the squire himself, or maybe other tenants, that both Gerald and an older brother, Howard, enlisted in the Royal Gloucestershire Hussars Yeomanry. Subsequently, Howard, Gerald and another brother, Leonard, all emigrated to Canada; in 1911, Gerald was working as a miller in Kenora, Ontario. He returned to England to visit his family at least once, as he sailed on the *Royal George* from Bristol on 4 October 1913, bound for Moose Jaw, Saskatchewan.

At the beginning of the war Gerald volunteered for the Canadian Mounted Rifles, but was discharged owing to a medical condition. However, he seemed determined to serve for, after an operation and whilst working at the Lake of the Woods Milling Company in Keewatin, Ontario, he enlisted in the Canadian Infantry on 3 November 1915 at Calgary. On 20 May 1916 he sailed for Europe with the 82nd Battalion of the Canadian Expeditionary Force on the *Empress of Britain*, but he was soon transferred to the 54th (Kootenay) Battalion, probably as a replacement for casualties. The men were billeted initially in the town of Albert until, on 13 November, they were moved up into the trenches near Courcelette, which had been the site two months earlier of a bitter battle that had marked the debut of the Canadian and New Zealand troops on the Somme.

It was on the very next day that Private Gerald Prout lost his life, when an enemy shell landed in his trench. He was first interred behind Regina trench, but in 1920 was reinterred at the CWGC Adanac Military Cemetery in Miraumont, along with eighteen of his comrades. His ultimate sacrifice is also commemorated both in Frampton, on the war memorial and the village hall plaque, and in Canada, on the Medicine Hat Cenotaph, Alberta, and a plaque in Keewatin commemorating staff of the Lake of the Woods Milling Company.

GEORGE HENRY R. PURNELL, 1894–1917
Driver TF1622, later T4/249085, Army Service Corps (3rd Company, 61st (2nd South Midland) Division Train)

George Henry R[owles?] Purnell was born in Gloucester in 1894 to George Henry Purnell, a bootmaker, and Eliza Mary née Rowles. The Rowles were an established family of seafarers in the Newnham, Arlingham and Frampton area; Eliza was born in Newnham at Quay Cottage and was the aunt of *Richard William and *Francis Edwin John Rowles. It is unclear when George's father died, and why Eliza, her children and mother were recorded in Ross-on-Wye in 1901. Eliza was certainly widowed by 1911 and living in Gloucester with some of her children and her mother. George has not been identified on the 1911 census so may have been at sea, but his eldest sister, Sophia, was a housekeeper to their great aunt, Mary Ann Rowles, in Frampton, and it is this connection which seems to lead to George's inclusion as a Frampton serviceman.

It would appear that George served in the Territorial Force, probably having volunteered for home service only as he was embodied into the supply train of the 61st (2nd South Midland) Division, which was initially part of the Army Reserve. He seems to have been posted to the Army Service Corps and given the rank of private, but later specialised as a driver. It is likely that he would have gone to France with his Division in May 1916, following which its first major engagement was the disastrous diversionary offensive at Fromelles when it suffered very heavy casualties without causing any diversion of enemy forces from the Somme. After that the 61st Division was used only to hold the line until 1917, when it was ordered to pursue the German Army as it withdrew to the fortified Hindenburg Line. It then captured the towns of Chaulnes and Bapaume.

On 3 June 1917, perhaps during a 'quieter' period between battles, George Henry Purnell was killed by enemy shell while proceeding with a supply convoy to the railhead at Arras, a colleague receiving a fatal shrapnel wound on the same duty. He was interred at the CWGC Faubourg D'Amiens Cemetery in Arras and is commemorated in Frampton, on both the war memorial and the plaque in the village hall. George was posthumously awarded the British War Medal and Victory Medal and was among the fallen who were remembered at a memorial service at St Mary's on 17 June 1917.

FRANCIS EDWIN JOHN ROWLES, 1897–1979
129th (Wentworth) Battalion, Canadian Expeditionary Force

Francis Edwin John Rowles, known as Frank, was the second son of Edwin John Rowles and Ellen Mary née Coole, his elder brother being *Richard William.

Frank's birth in Frampton was registered during the first quarter of 1897. In February 1913, at the age of sixteen, Frank sailed from Liverpool to Canada on the SS *Victorian* with the intention of being a farm labourer. His initial destination was Winnipeg, Manitoba, but family members believe that he lived rough and moved from place to place finding work scrub-clearing, on sheep farms and killing rabbits to protect crops.

On 29 January 1916 Frank attested for the 129th (Wentworth) Battalion of the Canadian Expeditionary Force at Dundas, Ontario, declaring that he was in farming and resident in Sheffield, in the same province. Frank gave his place of birth as Clonakilty, County Cork, Ireland, which is at variance with other records, and a date of birth some two years earlier. His battalion sailed to England in August 1916 and fought as part of the Canadian Corps on the Western Front. It is recorded that the Canadians were one of the most effective fighting forces in France, and were referred to as 'stormtroopers' by the Germans. Frank's service is commemorated on the plaque in Frampton Village Hall.

His future wife, Kathleen Doris Latty, emigrated to Canada in June 1920 and they were married at Galt, Waterloo, Ontario, on 25 March 1921; Frank was working as a machinist. They had two daughters, Diana Kathleen and Betty Joyce and the family visited Frampton in March 1932, sailing from New Brunswick to Liverpool on the SS *Montclare*. Francis Edwin John Rowles died in 1979 at Wentworth, Ontario.

RICHARD WILLIAM ROWLES, 1894–1958
Corporal TF1621, later T4/249084, Army Service Corps

Richard William Rowles, known as Dick, was born in Frampton on 23 March 1894, the eldest son of Edwin John Rowles, a master mariner, and Ellen Mary née Coole. Edwin was often away from home and on 8 December 1910, while captaining his ketch, *Atlas*, she was caught in heavy seas in the Bristol Channel and dismasted. Despite the assistance of another vessel, the *Atlas* and her three-man crew were lost. The family had lived at Clarence House, just below the Three Horseshoes on the village green, but by 1911 were at Blenheim House, near the Institute on The Street. Ellen used her dressmaking skills to provide an income, Dick was a grocery apprentice, his next brother, *Frances Edwin John, had no occupation, while their three younger siblings were still at school.

The date of Dick's enlistment into the Army Service Corps has not been traced, but while he served in France he came across a consignment of hay bales for one of the Hussars' regiments labelled 'Edgar Coole, Frampton on Severn'; they had been supplied by Dick's relative, *Robert Edgar Coole. Dick was awarded the British War Medal and Victory Medal and his service is commemorated on the plaque in the village hall.

Dick worked at Cadbury's as a milk condenser after the war, and remained there for the rest of his working life. On 16 January 1922 he married Effie, the sister of *Cyril Vick, at St George's, Nailsworth. They lived in Swindon Cottage, The Street, next to Cyril's butcher's shop at Ye Olde Cruck House. Dick and Effie had no children. Richard William Rowles died on 20 March 1958 and his ashes were interred in St Mary's churchyard.

FREDERICK GEORGE SIMMONS, 1896–1987
Petty Officer J23629, Royal Navy

Frederick George Simmons was born on 4 June 1896 in the King's Norton area of Birmingham to James Henry Simmons, a house decorator, and Mary Jane née Russell. His first job may have been a works messenger (the record is unclear), then a fitter and turner, a common trade in the many workshops of Birmingham. However, Frederick must have wanted a complete change, for on 6 March 1913, he enlisted into the Royal Navy at Devonport as a boy, essentially the equivalent of an apprenticeship for a trade.

During the latter part of his training he saw service at sea, first in the battleship *Venerable* and then the old cruiser *Leander*, by then a destroyer depot ship in the Mediterranean. It was there that Frederick attained the age of eighteen, signed for a twelve-year engagement and was appointed ordinary seaman. In November he was promoted to able seaman. From May to December 1915 he attended the Royal Navy Torpedo School in HMS *Defiance* at Devonport and after graduation served for a year at *Benbow*, a naval shore station on Trinidad. His next postings were to the submarine support ships *Dolphin* and *Vulcan*, which took him to the end of 1917, with a further promotion to leading seaman. He continued his submarine association in *Ambrose*, a merchantman converted to submarine depot ship and then based in Ireland, until the last day of the war.

Frederick was in a training environment, presumably as an instructor, for the next two years. However he seems to have considered leaving the Navy, possibly in connection with his forthcoming marriage, as in January 1919 he paid £18 to purchase his discharge, only to receive a refund in April and continue his career. He married Margaret Mary Hough at Devonport on 28 July 1919, and probably settled for a time into a more domestic life. This would not have changed dramatically even with an appointment in October 1920 to the 1911 battleship HMS *King George V* which by then was part of the Reserve Fleet based at Devonport, and in which he earned promotion to petty officer.

The end of his naval career came earlier than expected, at a time when the British government was trying to reduce service manpower and costs; on 27 July 1922 he was discharged with a bonus of £159 'on reduction'. Frederick and Margaret appear to have emigrated to Western Australia shortly afterwards, where Frederick worked as a fitter on the railways and their son, Edward Patrick, was born. Frederick George Simmons died on 20 March 1987 at Taree, New South Wales. His connection with Frampton had come while his parents were living at Buckholdt for a couple of years towards the end of the war and he was recorded as an absent voter in 1919–20. Frederick was awarded the 1914 Star, British War Medal and Victory Medal for his service, but is not remembered on the plaque in the village hall.

FRANK THOMAS SIMS, 1886–1951
Acting Farrier Corporal T4/042106, Army Service Corps

Frank Thomas Sims was born in Frampton on 10 March 1886 to Fanny Sims. He was brought up by his maternal grandparents David and Elizabeth Sims at their home on Perryway, and baptised privately alongside their youngest son on 7 February 1889. In 1891 his mother, Fanny, was working as a cook for General Francis Lock of the Bombay Staff Corps in Richmond. By 1901, Frank had also gone into domestic service, working as the hall boy at Fretherne Court. He later became an ostler at the Bell Hotel, Frampton, where his job was to look after the horses belonging to the guests.

Frank was a labourer when enlisting on 5 January 1915 at Stroud. He joined the Army Service Corps at Aldershot a week later and, with a reference from his previous employer at the Bell Hotel, was appointed on 25 May as a farrier/driver. By 14 June he had been promoted to acting farrier corporal, serving in the UK until the following year. He then embarked for France to join the 29th Division, which was being redeployed to France via Egypt after its evacuation from Gallipoli. He remained in France until 29 August 1918, later serving with the 3rd Division Supply Train, and at one stage was reprimanded for branding the wrong number on a horse. On his return to the UK he served with the Northern Command Supply Train, until being transferred to the Reserve on 17 July 1919. Frank received the British War Medal and Victory Medal and his service appears to be commemorated on the plaque in the village hall under 'T. Sims'.

He was granted leave from 28 October to 7 November 1917 and on 1 November he married Elizabeth Gertrude Mary Pearce at the Wesleyan Chapel, Eastington. Their home was at Cress Green in the same village. In 1939 Frank was a public works labourer. Frank Thomas Sims was buried in the parish churchyard at St Michael and All Angels on 16 October 1951.

THOMAS ERNEST SIMS, 1883–1960
Acting Sergeant 18137, 12th Reserve Cavalry Regiment; 11th (Prince Albert's Own) Hussars; 309643, Army Service Corps

Thomas Ernest Sims, known as Tom but perhaps later in life as Ernie, was born on 11 February 1883 in Discove, Bruton, Somerset, to Henry Sims and Edith Elizabeth née Wright. His parents had married in Frampton in 1878 and Henry's work, variously a coachman and a groom, took them to Painswick as well. They were living there when Henry died in 1885; Edith had him buried at Frampton where she returned to live with their children and among her family. She married

George Hewlett on 6 May 1889 at St Mary de Lode, Gloucester, and by 1891 Tom's home was on the village green, close to the Three Horseshoes. In 1901 he was working as a groom, and on 30 April 1910 he married Mary Elizabeth Hammond at St James, Cheltenham. Tom and Mary were living in Vicarage Lane with their daughter, Phyllis Beatrix Annie, in the spring of 1911. More children followed in quick succession: Eric Reginald, Henry John Hammond and Rita Delia.

Tom had already served for nearly four years in the Royal Gloucestershire Hussars Yeomanry when he enlisted for the First World War at the Colston Hall, Bristol, on 3 September 1914, signing as 'E. Thomas Sims'. The Sims family had been living on the edge of the Badminton Estate at Tresham. Tom was temporarily posted to 19th (Queen Alexandra's Own Royal) Hussars and a day later he was posted to the 12th Reserve Cavalry Regiment. By 19 September he was en route to join the Expeditionary Force in France where he would remain until well after the war ended. In the spring of 1915 Tom was posted to the 11th (Prince Albert's Own) Hussars and on 23 March 1916 he was appointed acting lance corporal. At some stage Tom appears to have spent time in No. 5 Base Hospital at Rouen as his name, number and this address was written in *Thomas Henry Griffin's war diary.

The following year Tom volunteered in response to an Army offer to transfer to the Remounts Service of the Army Service Corps. This organisation was responsible for providing horses and mules to all other Army units. Composed generally of older and more experienced soldiers, it obtained animals by compulsory purchase in the UK, and by purchasing from North and South America, New Zealand, Spain, Portugal, India and even China. A Remount Squadron would have been responsible for preparing and training some 500 horses. Although, when transferring to the Remounts Service at Rouen on 12 June 1917, he had to revert to his permanent rank of private, Tom quickly progressed to acting corporal on 8 September, and to substantive corporal (and foreman) on 9 December. He was promoted to acting sergeant in February 1919, and shortly afterwards had the only blot on his record when he was apparently absent from his unit from 21 February until being 'apprehended' on the 25th. However, as he was only reprimanded (and lost four days' pay) it seems likely that there had been some sort of misunderstanding. He returned to the UK and was demobilised on 31 May 1919. He was awarded the 1914 Star, British War Medal and Victory Medal.

His service papers record his name as Ernest Thomas Sims, and the plaque in the village hall has E. T. Sims. Anecdotal evidence suggests that a Sergeant Tom Sims assisted with the unveiling of the war memorial in 1920, and this seems to be the same man. The family grew further after the war following the births of Vera Evelyn, Brenda Mary, Bernard Thomas, Stella Edith and Barbara Jean. Tom was variously a groom, stoker and labourer during the 1920s. In 1939 he was a coal hoist labourer and the family were living at Florence Cottage, The Street (now demolished, but then to the north of Wild Goose Cottage). Thomas Ernest Sims was buried in St Mary's churchyard on 8 January 1960.

TIMOTHY JOHN SIMS, 1897–1981
Private 268002, 2nd, 7th and 6th Battalions,
Royal Warwickshire Regiment

Timothy John Sims was born on 25 July 1897 in one of the cottages at Tobacco Box. His parents were William Henry Sims, a groom and later a gardener, and Elizabeth née Barton. He was baptised with his older brother, *William, on 4 February 1907 at St Mary's, Fretherne, and after he left school Timothy was an errand boy for a grocer.

Only the documents relating to the awarding of Timothy's British War Medal and Victory Medal have survived; these were not stored with the main Army records and therefore survived destruction in the Second World War fire. They show that he enlisted, not before 1 January 1916, into the 2nd Battalion of the Royal Warwickshire Regiment as a private, subsequently being transferred to the 2/7th and finally the 2/6th Battalions. These units all served on the Western Front, but in 1917 the 2nd Battalion was redeployed to Italy. It may be that Timothy Sims was posted at that time to the 2/7th, a second-line battalion, which remained in France and was engaged in the battles of Langemarck (part of the third Ypres campaign), Cambrai, St Quentin (part of the 1918 Somme campaign), the Lys (where the Division suffered many casualties), and finally on the Selle during the final Allied advance. This is in accordance with the account of his daughter, who believes that he was a runner and saw action at Ypres and St Quentin. He was demobilised on 11 November 1919.

Timothy married Ethel Ivy Brocher at St Mary's on 18 September 1921. They had two daughters, Joy and Sibyl, and continued to live in the family home at Tobacco Box, which Timothy bought from Frampton Court Estate in 1924. He undertook various jobs including a gardener at The Denhalls (now Wisma Mulia) and a general labourer for the Estate. Timothy John Sims died at home on 2 September 1981 and was buried in St Mary's churchyard three days later. His war service is commemorated on the plaque in the village hall.

WILLIAM SIMS, 1895–1956
Rank and Service: Not known

William Sims, known as Bill, was born at Tobacco Box on 2 August 1895 to William Henry Sims and Elizabeth née Barton. He attended school in Frampton and on 23 March 1906 won first prize (a watch and chain) for the highest number of marks obtained in the weekly examinations held since Christmas. By 1911 he was working as an under gardener.

Although Bill's war service is commemorated on the plaque in the village hall alongside that of his younger brother, *Timothy John, no records have been traced. His family believe that he served in the Army.

Bill never married. He lived with his sister in Moreton Valence and used to cycle from there to work at the Royal Agricultural College, Cirencester, where he was employed as a waiter. On 22 September 1956, William Sims was killed in an accident on the main road between Stroud and Cirencester. He was buried in the churchyard of St Mary's, Fretherne.

WILLIAM SMITH, 1887–?
Sergeant, 1st Battalion, King's Royal Rifle Corps

It has not been possible to positively identify details of William Smith's early life beyond the fact that he was thirty-one years of age at the time of his marriage on 12 October 1918 at St Mary's, Frampton, and that his father was Thomas Smith. William's wedding to Catherine Sarah, sister of *George Edward and *Stephen John Dark, had evidently been planned for some time for their banns were read on three consecutive Sundays from 27 January that year, William's commitments with the King's Royal Rifle Corps presumably accounting for the subsequent delay.

The entry in the marriage register indicates that William was a sergeant with the 1st Battalion. While his period of service is not known, it must have been on the Western Front where his battalion formed part of the 6th Brigade, 2nd Division, taking part in most of the major actions. In 1918 they fought on the Somme, in the battles of the Hindenburg Line and the Battle of the Selle (17–25 October, shortly after William's marriage). The 2nd Division was selected to advance into Germany and formed part of the Occupation Force after the Armistice which no doubt accounts for William remaining an absent voter at Fromebridge in the spring of 1919.

After the war, William and Catherine settled in Fromebridge, later living at the Pike House, Perryway, before moving away. During this time, four children were born: William, George, Harold and Gerald. William Smith's war service has not been remembered on the plaque in the village hall.

CHARLES WILLIAM SPARRY, 1894–1991
Driver TF1585, later T4/249060, Army Service Corps

Charles William Sparry was born on 26 November 1894 in Leamington Hastings, Warwickshire, a small village north-east of Leamington Spa. His parents, John Sparry, a coachman, and Elizabeth née Price, originated from Worcestershire, and it seems likely that John's work led them to Frampton during the 1890s.

The Sparry family lived on Perryway by 1911, Charles seemingly without work at the time of the census. In the following August, the Gloucester papers reported that Charles was one of several Frampton lads in trouble for scrumping pears from an orchard, the property of John James Broad who farmed at Advowsons. Frank Halling, *David George Herbert, Charles William Sparry, *Christopher Charles Fryer, Archibald Dunford, *Sidney Charles Mills, *Walter Harold Mills, Walter Wright and Wallace Rowles were all summoned and the first five were each fined 1s to make an example of them, with the rest let off on a caution.

Charles joined the Territorial Force as a transport driver in the Army Service Corps. His early career was certainly focussed on horses, no doubt following the calling of his father and elder brother. As a territorial it is likely that he was part of the 61st (2nd South Midlands) Division, which left for France on 21 May 1916, and Charles would have been in the supply or ammunition trains responsible for keeping the forward units sufficiently provisioned for combat. His family recall being told that on one occasion his mate and his mate's horse were both killed, but Frampton servicemen, like most others, spoke only briefly of these terrible occurrences.

Charles was later awarded the British War Medal and Victory Medal and is commemorated on the plaque in the village hall. It is interesting to note that the medal roll lists in sequence the Territorial Force (TF) soldier numbers of those who must have joined with him, almost all of whom transferred together to the Regular Army on 1 September 1916, and were therefore given new soldier numbers, again in sequence. This exemplified the spirit and the commitment of the British Army at that time, working together within their units.

Charles remained an absent voter throughout 1919 but was back in Frampton, and working as a groom, at the time of his marriage to Margaret Susan Kate Lawrence at St Luke the Less, Gloucester on 11 March 1920. Charles started work at Cadbury's the following month and the couple had two sons and four daughters. Charles William Sparry ended his days at the Old Vicarage Nursing Home in Frampton, and died at the age of ninety-seven in 1991.

ALFRED STAPLEHURST, 1881–1915
Private 16127, 7th (Service) Battalion, Gloucestershire Regiment

Alfred Staplehurst was born to Henry, a farm labourer, and Ruth Staplehurst at Little Horsted, Sussex, in 1881. By 1901 Alfred was a chicken crammer. He married Annie Maria Hammond in 1906, and it was presumably work that brought them to Gloucestershire, for Alfred was employed as a poultryman at Churchdown in 1911. A move to Frampton followed, where he was recorded on the 1915 electoral register living on The Green.

Alfred enlisted into Lord Kitchener's Army on 27 November 1914 and was posted to the Gloucestershire Regiment. After training he embarked with the 7th (Service) Battalion at Avonmouth, landing first at Alexandria, and entering the Balkans theatre on 19 June 1915, probably at Mudros, on the Greek island of Lemnos. The next month they were deployed to Gallipoli, to be immediately involved in the aftermath of the Battle of Gully Ravine. They were located at Geoghan's Bluff. Owing to the very cramped area held at Cape Helles (only about 4 miles long) there was no place of safety, and the unit diaries record that casualties were suffered on 19 July (four wounded), 20 July (one killed, four wounded), 22 July (three wounded) and, in repelling a Turkish attack, on 23 July (two killed, one wounded). One of these casualties was almost certainly Private Alfred Staplehurst who died on 23 July of wounds received.

Although he has no known grave, Alfred's body may have been one of the 925 reinterred from Geoghan's Bluff cemetery to that at Cape Helles, Turkey, where he is commemorated at the CWGC Helles Memorial. His ultimate sacrifice is also remembered in Frampton on the war memorial and on the village hall plaque. He was posthumously awarded the 1914–15 Star, British War Medal and Victory Medal.

WILLIAM HENRY STONE 1895–?
Rank and Service: Not known

William Henry Stone was born at Cambridge in the parish of Slimbridge, and his birth was registered during the first quarter of 1895. In 1901 he was living near the White Lion Hotel, Cambridge, with his parents Henry Stone, a coachbuilder, and Mary née Savage, together with his elder sisters, Elizabeth and Laura. His mother died in 1904, and by 1911 William was working with his father as a coachbuilder and they were living at The Lake, Frampton, with Mary's sister Laura as their housekeeper.

Soon after the government introduced conscription William appealed to the Gloucester tribunal as a conscientious objector, requesting exemption from service on the grounds of his pacifist beliefs. His case was heard on 31 March 1916 when he was closely questioned. He said that his feelings had started in about November 1914, and that he certainly had not been an objector before the war. After also admitting that he did not belong to any organisation such as the Society of Friends, his request for exemption was dismissed and he was refused the right to appeal.

William's service during the war, which is commemorated on the plaque in the village hall but has not otherwise been traced, would doubtless have involved duties that did not include anything related to active combat, for many conscientious objectors did serve their country. It is interesting to note that he was not recorded as an absent voter during 1918–19. After the war he continued to live at The Lake until 1922. In 1944 William was a postman when he was granted probate for his father's estate; his address at the time was not given.

PERCY STRAHAN 1874–?
Major, 8th (Service) Battalion, Border Regiment

Percy Strahan was born in Simla, India, on 1 February 1874. His father, Lieutenant G. Strahan of Bengal, sent Percy to England for his education, boarding at a school in Alvescot, Oxfordshire, run by a Strahan relative. An Army career followed, with Percy being commissioned into the 1st Battalion of the South Staffordshire Regiment on 4 August 1900 and probably joining it immediately in South Africa for the Boer War. After hostilities ceased he was transferred to the 3rd Battalion of the Royal Garrison Regiment in Malta from which, on 25 July 1903, Lieutenant Percy Strahan married Beatrice Ferens at St Mary's, Huxham, Devon, a wedding hastily arranged to allow him to return to his regiment. He completed his first military career in South Africa, where the reservists of the Royal Garrison Regiment had taken over from Regular line regiments. By 1911 Captain Strahan had retired from the Army and was living with Beatrice in Hereford Road, Paddington, and engaged in the motor trade.

Recommissioned into the 8th (Service) Battalion of the Border Regiment for the war, on 3 November 1914 Percy was appointed Temporary Major, the battalion forming at Carlisle as part of the Third New Army raised by Lord Kitchener. By 27 September 1915 they had landed at Boulogne and were then engaged in action on the Western Front, including Vimy Ridge, Albert, and Pozières in 1916; Messines and Pilckem in 1917 and St Quentin, Bapaume, Messines, and Bailleul in 1918. Although we cannot be sure that Major Strahan took part in these actions, he was mentioned in Sir Douglas Haig's despatch of 9 April 1917, which would have covered the operations on the Ancre during the German withdrawal to the Hindenburg Line. Percy was later awarded the 1914–15 Star, British War Medal and Victory Medal.

Percy Strahan became the Commandant of the German prisoners of war camp associated with the gravel workings at Frampton in March 1918, living with his wife, Beatrice, on The Green where they were included in both the spring and autumn electoral registers of 1919, Percy as a military voter. The Strahans integrated into local society, counting the Clifford and Darell families among their friends. Afterwards they settled at Sirmoor Lodge, Bexhill-on-Sea, Sussex. Percy Strahan's service during the war has not been remembered on the plaque in Frampton Village Hall.

ARTHUR HARRY SUTTON, 1892–1957
Battery-Sergeant-Major 45661, 42nd Brigade, Royal Field Artillery

Arthur Harry Sutton was born in York on 30 November 1892 to John, a regular soldier but later a draper, and Alice Sutton. In 1913 he married Bessie Gladys, the older sister of *Thomas Hart Brinkworth, in the Farnham area.

Harry followed the family tradition of enlisting in the Army at the age of fourteen and was one of five brothers to serve his country. He was an accomplished horseman and shared first prize in the rough riders display at the 1914 Naval and Military Tournament.

Following the outbreak of war Harry was deployed to France on 19 August 1914 with the 42nd Brigade of the Royal Field Artillery, and already a corporal. A month later he was awarded the Distinguished Conduct Medal: 'For gallantry and good work throughout the campaign. On two occasions he repaired the telephone under heavy shell and rifle fire'. Harry's actions, which earned him promotion to sergeant, included him leaving his trench while under fire, and without regard for his own safety, to rescue three wounded Gurkhas. The medal was presented twice, first by the Divisional Commander, and then on 2 December 1914 by King George V during a visit to the Western Front.

Further promotion followed. During the Battle of Pilckem Ridge (31 July–2 August), the opening attack of the main part of the Third Battle of Ypres, Battery-Sergeant-Major Harry Sutton was in sole charge of the battery wagon lines close to the Yser Canal. His 'untiring energy, courage and power of command' enabled the ammunition supply to be maintained despite heavy shelling and he also organised the successful evacuation of casualties to a place of safety. For this work Harry received a Certificate of Bravery from the General Officer Commanding 38th (Welsh) Division and was commended for his 'conspicuous gallantry and devotion to duty'. By February 1918 Harry had also been awarded the Belgian Croix de Guerre.

Harry was transferred to the Army Reserve on 8 August 1919, and later received the 1914 Star, British War Medal and Victory Medal. His medals and their provenance were auctioned in 2000, a rare set which fetched £1,150.

While Arthur was serving his country, Bessie returned to Frampton to live with her parents, William James Hart Brinkworth and Patience Elizabeth née Williams, in Hart's Cottages, from where Arthur was recorded as an absent voter in 1918. He is not remembered on the village hall plaque. In 1934 they lived in Kilburn and by 1939 were in Willesden, with Arthur a ganger (foreman) on the London Transport railways. Arthur Harry Sutton died on 17 July 1957 in the Hampstead area.

ERNEST WALTER HENRY TAINTON, 1895–1979
Private 15464, 9th (Service) Battalion, Gloucestershire Regiment

Ernest Walter Henry Tainton was the eldest of the five sons of *Walter Henry Tainton, a farm labourer and cowman, and Clara Jane née Farmiloe. He was born in Horsley on 31 January 1895 but by 1901 the family had moved to Owlpen. In 1911 Ernest was a mill hand in a cloth factory and still living at home, which was then in Newington Bagpath. By the time war was declared the Taintons had settled in Frampton and Ernest was working as a labourer.

Ernest volunteered early to join the Army, attesting on 11 November 1914. Details of the place of his attestation have not survived the partial destruction of his records, but the next day he was at the Bristol depot of the Gloucestershire Regiment, to be posted a few days later to the 9th (Service) Battalion as a private. He left the UK for France on 19 September 1915 (by which time his father Walter had been killed in action near Ypres), serving with *Francis William Aldridge and *William George Birch throughout the war, and also initially with *Christopher Charles Fryer and *Thomas Henry Griffin. The 9th Glosters did not remain in France long, being redeployed in November to the Mediterranean Expeditionary Force which landed at Salonika in Greece, and then moved north to strengthen Serbian resistance against Bulgarian forces. The battalion spent two and a half years in the Balkans, and would have taken part in the battles of Horseshoe Hill and Doiran.

The Austro-Hungarian and Bulgarian forces opposing them weakened, and the 9th Glosters were withdrawn from Greece in July 1918 and moved to France, where they joined the 66th (2nd East Lancashire) Division which was being reformed following losses in the early 1918 Somme campaign. They came into the field in October for the Battle of Cambrai, followed by the Pursuit to the Selle and the offensive against the Hindenburg Line. With only a week's rest before, as Divisional Pioneers, they bridged the Selle, they were again in action for some sharp engagements near Le Cateau in the final days of the war after which they were ordered to occupy the Rhine bridgeheads until February 1919. Ernest's service earned him the 1914–15 Star, British War Medal and Victory Medal and he is commemorated on the plaque in the village hall.

After demobilisation in March 1919 and transfer to the Reserve, Ernest returned to Frampton to live at Ward's Court, marrying Lily Gertrude Twinning in 1922. Four children followed: Stanley, Ronald, Ilene and Gordon. Their home was later next to the garage (now Frampton Autos), and Ernest worked in engineering. At the beginning of 1960 Ernest lost his mother and wife within three days of each other; both were buried at St Mary's. Ernest Walter Henry Tainton moved to 22 Phillimore Gardens to live with his son, Stanley, and was himself buried in the churchyard on 13 January 1979.

WALTER HENRY TAINTON, 1874–1915
Private 2869, 2nd Battalion, Gloucestershire Regiment

Walter Henry Tainton was born on 27 September 1874 in Horsley, the eldest son of Henry Tainton and Charlotte née Guy. He was baptised at the Church of the Holy Cross, Avening, on 31 January the following year. Henry had a variety of occupations, variously a labourer, maltster and baker and was supporting a family of eight young children in 1891, by which time Walter was already a farm labourer. Walter's marriage to Clara Jane Farmiloe was registered during the first quarter of 1895 and by 1901 they were living in Owlpen, in a cottage close to Luggershall Farm with their two eldest sons, *Ernest Walter Henry and William. In 1911 the family, now completed by Albert, Charles and Percy, were at Newington Bagpath, in a cottage comprising two rooms and a kitchen; Walter a cowman on a farm, and Ernest working in a cloth mill. Walter and Clara later moved to Park Corner, Frampton.

Walter's enlistment into Lord Kitchener's Army appears in the weekly report of the *Gloucester Journal* on 26 September 1914. He completed his training in time to arrive in France and join the regular soldiers of the 2nd Battalion of the Gloucestershire Regiment on 25 March 1915, just after the fighting at St Eloi, where the Germans had exploded a huge underground mine. There was much underground work with counter-mining, but another German mine exploded in April. On 11 May the 2nd Battalion was shelled in their trenches nearly all day, and after being sent to rest in a field were ordered to Sanctuary Wood, and decided to drive the Germans off a hill, a position from which they could fire into the British trenches. This was eventually successful and, although the hill could not be held owing to enemy shellfire, the time was used to retrench in better positions. These actions resulted in twelve men killed, including Private Walter Henry Tainton, eight missing and eighteen wounded; great praise was earned from General Joffre and their Corps Commander.

Walter was posthumously awarded the 1914–15 Star, British War Medal and Victory Medal, and is commemorated on the CWGC Ypres (Menin Gate) Memorial in Belgium, as well as on Frampton's war memorial and village hall plaque. Clara continued to live in Frampton at Ward's Court, and was buried at St Mary's on 23 January 1960.

ALBERT EDWARD TOWNSEND, 1884–1917
Gunner 29001, 28th Brigade, Royal Field Artillery

Albert Edward Townsend was born in Leigh (near Cricklade), Wiltshire, in 1884, to George Townsend, a farm labourer, and Mary Ann née Richens. The household included not only Albert and his many siblings, but also extended family too. By 1901 they were living in Frampton where George was a cattleman; Albert, however, was then a stable boy for the railways in Staffordshire. In 1911 he was working in a Wolverhampton iron foundry.

Albert must have joined the Army before the war: Britain was only in a formal state of war from midnight on 4 August 1914, but he arrived in France on

19 August as a gunner with the 28th Brigade Royal Field Artillery, and almost certainly took part in the Battle of Mons, the first to involve the British. As part of the 5th Division they would have been involved in many of the major battles afterwards, from the 'Race to the Sea', to Ypres, and the Somme. In 1917 the Division fought in the Arras offensive until the end of June, and was recorded as at rest from 30 July. It is not known where or when Albert Edward Townsend suffered the wounds that caused his death on 3 August, but as he was at a military hospital in Rouen, a considerable distance from the front line, it must have been at least some days beforehand. He was interred at the CWGC St Sever Cemetery Extension in Rouen.

Albert was posthumously awarded the 1914 Star, British War Medal and Victory Medal and his ultimate sacrifice is commemorated in Frampton on the war memorial and the plaque in the village hall.

MILTON TUDOR, 1898–1967
Acting Corporal 42043, 23rd (Service) Battalion (Welsh Pioneers), Welsh Regiment; 89322, 18th (Service) Battalion (2nd City), King's (Liverpool Regiment)

Milton Tudor was baptised on 10 April 1898 at St Mary's, Berkeley, the son of Maurice Tudor, an engine driver, and Emma née Lyes, having been born on 16 January. They were at Sharpness at the time of his baptism, but by 1901 Maurice and Emma were living at Purton with their five children. Moving again, and with the addition of another daughter, 1911 found them back at Sharpness where Maurice worked as a dock labourer, and Milton was an office boy for the Steam Packet Company. The company, which also employed Milton's older brother, Clifford, as a cabin boy, operated regular passenger services on the *Wave* and *Lapwing* between Gloucester and Sharpness.

So far as Milton's war service is concerned, it is certain that he served first in the 23rd (Service) Battalion (Welsh Pioneers) of the Welsh Regiment; formed at Porthcawl in September 1915, they embarked at Devonport in July 1916 for Salonika. In the Balkans theatre the battalion was attached to the 28th Division as Pioneers. After earning appointment to acting corporal, Milton is recorded as having been transferred at some point to the 2nd (Garrison) Battalion of the King's (Liverpool Regiment); this is likely to have happened when they arrived in theatre in August 1917 when experienced soldiers would often have been transferred in to guide the newcomers. It is noteworthy that Milton was also considered suitable for the infantry, rather than the Pioneers (who were essentially labourers). He would have taken part in the Battle of Doiran in 1918, which failed owing to lack of artillery support combined with a reckless attack by a Greek division. He remained in the Balkans until the end of the war. Following demobilisation Milton received the British War Medal and Victory Medal and his service is commemorated on the plaque in Frampton Village Hall.

After the war Milton worked as a chocolate maker for Cadbury's, and on 15 August 1921 he married Thora Annie Niblett Cook (sister of *Raymond George) at St Mary's; their son, Howard George, was born the same year. Milton and his family lived at The Shrubs, The Street, in Frampton, and he ran the newsagents and was also a churchwarden. Milton Tudor was buried in St Mary's churchyard on 23 March 1967.

CYRIL VICK, 1890–1960
Gunner 239656, Royal Field Artillery

Cyril Vick was born on 24 August 1890 at Kidnam's Farm, Hyde Lane, Whitminster, and baptised in the parish church of St Andrew on 23 November the same year. He was the only son of John Richard and Stella née Vick (both of the same surname) and was brought up on the farm with his four sisters. Despite helping alongside his father during his early years, Cyril decided not to follow the family tradition of farming and in 1911 was living in Gloucester and working as a butcher; his sisters, Ruby and Effie, and a cousin, Reginald, were also in his household and seemingly employed in the city.

Family recall that Cyril enlisted into the Royal Field Artillery as a gunner, serving on the Western Front. Artillery, such as heavy guns and howitzers, played a huge role in the First World War. Although they were perhaps too often used as a blunt weapon and were then not very effective, until the introduction of tanks artillery were the only means of cutting gaps in enemy defences, especially the barbed wire and machine-gun posts, ready for an infantry attack. They would also drive enemy troops into their deepest shelters, but the soldiers could then emerge quickly as soon as the barrage stopped. A gunner's life must have consisted of much hard work in loading and firing huge shells continuously for days, and of course they (and the railways which carried the shells to the front) were also a prime target for enemy artillery. For his service Cyril was awarded the British War Medal and Victory Medal, and is commemorated on the plaque in Frampton Village Hall.

After the war Cyril lived at Advowsons Farm (also known as The Gables), Frampton, and married Frances Ann Nash at St Mary's on 21 April 1920. He set up in business as a butcher in The Street, firstly in Ye Olde Cruck House where the pork butcher's shop had been in previous times, and then on the corner of Ward's Court. They had one daughter, Mary. Cyril Vick died at The Gables on 21 April 1960 and was buried at St Peter's, Bentham, where he was joined by his widow, Frances, in 1976.

WELLS ALEXANDER WATKINS, 1891–1965
Private 183207, Canadian Expeditionary Force

Wells Alexander Watkins Long, known as Alec, was born in Frampton on 18 August 1891 to George Alexander Watkins Long, a mariner, and Agnes née Ayland. The family, who used the name Watkins rather than Long, lived in Lake House; Alec was the fourth child of five. The 1911 census records him as a grocery assistant, and this photograph, probably taken a little earlier, shows Alec outside the shop run by William Henry Goodman at the top of the village green.

The Goodman and Watkins families were well known to one another for both were heavily involved in the running of the Congregational church at Frampton. However, in April 1913, Alec decided to leave his roots and he sailed from Bristol to Halifax, Nova Scotia, on the RMS *Royal Edward*, a passenger ship belonging to the Canadian Northern Steamship Company. It seems that he intended to make his life in Canada, travelling on to Calgary where he settled and found work.

As the war progressed, Alec was keen to help his new country in its support of Great Britain, and he enlisted on 5 November 1915 at Calgary to serve with the Canadian Expeditionary Force in France. Unfortunately, no records of his wartime service have been found, but it is worth noting that the Canadians formed a separate Corps and fought together; therefore it is likely that Alec was involved in the battles of the Somme, the major Canadian victory at Vimy Ridge and at Passchendaele. Alec's war service is commemorated on the plaque in Frampton Village Hall.

He is known to have been back in Frampton by September 1921 when he was fined 5s for riding his bicycle without lights and was described as a coal merchant. In the summer of 1922 Alec married Lottie Evelyn Rowles, their marriage being registered in the Bristol area. They settled first at 12 Whitminster Lane (one of the newly built council houses) with their two daughters, Wynne Alexandra and Alexandra Marguerita, before moving to Westmont, Bridge Road, from where Alec ran a haulage business, W. A. Watkins & Son. Wells Alexander Watkins died at home on 15 December 1965 and was cremated at Gloucester Crematorium.

FRANK WEAVER, 1880–1924
Private 26975, 11th (Labour) Battalion, Royal Berkshire Regiment; 52678, Devonshire Regiment

Frank Weaver was born in 1880 to Elijah Weaver, a general labourer, and Eliza née Barnes and baptised in his parish church of St Andrew's, Whitminster on 19 September the same year. In 1901 both Frank and his father were working on the roads. On 14 April 1909 Frank married Elizabeth Caroline Mary, sister of *Victor Charles Lawrence, at St Mary's, Fretherne, by which time Frank had become a gardener. Their first son, Charles Elijah, was born the next year, and Francis followed in 1914.

On 24 November 1915 Frank volunteered to join the Army, and was posted as a private to the 11th (Labour) Battalion of the Royal Berkshire Regiment, which served in France from July 1916; their role would have been to dig trenches, build fortifications, and build and maintain roads and light railways. At some stage he was transferred to the Devonshire Regiment. According to family members, Frank suffered from shell shock, and spent time in the sanatorium at Cranham from where he wrote a postcard home to his son, Charlie. On 7 June 1917 Frank was discharged from the Army as no longer fit for military service and awarded the Silver War Badge. He later received the British War Medal and Victory Medal and is commemorated on the plaque in the village hall.

Home for the Weaver family was at The Lake, in Frampton, and two more sons were born, Leslie and Hubert. Frank Weaver died at the age of forty-four and was buried at St Mary's on 25 June 1924. His widow later married another war veteran, her widowed brother-in-law, *Victor William Wilks.

CHARLES ALEXANDER WELLER 1888–1961
Major, Royal Army Medical Corps

Charles Alexander Weller was the second child of Frampton's doctor, Charles Joseph Weller and his wife, Ellen Frances Louisa née Severne. His arrival late in 1888 was marked by a private baptism on 10 January the following year. The first part of his childhood was spent at Russell House, The Green, with his older sister, Frances Alice Maud. While she was educated at home by a governess, Charles was sent to St Cuthbert's preparatory school in Malvern, later matriculating for Clare College, Cambridge, from where he graduated in 1910 with a BA. The 1911 census records Charles in London as a medical student, which led to his registration on 14 February 1913 and qualifying in that year as both physician and surgeon.

Having volunteered to serve in the Army, on 10 August 1914 Charles was commissioned in the temporary rank of lieutenant in the Royal Army Medical Corps. He was assigned to the British Expeditionary Force, arriving in France on 15 August, but we do not know whether he spent the entire war there. Charles was in due course promoted to captain, and finally to major. He received a mention in despatches and was later awarded the 1914 Star, British War Medal and Victory Medal. By August 1919, he was at Birmingham General Hospital, probably still as an Army surgeon as the hospital is given as his address, but by November 1920 his address was Frampton, where his service is commemorated on the plaque in the village hall.

At the time of his marriage, on 20 April 1922, to Jane Drew Harris at St Matthias', Richmond, Charles was practising as a doctor. They made their home at Aldborough House, Thaxted, Essex, and their sons, Allan and Michael, were born shortly afterwards. It was still the residence of Charles Alexander Weller when he died on 17 September 1961.

ARTHUR GEOFFREY WHITE, 1892–1975
Rank and Service: Not known

Arthur Geoffrey White was born on 16 April 1892 to Charles White, the miller at Fromebridge, and Elizabeth née Workman. The grist mill (which ground grain into flour) was a family business and he was soon involved. The commemoration of 'G. White' on the village hall plaque is believed to refer to Arthur, who was listed as A. Geoffrey White on the 1911 census and he is probably shown as an organiser of Frampton Horse Show on page 23. In later life he was certainly known as Arthur. Although an experienced miller would have had a key role in food production, and could well have been exempt from conscription, it is entirely possible that Arthur served his country, perhaps even taking on duties at another mill. No records of his wartime service survive and it is perhaps interesting to note that he is not recorded on the electoral registers in Fromebridge at this time, thus reinforcing the suggestion of his deployment to another mill.

On 12 November 1917 Arthur married Mabel Gertrude, the daughter of Richard Ward, whose grocer's shop was situated at the south end of the village green (in recent years a restaurant). Their son, Stanley Arthur, was born in 1918 and later ran the mill. Arthur Geoffrey White's ashes were interred in St Mary's churchyard on 4 October 1975.

WILLIAM WHITHORN, 1890–1976
Private SE 25722, Army Veterinary Corps

William Whithorn was born in Berkeley on 27 May 1890 to William Whithorn, a farm labourer, and Ruth née Young. His parents had married in 1885, somewhat late in life, but they had five children; their youngest child, Percy John, was killed in action in 1916. William found work as a waggoner on a farm in Woodford, near Berkeley, and in 1915 became the second husband of Louisa Ellen Bray (née Hayward). Louisa's first husband, William Bray, had been a Great Western Railway platelayer who had died in 1913. William became stepfather to two daughters, Betty Louisa and Beatrice May, and his first child with Louisa, Cyril, was born in 1916.

On 8 February 1917, with his experience of working with horses, William joined the Army Veterinary Corps. He did not see overseas service. Later that year, on 9 November, he was discharged as physically unfit due to myalgia that was 'Not a result of, but aggravated by military service during the war and exposure to Service conditions'. This condition was assessed as permanent and preventing 30 per cent of normal activity, but no treatment was required. As a result he had a disability pension, initially at 12s 6d per week for support of three children; after a later medical review reported 50 per cent disability, the pension was increased to 13s 9d, with an additional 7s 11d for the children. He was awarded the Silver War Badge in recognition of his disability and his service is commemorated on the plaque in the village hall.

After his discharge, William and Louisa lived in The Street, Frampton, where they had five more children: Geoffrey, Winifred, Ralph, Sidney and Leslie. They later moved to 5 Bridge Road and then to 17 The Oval. Louisa died in 1961, and William married Lilian Summers in 1964. Latterly they lived at 7 Bridge Road. William Whithorn died in 1976 and Lilian three years later.

ERNEST HENRY WILKS, 1889–1949
Able Seaman 783580, Mercantile Marine

Ernest Henry Wilks, born in 1889 in Frampton, was the second son of Henry Wilks and Martha née Hazell; his older brother, George John, had died five years earlier, at just one day old. Henry was a waterman, and the family lived close to the canal in Splatt Lane during Ernest's childhood. By 1911 they had moved to one of the cottages at Buckholdt, in The Street, increasing the family's accommodation from four to eight rooms. Ernest was by this time working as a labourer, with *Victor William, his younger brother, a fireman or stoker. On 29 August 1914, just after the onset of war, Ernest married Fanny White at St Mary's; one of their witnesses was *Henry Elphinstone Guy.

During the war Ernest appears to have served as an able seaman in the Mercantile Marine, despite his appearance in this photograph wearing a hat with 'HMS' on the band (in wartime ships' names did not appear on sailors' hatbands). His record card bears a 1923 statement 'All Naval service Rejected by letter', implying that he had made a claim for such service. Nevertheless, as he qualified for both the British War Medal and Mercantile Marine War Medal he must have made one or more voyages through a danger zone (a definition which would have included all offshore areas of the sea, and also all coastal waters on the south and east coasts of Britain). No records have been found of the ships on which he sailed, or the ports that he visited but his service is commemorated on the plaque in the village hall.

Ernest does not appear to have lived in Frampton after the war. Latterly his home was at Brooklyn, Stanley Downton, near Stonehouse, the address given when he was buried in St Mary's churchyard, Frampton, on 17 December 1949.

VICTOR WILLIAM WILKS, 1891–1955
Greaser 783583, Mercantile Marine

Victor William Wilks, the youngest son of Henry Wilks and Martha née Hazell, was born in Frampton on 13 November 1891. The canal featured heavily in Victor's life from an early age, for not only was his father a waterman, but his grandfather was the bridgekeeper at Hardwicke. In September 1904 the school logbook reported that Victor was absent, apparently being employed in the carrying trade to Gloucester by his mother. The family's business was seemingly flourishing for they were able to move from their small cottage in Splatt Lane to The Street, into one of the cottages beside Buckholdt. By 1911 Victor was working as a fireman or stoker, perhaps on one of the canal barges. On Christmas Day 1913 he married Ruth Beatrice, the sister of *Victor Charles Lawrence, at St Mary's, Fretherne. The birth of their son, Frederick Victor, came exactly one year later.

Victor, like his brother, *Ernest Henry, served in the Mercantile Marine during the war, the closeness of their formal numbers suggesting that they may have joined together, and indeed they may even have worked on the same vessels. Victor was rated as a greaser, working below deck in the engine room, so his service appears to have been on registered merchantmen. He was awarded the British War Medal and Mercantile Marine War Medal and his service is commemorated on the plaque in the village hall.

Victor's wife Ruth died in 1921, aged twenty-six. On 3 August 1931, he married her sister, Elizabeth Caroline Mary, the widow of *Frank Weaver, at St James the Great, Saul. At the time of this marriage Victor was an engineer; by 1939 the family were living at 3 Dinmore Road, Sharpness and his occupation was more precisely given as an engineer on a river tug. Victor William Wilks died on 28 February 1955 at Bristol Royal Infirmary and was buried on 4 March at St Mary's, Berkeley.

RICHARD SIDNEY WINTER
1884–1917
Able Seaman R/4635, 3rd Reserve Battalion Royal Naval Division; Anson Battalion, 63rd (Royal Naval) Division

Richard Sidney Winter, known as Sidney, was born on 11 August 1884 in Frampton to Richard James Winter, a grocer's porter, and Annie Sophia née Masters. He was one of six children. In 1901 Sidney was a bricklayer's labourer, but was later in the Gloucestershire Constabulary in Cheltenham. When he married Lucy Amy Brocher at St Peter's, Framilode, on 17 July 1915, he was an agent for Pearl Assurance at Stroud. Their daughter, Kathleen, was born around eighteen months later while he was working at Cadbury's.

Sidney appears to have first volunteered for the Army, being placed in the Army Reserve on 31 January 1916. However, he must also have applied for the Royal Naval Volunteer Reserve for he was mobilised on 2 July 1917 and reported to the 3rd Reserve Battalion Royal Naval Division at Blandford for training. On completion he was rated as an able seaman and posted to France on 30 October to join Anson Battalion of the 63rd (Royal Naval) Division. This had previously been formed from Royal Navy and Royal Marine personnel who were not needed for service at sea. However, after sustaining many losses at Antwerp and Gallipoli, it had been transferred to the Army in 1916 and served on the Western Front for the remainder of the war.

The Second Battle of Passchendaele had been raging as Sidney arrived at the front, in which the Royal Naval Division had suffered over 3,000 casualties, but his timing was good and he would have taken part in the considerably more successful second phase – by attacking at night they took much more ground with few losses. This battle was followed for the Division by the Action of Welsh Ridge, a part of the Battle of Cambrai, in the first half of December. Although the front was then quieter for a time, it was always dangerous and, according to his Commanding Officer when later writing to his mother, Richard Sidney Winter was

> shot through the head and instantly killed while gallantly advancing with the Company (A) on December 30th last [1917]. The action was a particularly hard one and the men did splendidly and well, especially your son, of whom, as a Gloucestershire man myself, I was very proud. His loss was a grief to me, as I had come to know and appreciate the lad very well. He was seen by several men to fall during the advance … I need hardly say that I extend to you my deepest sympathy. It may be some slight consolation to know that A.-B. [Able Seaman] Winter died bravely and that he was a splendid Gloucestershire lad.

Sidney was posthumously awarded the British War Medal and Victory Medal and is commemorated on Frampton's war memorial and the village hall plaque. He is also remembered on the CWGC Thiepval Memorial to the Missing of the Somme, the largest British war memorial in the world.

SELECT BIBLIOGRAPHY

WEBSITES

1915crewlists.rmg.co.uk
grandeguerre.icrc.org
www.ancestry.co.uk
www.cwgc.org
www.findmypast.co.uk
www.forces-war-records.co.uk
www.glosters.org.uk
www.iwm.org.uk
www.longlongtrail.co.uk
www.thegazette.co.uk
www.wikipedia.org

PRINT PUBLICATIONS

Clifford, Rollo, *The Royal Gloucestershire Hussars* (Stroud: Alan Sutton Publishing Ltd, 1991).

Darell, Sir Lionel, *Ratcatcher Baronet* (London: Sir Joseph Causton & Sons Ltd, 1952).

Edwards, Brian, 'Frampton-on-Severn Gravel Pits and their Transport Links', *Archive: The Quarterly Journal for British Industrial and Transport History* (Issue 37, March 2003), 15–29.

Edwards, Brian, 'National Filling Factory No 5 Quedgeley', *Gloucestershire Society for Industrial Archaeology Journal* (1994), 32–52.

Edwards, Brian, 'The Slimbridge Munitions Depot', *Gloucestershire Society for Industrial Archaeology Journal* (1995), 13–21.

Fox, Frank, *The History of the Royal Gloucestershire Hussars Yeomanry 1898–1922: The Great Cavalry Campaign in Palestine* (London: Philip Allan, 1923).

Hewlett, Rose and Jean Speed, *Frampton on Severn: An Illustrated History* (Nailsworth: Hathaway Press, 2007).

Lloyd, T. O., *Empire, Welfare State, Europe,* 4th Edition (Oxford: Oxford University Press, 1993).

Marwick, Arthur, *The Deluge,* 2nd Edition (Basingstoke: Palgrave Macmillan, 1991).

Read, Donald, *Edwardian England 1901–15, Society and Politics* (London: History Book Club, 1972).

Spence, Rose, *Frampton on Severn: Portrait of a Victorian Village* (Chichester: Phillimore & Co. Ltd, 2000).

Taylor, A. J. P., *English History 1914–1945* (Oxford: Oxford University Press, 1966).

Williamson, Debbie, *Broadway Remembers* (Broadway: Debbie Williamson, 2014).

The following repositories have provided access to numerous records:
Cadbury Archives
Frampton Archive
Gloucestershire Archives
Soldiers of Gloucestershire Museum
The National Archives

Material has also been drawn from the collections of private individuals.

INDEX